Music

IN THEORY AND PRACTICE

VOLUME II

Tenth Edition

Bruce Benward
Late of the University of Wisconsin–Madison

Marilyn Saker
Eastern Michigan University

Mc
Graw
Hill

MUSIC IN THEORY AND PRACTICE: VOLUME 2, TENTH EDITION

1 2 3 4 5 6 7 8 9 LMN 25 24 23 22 21 20

ISBN 978-1-260-49355-9 (bound edition)
MHID 1-260-49355-5 (bound edition)
ISBN 978-1-260-49346-7 (loose-leaf edition)
MHID 1-260-49346-6 (loose-leaf edition)

Portfolio Manager: *Sarah Remington*
Product Developers: *Mary Ellen Curley, Elizabeth Murphy*
Marketing Manager: *Meredith Leo DiGiano*
Content Project Managers: *Rick Hecker, Katie Reuter*
Buyer: *Susan K. Culbertson*
Design: *David W. Hash*
Content Licensing Specialist: *Brianna Kirschbaum*
Cover Image: *©Robert Kyllo/Shutterstock*
Compositor: *Aptara, Inc.*

Library of Congress Control Number: 2019955991

Contents

Preface

To the Student

Volume 1 of *Music in Theory and Practice* was a general introduction to music theory. You spent time mastering the details of music syntax and discovering how small patterns, such as scales, intervals, and triads, combine to create larger units—phrases, periods, two-part form, and three-part form. This volume focuses on musical styles from the Renaissance to the present. It includes more complex chords, an emphasis on larger forms, and strategies to help you analyze the compositions you perform.

The goal of this volume is the practical application of information. The analytical techniques presented here are carefully designed to be clear, uncomplicated, and readily applicable to the repertoire you will develop during your career as a musician. The thorough understanding of the musical structure of a composition that you gain through analysis considerably reduces the time required for preparing a performance of that work.

New to This Edition

The tenth edition of *Music in Theory and Practice* includes the following enhancements:

1. Both core texts and workbooks are now available in the McGraw-Hill eBook. The eBooks are included in Connect or can be purchased via the ReadAnywhere app. When accessed in the app, students can read off-line and data-free by downloading the entire text or only the chapters they need. They can also highlight and take notes in the eBook, and their highlights will sync between the app and Connect.
2. A significant number of new audio files (MP3s) are available for music appearing in the books. These audio files are embedded in the eBooks but are also available to purchasers of print copies through the Connect Online Learning Center.
3. Chapters are now numbered continuously across volumes 1 and 2 of *Music in Theory and Practice* and its workbooks, in both print and eBook formats.
4. New examples have been added throughout the chapters to augment and demonstrate explanations.
5. Several new assignments provide additional practice for students and allow instructors greater flexibility in course planning.

Texts and Supplements

This two-volume series is a part of a carefully integrated package. The following texts and ancillaries are available for the tenth edition:

For students and instructors:
Music in Theory and Practice, Volume 1
Music in Theory and Practice, Volume 2
Workbook to Accompany *Music in Theory and Practice,* Volume 1
Workbook to Accompany *Music in Theory and Practice,* Volume 2
eBook
SmartBook® 2.0, an adaptive study resource available within Connect
Connect Access card + Volume I Workbook + Volume II Workbook
Connect Access card + Volume I Workbook:
Connect Access card + Volume II Workbook

For instructors:
Instructor's Manual to Accompany *Music in Theory and Practice,* Volume 1
Instructor's Manual to Accompany *Music in Theory and Practice,* Volume 2
Workbook Solutions Manual to Accompany *Music in Theory and Practice,* Volume 1
Workbook Solutions Manual to Accompany *Music in Theory and Practice,* Volume 2

Resources available from the Connect Online Learning Center include printable versions of the Instructor's Manuals and Workbook Solutions Manuals, audio files, assignment templates compatible with Finale® Music Notation software, supplementary drill assignments, testing materials, and recordings. Audio files available for this edition of *Music in Theory and Practice* are identified throughout the texts and workbooks with the ♪ graphic.

Acknowledgments

I am indebted to my multitalented colleague, Samuel Joshua, for producing the large number of audio files new to the tenth edition. The thoughtful care with which he approached this enormous task, and his expansive knowledge of music production, significantly benefitted *Music in Theory and Practice*. Thank you, Sam.

It is with sincere gratitude that I thank jazz musician Mark Pappas for his intelligent advice regarding the jazz and popular-music elements appearing throughout the text. His guidance has proven time and again to be invaluable.

Grateful acknowledgment is extended to the highly professional staff at McGraw-Hill. It was a sincere honor to work with Elizabeth Murphy, Sarah Remington, Rick Hecker, Brianna Kirschbaum, Barbara Hacha, and Betty Chen. The helpful suggestions made by reviewers for the tenth edition are also acknowledged:

Reginald Klopfenstein, *Bethel University*
Brian Kubin, *Truman State University*
Timothy Nutting, *Navarro College*
Leslie Odom, *University of Florida*
J. Whitney Prince, *Eastern Michigan University*
Anne Watson, *Northeastern State University*

Most importantly of all, I am genuinely grateful for the extraordinary set of circumstances that led me to study with the incomparable Bruce Benward. It's funny how the truly talented teachers never really leave you. Thank you, Bruce.

Marilyn Saker

You're in the driver's seat.

Want to build your own course? No problem. Prefer to use our turnkey, prebuilt course? Easy. Want to make changes throughout the semester? Sure. And you'll save time with Connect's auto-grading too.

65%
Less Time Grading

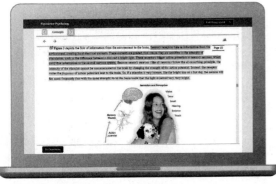

Laptop: McGraw-Hill; Woman/dog: George Doyle/Getty Images

They'll thank you for it.

Adaptive study resources like SmartBook® 2.0 help your students be better prepared in less time. You can transform your class time from dull definitions to dynamic debates. Find out more about the powerful personalized learning experience available in SmartBook 2.0 at **www.mheducation.com/highered/connect/smartbook**

Make it simple, make it affordable.

Connect makes it easy with seamless integration using any of the major Learning Management Systems—Blackboard®, Canvas, and D2L, among others—to let you organize your course in one convenient location. Give your students access to digital materials at a discount with our inclusive access program. Ask your McGraw-Hill representative for more information.

Padlock: Jobalou/Getty Images

Solutions for your challenges.

A product isn't a solution. Real solutions are affordable, reliable, and come with training and ongoing support when you need it and how you want it. Our Customer Experience Group can also help you troubleshoot tech problems—although Connect's 99% uptime means you might not need to call them. See for yourself at **status.mheducation.com**

Checkmark: Jobalou/Getty Images

FOR STUDENTS

Effective, efficient studying.

Connect helps you be more productive with your study time and get better grades using tools like SmartBook 2.0, which highlights key concepts and creates a personalized study plan. Connect sets you up for success, so you walk into class with confidence and walk out with better grades.

Study anytime, anywhere.

Download the free ReadAnywhere app and access your online eBook or SmartBook 2.0 assignments when it's convenient, even if you're offline. And since the app automatically syncs with your eBook and SmartBook 2.0 assignments in Connect, all of your work is available every time you open it. Find out more at **www.mheducation.com/readanywhere**

"I really liked this app—it made it easy to study when you don't have your text-book in front of you."

- Jordan Cunningham,
Eastern Washington University

No surprises.

The Connect Calendar and Reports tools keep you on track with the work you need to get done and your assignment scores. Life gets busy; Connect tools help you keep learning through it all.

Calendar: owattaphotos/Getty Images

Learning for everyone.

McGraw-Hill works directly with Accessibility Services Departments and faculty to meet the learning needs of all students. Please contact your Accessibility Services office and ask them to email accessibility@mheducation.com, or visit **www.mheducation.com/about/accessibility** for more information.

Top: Jenner Images/Getty Images, Left: Hero Images/Getty Images, Right: Hero Images/Getty Images

The Renaissance and Baroque Periods

Renaissance Period (1450–1600)

The term *Renaissance* refers to the era of the flowering of the arts and literature that followed the Middle Ages. The overriding function of music in the Renaissance period was to contribute to worship. Although greatly overshadowed by the sacred music of the period, secular works did exist and were an important part of the literature.

Vocal music was far more common than instrumental music during the Renaissance. Choruses came into being shortly before the beginning of the Renaissance but did not reach full flower until well into the era. Choruses of the time were usually small groups of perhaps 12 to 15 singers. The choral group was often divided into four parts—the familiar soprano, alto, tenor, and bass. Late Renaissance music often required a fifth part, either a second soprano or a second tenor, and works for six, eight, and even 16-part choruses were not unusual. Instrumental groups frequently accompanied choruses and usually doubled the voice parts. In chapels, however, the groups sang *a cappella,* or unaccompanied.

As an introduction to the music of the late Renaissance, we will study two- and three-part vocal polyphony, concentrating our attention on the works of Orlande de Lassus, Josquin Desprez, Giovanni Pierluigi da Palestrina, and Tomás Luis de Victoria.

Baroque Period (1600–1750)

The *baroque* was a period of great change. Baroque composers preferred new tonality systems to the modality of the Renaissance. Their compositional style made it possible to hear the words of sung texts more easily. Instrumental music began to assume more importance than vocal music for the first time in history. Improvisation of music was a common practice, particularly in the performance of accompaniments and in the performance of opera singers, who were expected to improvise embellishments at certain points in their arias. Much of the music of the baroque included a figured bass that served as a basis for improvising accompaniments.

We will examine instrumental works of the baroque period in contrapuntal texture, principally the two-part inventions and fugues of J. S. Bach.

CHAPTER 18

Late Renaissance Polyphony

Topics			
	Modes	Musica Ficta	Consonant 4th
	Dorian Mode	Unaccented Passing Tone	Hocket
	Phrygian Mode	Accented Passing Tone	Clausula Vera
	Lydian Mode	Lower Neighboring Tone	Plagal Cadence
	Mixolydian Mode	Suspensions	Weak Interior Cadences
	Aeolian Mode	Portamento	Text Setting
	Ionian Mode	Nota Cambiata	Agogic Accent
	Final	Six-Five Figure	Imitation

Important Concepts

Late Renaissance polyphony refers to music from approximately 1550 to 1600. The polyphony of this period is perhaps the purest ever written because it is not influenced by the functional harmony of later periods. Interacting melodic lines characterize the compositional style of this period.

Modes

Sixteenth-century music is essentially modal. The *Dorian, Phrygian, Lydian,* and *Mixolydian modes* were in common use. The *Aeolian* (natural minor scale) and *Ionian* (major scale) modes were used occasionally. Each mode is identified by its beginning tone, called the *final.*

Mode	Piano White Keys	Final
Dorian	D to D	D
Phrygian	E to E	E
Lydian	F to F	F
Mixolydian	G to G	G
Aeolian	A to A	A
Ionian	C to C	C

Musica Ficta

Altered tones were frequently added to the pure modes. This practice became known as *musica ficta.* Musica ficta accidentals were not written in the original manuscripts but were sung by the performers according to performance practices of the period. In modern editions the musica ficta accidentals are often indicated above the staves. The melodic tritone between F and B was avoided by lowering the B to B-flat (Figure 18.1).

Figure 18.1

Lassus: *Beatus homo* (Happy Is the Man), mm. 24–26.

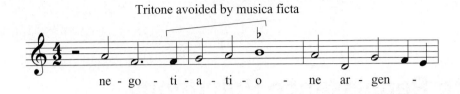

In the Dorian and Mixolydian modes, a "leading tone" was created at cadences by raising the seventh scale degree. The Phrygian and Lydian modes required no alteration at cadence points (Figure 18.2).

Figure 18.2

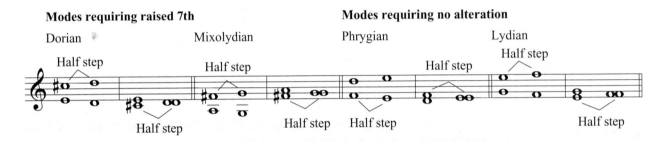

Transposed Modes The modes were often transposed a perfect fifth lower, creating a key signature of one flat (Figure 18.3).

Figure 18.3

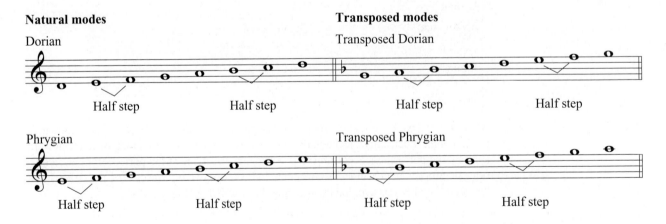

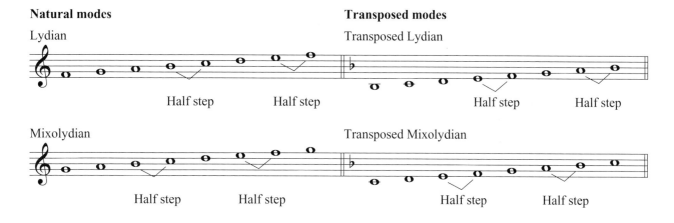

Natural modes

Lydian

Half step   Half step

Mixolydian

Half step   Half step

Transposed modes

Transposed Lydian

Half step   Half step

Transposed Mixolydian

Half step   Half step

Consonance

In late Renaissance polyphony, vertical structures were organized according to the consonant intervals above the lowest-sounding tone (Figure 18.4).

Figure 18.4

Consonant intervals in the sixteenth-century style

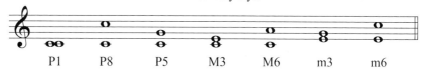

P1   P8   P5   M3   M6   m3   m6

The lowest-sounding tone may not always be the lowest voice in the score because voice crossing was quite common (Figure 18.5).

Figure 18.5

Palestrina: *Missa Inviolata*, Credo, mm. 14–15.

☐ = Lowest-sounding tone

The numbers between the staves in Figure 18.5 refer to the interval above the lowest-sounding tone. This method of analysis is employed throughout this chapter.

The concept of tonal harmony was unknown during the Renaissance period. Composers thought only in terms of consonances and dissonances.

Dissonance

Vertical dissonance was treated with considerable care. The dissonant intervals are: P4, M2, m2, M7, m7, and all diminished and augmented intervals.

Dissonance Types in Two-Voice Writing

Passing tones, lower neighboring tones, suspensions, portamentos, and cambiatas are the only dissonances found in two-voice writing.

Unaccented Passing Tone

Unaccented passing tones in half notes are found on beats 2 and 4 in $\frac{4}{2}$ meter, in quarter notes on the second half of any beat, and in eighth notes in unstressed locations. Unaccented passing tones are used in ascending and descending directions (Figure 18.6).

Figure 18.6

Josquin Desprez: *Missa "L'homme armé super voces musicales"*
(Mass based on "The Armed Man"), Benedictus, mm. 26–27.

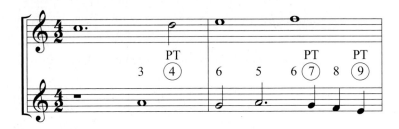

Accented Passing Tone

Accented passing tones in quarter notes occur only on beats 2 and 4 in $\frac{4}{2}$ meter, and only in a descending direction. Half-note accented passing tones were not allowed (Figure 18.7).

Figure 18.7

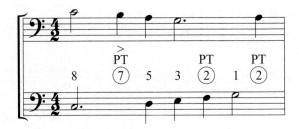

Lower Neighboring Tone

Lower neighboring tones occur in quarter notes in unstressed locations (Figure 18.8).

Figure 18.8

Josquin Desprez: *Missa Da pacem*, Credo, mm. 9–10.

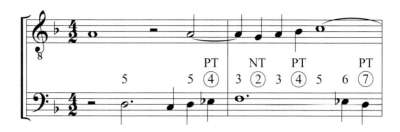

Suspensions

In two-voice writing, the only suspensions available are 7–6 and 2–3. The suspension occurs on beats 1 or 3 in $\frac{4}{2}$ meter and the resolutions on beats 2 or 4 (Figure 18.9).

Figure 18.9

Lassus: *Beatus vir in sapientia* (Blessed Is the Man), mm. 23–24.

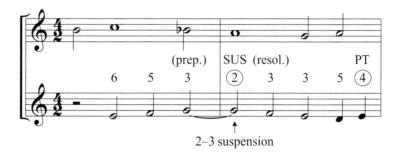

2–3 suspension

Decorated suspensions are common. The decorations usually consist of a portamento (discussed in the following section) or with double eighth notes where the second eighth note is a lower neighboring tone (Figure 18.10).

Figure 18.10

Lassus: *Serve bone* (Well Done), mm. 5–6.

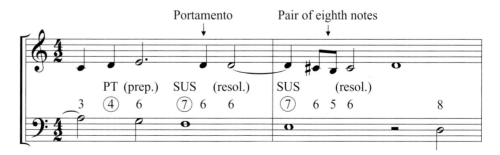

Portamento

The *portamento* is a common device of the late Renaissance that resembles the anticipation found in later periods. The portamento figure consists of three notes—often a dotted half note (or a half note tied to a quarter note), a quarter note, and a half or quarter note. The portamento tone is the second of the three (Figure 18.11).

Figure 18.11

Portamento figure as suspension decoration

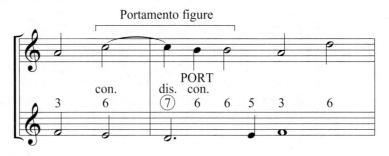

Dissonant portamento

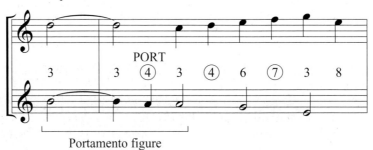

Portamento figure

Nota Cambiata

A forerunner of the eighteenth-century changing tones, the *nota cambiata* is a four-note melodic figure. The second note of the four is the nota cambiata itself. The first and third notes are always consonant with the lowest-sounding tone, whereas the second and fourth may or may not be dissonant (Figure 18.12).

Figure 18.12

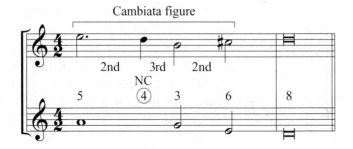

Suspensions

In polyphony with three or more voices, the 9–8 (2–1) and 4–3 suspensions occur, as well as the 7–6 and 2–3 suspensions described on page 419 (Figure 18.13).

Figure 18.13

Palestrina: *Missa Inviolata,* Credo, mm. 20–21.

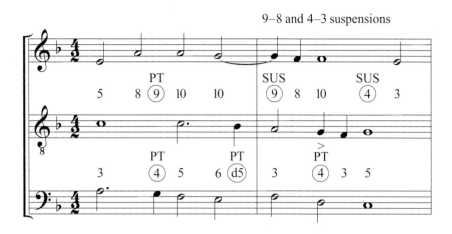

9–8 and 4–3 suspensions

The Six–Five Figure

Occasionally one voice will sing a 5th above the lowest-sounding tone at the same time that another voice sings a 6th. Although both of these intervals are consonances, a dissonance occurs between them that requires resolution. The 5th resolves downward as a suspension, whereas the lowest-sounding voice moves upward, creating a 3rd (Figure 18.14).

Figure 18.14

Palestrina: *Missa Jam Christus astra ascenderat,* Credo, m. 24.

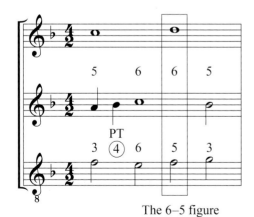

The 6–5 figure

The Consonant 4th

The 4th is normally considered to be a dissonance, but at cadence points a figure similar to the cadential six-four chord in tonal music sometimes occurs. The 4th in this case is considered to be consonant (Figure 18.15).

Figure 18.15

Victoria: *Magnificat Septimi Toni: De posuit potentes,* mm. 11–12.

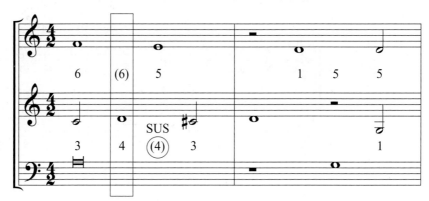

The consonant 4th

Melody

The melodic lines in sixteenth-century choral music have the following characteristics:

1. Melodic movement is predominantly stepwise.
2. Although skips occur, the following intervals are avoided:
   Ascending M6ths
   All descending 6ths
   All 7ths
   All diminished and augmented intervals
   Skips greater than an octave
3. Triads are sometimes outlined in the melody.
4. Two or more successive skips in the same direction (other than skips that outline a triad) are rare.
5. A skip greater than a 3rd is preceded and followed by an interval that is in the opposite direction to the skip and most often stepwise. For example, the approach to, and departure from, an ascending skip is by a descending interval (usually a step) (Figure 18.16).

Figure 18.16

6. Melodic sequences, so common in the eighteenth century, are infrequent in this style.

Rhythm and Meter

The two common meters in late Renaissance polyphony were quadruple meter and triple meter. This chapter deals only with quadruple meter. The rhythms in quadruple meter were limited to the following note values:

Breve (double whole note)
Half note
Dotted half note
Eighth note (used sparingly and in pairs)
Whole note
Dotted whole note
Quarter note

1. Note values were tied only to a succeeding note of equal or next shorter value (Figure 18.17).

Figure 18.17

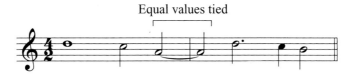

Equal values tied

Note tied to next shorter value

Unstylistic   Unstylistic

2. Quarter rests were not used at all, and half rests are found only on beats 1 and 3 (Figure 18.18).

Figure 18.18

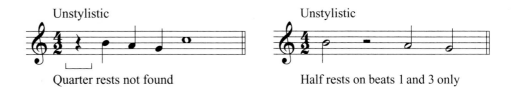

Unstylistic   Unstylistic

Quarter rests not found   Half rests on beats 1 and 3 only

3. Eighth notes occur only on the second half of a beat and always in pairs (Figure 18.19).

Figure 18.19

Unstylistic

Eighth notes not found on
accented portion of the beat

4. Compositions generally begin with a note of at least a dotted half-note value. More often the beginning note is a whole note or breve.
5. The final note is at least a whole-note value and most often a breve.
6. There was considerable rhythmic variety in late Renaissance polyphony. Two simultaneous voices never have the same rhythm, and rhythmic figures were not repeated in successive measures (Figure 18.20).

Figure 18.20

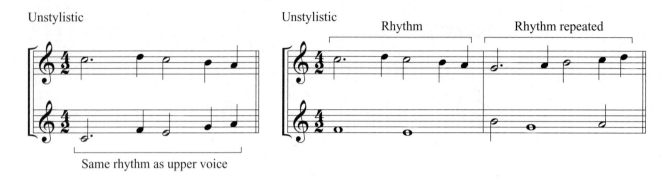

7. To keep the rhythmic flow from being interrupted at interior cadence points, one voice usually rests and then begins the next phrase immediately. This staggering of rests is referred to as *hocket* (Figure 18.21).

Figure 18.21

Lassus: *Beatus homo* (Happy Is the Man), mm. 23–24.

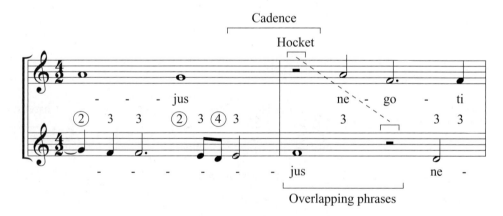

8. Original manuscripts of the period did not contain bar lines. However, for the sake of twentieth-century musicians, most modern editions include bar lines.
9. The rhythms in individual voices sometimes suggest meters other than the meter signature. Most modern editions place the bar lines according to the prevailing meter, regardless of the meter suggested in individual voices, to avoid notational complexity (Figure 18.22).

Figure 18.22

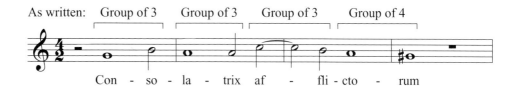

As written:　Group of 3　Group of 3　Group of 3　Group of 4

Con - so - la - trix af - fli - cto - rum

Rewritten to show rhythmic groupings more clearly

Con - so - la - trix af - fli - cto - rum

Cadences

Clausula Vera

Most final cadences in two-voice writing are of the *clausula vera* type, in which the two voices approach an octave or unison through stepwise motion (Figure 18.23).

Figure 18.23

Lassus: *Beatus homo* (Happy Is the Man), mm. 34–35.

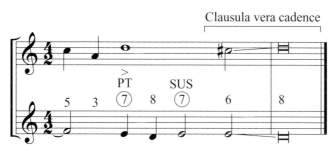

Clausula vera cadence

PT　SUS

5　3　⑦　8　⑦　6　8

Expands out to octave

In three-voice writing the third voice often adds falling 5th motion to the clausula vera, creating a cadence similar to the authentic cadence in tonal music (Figure 18.24).

Figure 18.24

Palestrina: *Magnificat Secundi Toni: Deposuit potentes,* mm. 27–28.

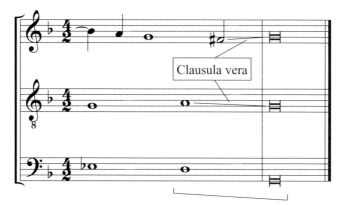

Clausula vera

Decending 5th in the bass

Plagal Cadence

A *plagal cadence* is occasionally found at interior cadence points. In a two-voice plagal cadence, the lower voice moves up a P5th or down a P4th (Figure 18.25).

Figure 18.25

Plagal cadences

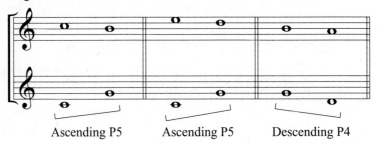

Ascending P5   Ascending P5   Descending P4

Weak Interior Cadences

Pauses often occur in individual melodic lines in compositions of this period. These momentary breaks in rhythmic activity sometimes have the effect of cadences (Figure 18.26).

Figure 18.26

Lassus: *Qui vult venire post me* (He Who Would Follow Me), mm. 3–5.

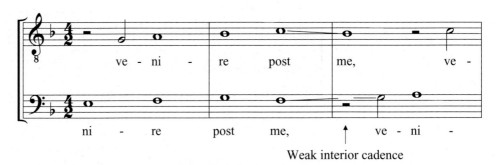

Weak interior cadence

Parallel Motion

As in eighteenth-century style, parallel P8ths, P5ths, and P1s were prohibited during this period (Figure 18.27).

Figure 18.27

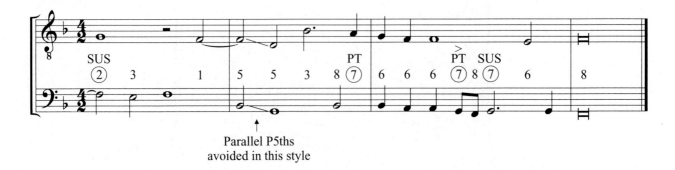

Parallel P5ths
avoided in this style

Parallel M3rds, m3rds, M6ths, and m6th intervals were common, though these were usually limited to four or five notes in succession (Figure 18.28).

Figure 18.28

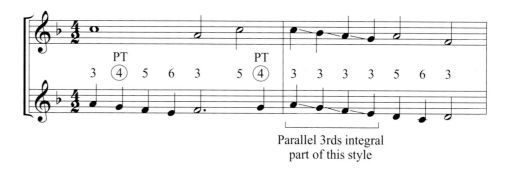

Parallel 3rds integral
part of this style

Text Setting

In late Renaissance polyphony there were a number of conventions for the setting of texts, including the following:

1. Syllables are assigned only to half-note (or larger) values. A single quarter note may carry a syllable only when preceded by a dotted half note and followed by a half or whole note.
2. After a series of quarter notes, a syllable is not changed until after a white note value occurs (Figure 18.29).

Figure 18.29

Palestrina: *Alleluja tulerunt* (Hallelujah, They Had Borne), mm. 1–3.

Syllable changes on
2nd white note

3. The rhythms follow the accents of the words quite closely. Accented syllables are often given *agogic* (durational) stress (Figure 18.30).

Figure 18.30

Palestrina: *Alleluja tulerunt* (Hallelujah, They Had Borne), mm. 1–3.

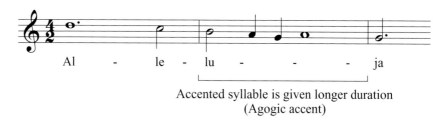

Accented syllable is given longer duration
(Agogic accent)

Form

Late Renaissance vocal compositions have a formal design that parallels the text.

1. Each phrase of text is considered a section and is set musically so that a cadence or at least a pause will occur at the end of the line.
2. Each section of music begins with imitation that is usually abandoned before the end of the section.
3. After each interior cadence a new imitation begins.

History

The four composers—Josquin Desprez (ca.1440–1521), Giovanni Pierluigi da Palestrina (ca. 1525–1594), Orlande de Lassus (ca. 1530–1594), and Tomás Luis de Victoria (1548–1611)—whose music is presented in the examples in this chapter, are the best-known composers of sacred music in the Renaissance. The works of these composers are remarkable for their stylistic consistency and musical value. They continue to appear in concerts of choral music today.

Josquin Desprez (ca. 1440–1521)

Josquin Desprez was born in the north of France, performed as a singer in the papal chapel choir in Rome, and returned to France to serve in the court of Louis XII. He perfected the technique of pervasive imitation (imitation at the beginning of each section) during his stay in Rome. His works were known throughout Europe and influenced many later composers, including Palestrina, Lassus, and Victoria. In addition to sacred music, Josquin composed a number of secular chansons.

Giovanni Pierluigi da Palestrina (ca. 1525–1594)

Born in Palestrina, Italy, Giovanni Pierluigi da Palestrina became the master of the chapel choir in several of Rome's greatest churches. His reputation as a composer of sacred music was so great that he was asked to rewrite the church's plainchant books to bring them in line with the reforms instituted by the Council of Trent. (The Council of Trent required that the text of the Mass always be understandable by a congregation.) In the twentieth century, Palestrina's music has been studied extensively. The stylistic norms described in this chapter are based on Knud Jeppesen's monumental work *The Style of Palestrina and the Dissonance*.

Orlande de Lassus (ca. 1530–1594)

Orlande de Lassus was a Franco-Flemish composer who also learned his craft as a composer in the churches in Rome. Returning to his native Mons (now a part of Belgium), he began publishing works that became known throughout Europe. In 1556 he joined the court of Duke Albrecht V of Bavaria, where he spent the remainder of his life. In addition to sacred music, Lassus composed more than four hundred secular works, including madrigals, villanellas, chansons, and lieder.

Tomás Luis de Victoria (1548–1611)

Born in Avila, Spain, where he became a choirboy at the Avila Cathedral, Tomás Luis de Victoria moved to Rome in 1565 and studied composition with Palestrina. Victoria became a priest and returned to Spain as chaplain to Philip II's sister in Madrid, where he spent the remainder of his life. He is considered to be the greatest Spanish composer of the Renaissance. Victoria composed only sacred music and is known for dramatic and emotional interpretation of the texts.

Applications

Beatus homo, analyzed in Figure 18.31, is from a group of two-voiced motets by Orlande de Lassus. The text for this motet is taken from Proverbs 3:13–14.

Figure 18.31

Lassus: *Beatus homo* (Happy Is the Man) from *Cantiones Duarum Vocum.*

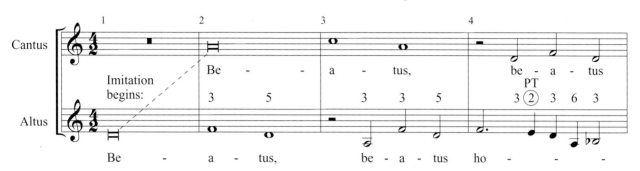

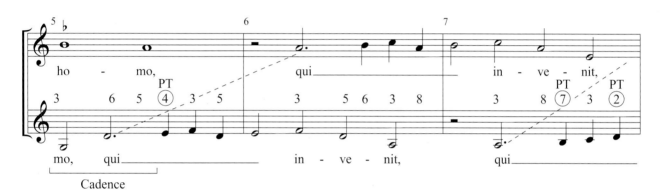

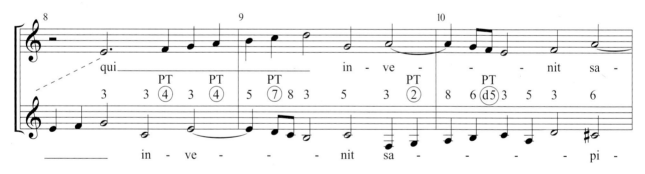

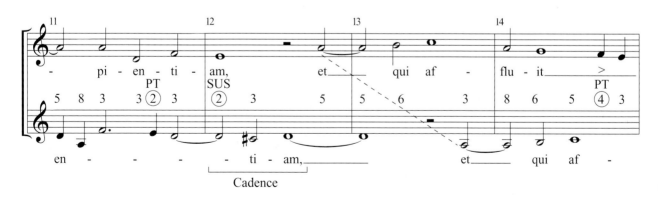

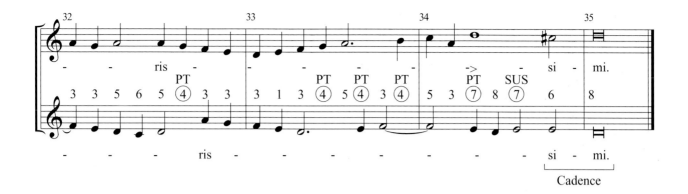

ris - - si - mi.

PT PT PT PT -> PT SUS si - mi.

3 3 5 6 5 ④ 3 3 3 1 3 ④ 5 ④ 3 ④ 5 3 ⑦ 8 ⑦ 6 8

ris - - - - - - si - mi.

Cadence

Mode

Beatus homo is in the Dorian mode. Four of the five cadences are on D. The few accidentals that appear are C♯ (three times) and B♭ (six times). Their purpose is clear: the former provides a leading tone at cadence points, and the latter corrects tritones (Figure 18.32).

Figure 18.32

Dorian mode with musica ficta tones

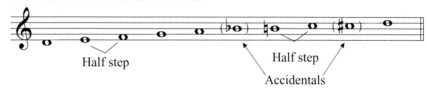

Half step

Half step

Accidentals

Melody

Eighty-eight percent of the melodic intervals in *Beatus homo* are seconds. Triad outlines appear in measures 6, 7, 8, 11, and 20 (Figure 18.33).

Figure 18.33

Measure 7

Outlined triad

There are no sequences or repetitions in the melodic lines. However, the opening part of each phrase is treated in *imitation*. Much of the imitation is strict, but sometimes modifications of intervals occur (Figure 18.34).

Figure 18.34

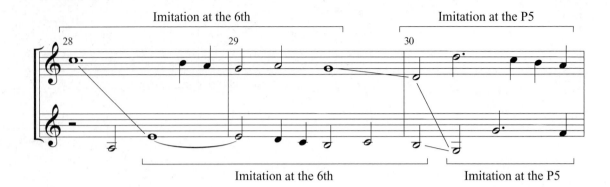

Vertical Intervals

Consonance

Vertical intervals are primarily the consonances: the perfect unison, 5th, and octave, as well as the major and minor 3rds and 6ths. These intervals account for the vast majority of the vertical intervals in the composition.

Dissonance

The composition contains 27 dissonant intervals. The unaccented passing tone appears as the most frequently occurring single dissonance in the composition. The following frequency chart shows the dissonant types represented in the composition:

Unaccented passing tones	20
Accented passing tones	2
7–6 suspensions	1
2–3 suspensions	3
Lower neighbor tone	1

Cadences

Beatus homo contains three clausula vera and two plagal cadences as shown in the following table:

Measure(s)	Ending On	Cadence Type
5	D	Plagal
11–12	D	Clausula vera (with hocket)
16–17	D	Plagal (with hocket)
23–24	F	Clausula vera (with hocket)
34–35	D	Clausula vera

Text Setting

Both melismatic (one syllable of text to two or more notes of music) and syllabic (one syllable of text to one note of music) treatments are found in *Beatus homo,* although melismatic style predominates (Figure 18.35).

Figure 18.35

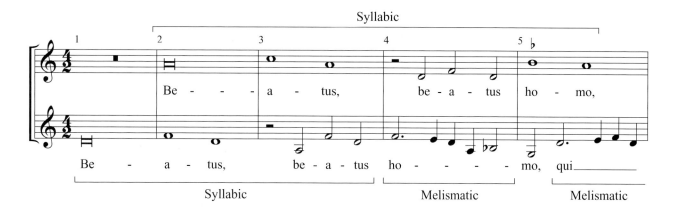

Form

The five phrases of the text create the form of the composition:

Phrase	Text	Measures
1	*Beatus homo* Happy is the man	1–5
2	*Qui invenit sapientiam* Who finds wisdom	5–12
3	*Et qui affluit prudentia* And who is rich in understanding	12–17
4	*Melior est acquisitio ejus* The acquiring of it	17–24
5	*Negotiatione argenti et auri primi et purissimi* Is better than the purchase of silver and the finest and purest gold	24–35

The clausula vera cadences divide the composition into three equal parts: measures 1 to 12, 12 to 24, and 24 to 35. Such symmetry is typical of the Renaissance.

Summary

The polyphonic music of the late Renaissance is rooted in modality and characterized by rhythmically varied melodic lines occurring in imitation. An organized system of vertical consonances and dissonances accompanies sixteenth-century counterpoint with the unaccented passing tone dominating as the most common type of dissonance. In two-voice writing, accented passing tones, lower neighboring tones, the 7–6 and 2–3 suspensions, and the portamento and nota cambiata figures are the only other allowable dissonances.

Compositions with three or more voices also include the 4–3 suspension, the six-five figure, and the consonant 4th.

Cadences in late Renaissance polyphony include the clausula vera, the plagal cadence, and weak interior cadences. Texts were set following a series of conventions, and in turn, formal designs reflect the organization of the text. Each text phrase begins in imitation and each phrase ends with a cadence.

Practice

As you begin your study of the sixteenth-century style, a review of the modes is advised. Chances are that you understand the organization and sound of tonal major and minor scales well, but the modal scales may be less familiar. If you have forgotten the basic construction of the modal scales, review the information provided in volume 1 (see Chapter 2, pages 46–47, and Chapter 8 pages 170–171).

Not only will you need to be able to write and identify the modes, you will also need to be familiar with the subtle differences between the modal and tonal scales. Play and sing the modes. Contrast the similarities and differences between modal and tonal scales by playing the two in succession (see Figure 18.36).

Figure 18.36

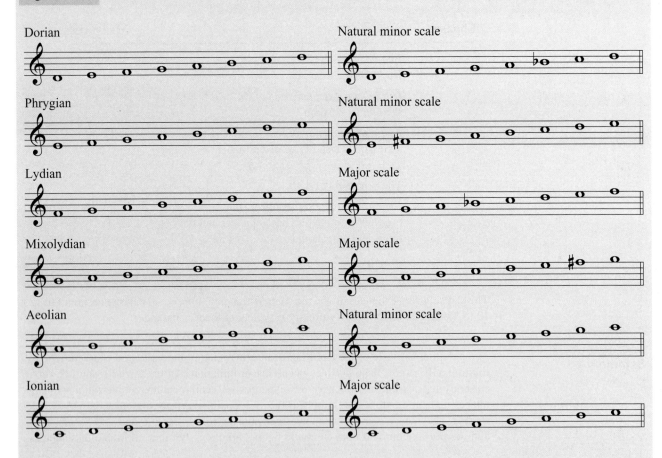

When you are confident that you can identify, write, and hear the modal scales accurately, listen to several examples of two-voice late Renaissance polyphony (motets from the *Cantiones Duarum Vocum* by Lassus are recommended for this type of aural assessment). By ear, attempt to identify the mode or modes occurring in the composition.

Assignment 18.1

Analyze the following two-voice, sixteenth-century motet in the same way as the specimen analysis in this chapter (pages 429–433). Note that the tenor voice contains an octave treble clef, meaning that the pitches are an octave lower than printed.

1. Indicate the harmonic intervals between the two voices.
2. Circle each dissonant number and name it.
3. Mark the beginning pitches of each imitation with a dotted line.
4. Identify and label the cadences.
5. Name the mode of the composition.

Lassus: *Missa ad imitationem moduli Iager (Jäger),* Benedictus. ♪

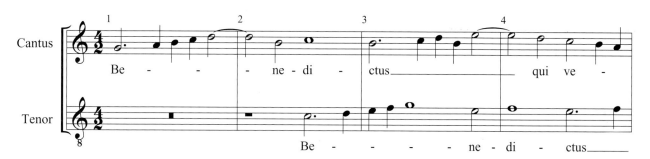

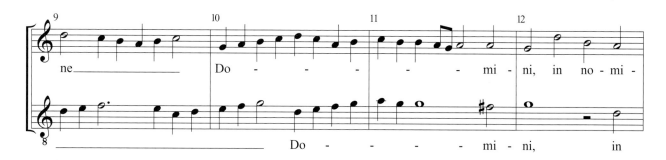

Translation: Blessed is he that cometh in the name of the Lord.

Assignment 18.2

In each exercise that follows, there is at least one error in style. Circle the note or notes that constitute the error, and pencil in a correction.

Suggested Procedure:

1. Analyze the harmonic intervals in each exercise. Adjacent repetitions of the numbers 1, 5, and 8 can reveal unstylistic parallels.
2. Assess the use of dissonance. Check for melodic shapes and rhythmic applications not common to this style.
3. Analyze the melodic intervals in each individual voice. The melodic tritone, as well as the outline of a tritone, are considered errors in this style.
4. Examine the tied notes. Specific note-value pairings are an integral part of this style.

Assignment 18.3 Analyze the following example of three-voice polyphony. Note that the interval between the lowest-sounding tone and each of the upper two voices should be named. Label each dissonance with a circle and name it.

Palestrina: *Missa Jam Christus astra ascenderat,* Credo. ♩♩

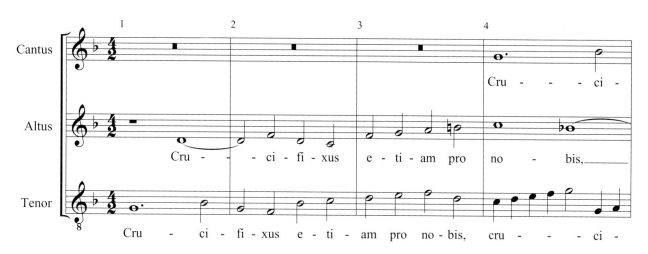

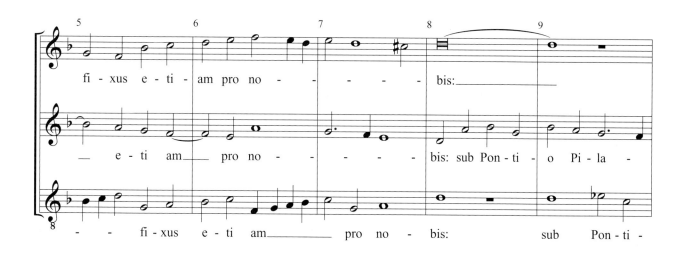

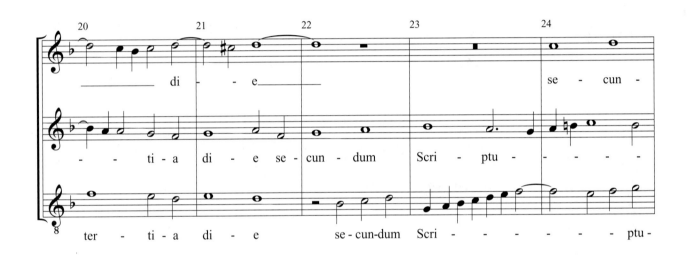

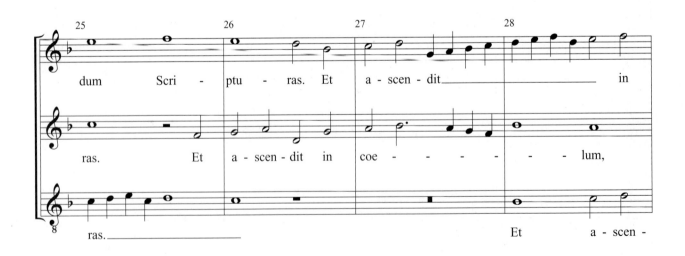

PART C   The Renaissance and Baroque Periods

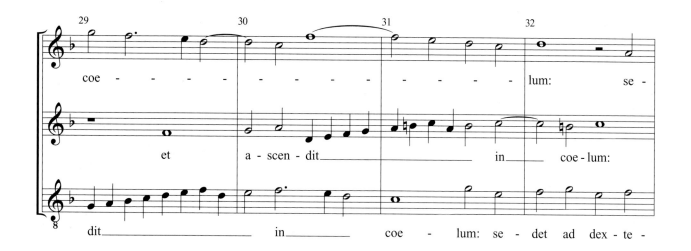

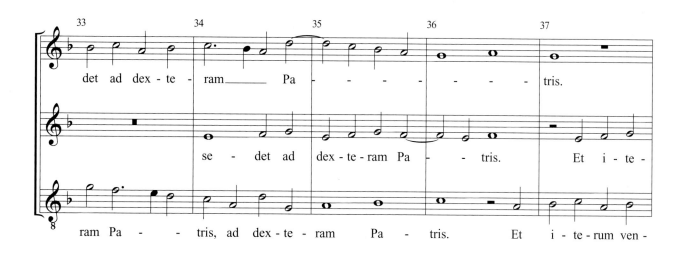

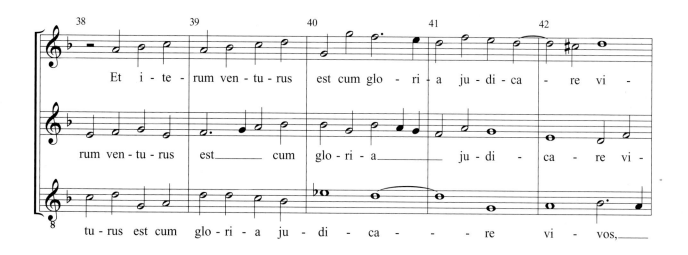

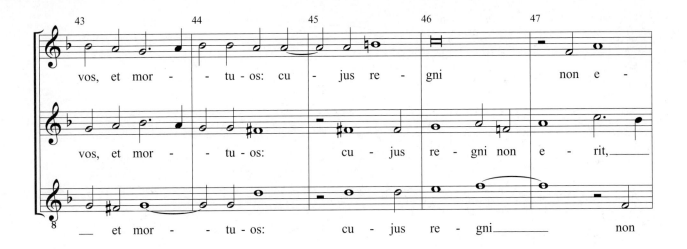

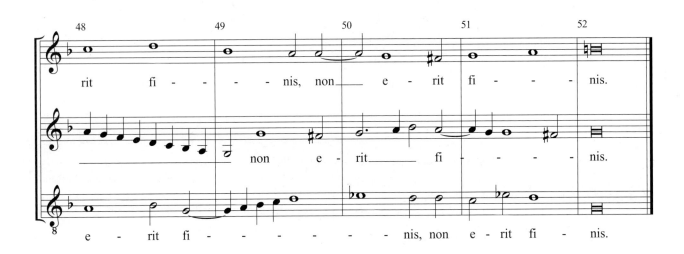

Translation: He was crucified also for us, suffered under Pontius Pilate, and was buried. And the third day He rose again according to the Scriptures; and ascended into heaven. He sitteth at the right hand of the Father; and He shall come again with glory to judge the living and the dead; and His kingdom shall have no end.

CHAPTER 19

Two-Voice Eighteenth-Century Counterpoint

<table>
<tr><td>**Topics**</td><td>Counterpoint
Polyphony
Two-Part Invention
Motive</td><td>Countermotive
Sequence
Sectional Form</td><td>Harmonic Rhythm
Hidden 5ths
Hidden Octaves</td></tr>
</table>

Important Concepts

This chapter covers approximately the years 1675 to 1750. Although the time span is somewhat at odds with this chapter's title, the label is traditional and probably due to the overpowering influence of J. S. Bach (1685–1750).

Counterpoint

Counterpoint literally means "point-against-point," but the term has come to mean the combination of two or more melodic lines. Both terms *polyphony* and *counterpoint* refer to textures that consist of more than one melodic line. The term counterpoint is generally associated with the eighteenth century, and polyphony with the sixteenth.

Two-Part Invention

This chapter is devoted to the study of two-voice counterpoint, especially that of J. S. Bach. A *two-part invention* is a two-voice composition in which a short musical idea, called the *motive,* and its counterpoint, called the *countermotive,* form the basis for the entire work. By far the best-known two-part inventions are the 15 inventions of J. S. Bach.

Bach Inventions

The distinguishing features of two-part inventions by Bach are as follows:

1. Contrapuntal texture is employed throughout.
2. A single motive, unaccompanied, usually occurs first in the composition. See Figure 19.1, Bach: Invention no. 4, measures 1 and 2 (p. 442).
3. After the unaccompanied statement of the motive, it is imitated in the other voice along with the countermotive. This may be seen in Figure 19.1, Bach: Invention no. 4, measures 3 and 4 (p. 442). In this particular invention, the motive and countermotive occur again, this time with the voices switched in mm. 5 and 6 (p. 442).
4. Both the motive and countermotive are based on distinctive melodic, rhythmic, and/or harmonic ideas, and recur repeatedly throughout the composition in both straightforward and developed presentations. Invention motives and countermotives are typically short—from a half measure to two measures long—and may be identified as the primary opening melodic ideas.

Figure 19.1

Bach: Invention no. 4 in D Minor, BWV 775, mm. 1–6.

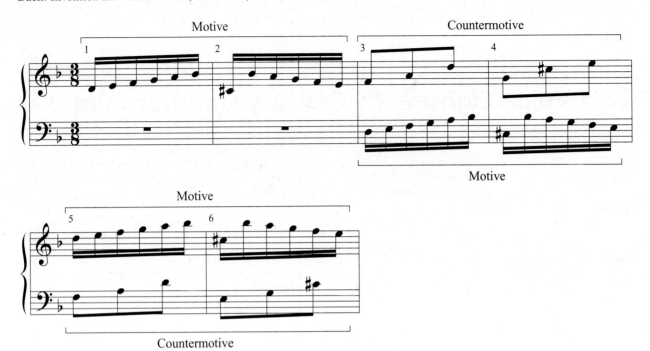

5. After the motive has appeared in both voices (the second statement accompanied by the countermotive), most inventions continue with one or more *sequences*. A sequence is the immediate restatement of a melodic motive or figure at a higher or lower pitch. In Invention no. 4 (Figure 19.1), a sequence occurs in measures 7 to 10. The upper voice is derived from the motive, whereas the lower voice comes from the countermotive. The purpose of sequences is to facilitate a modulation to the key of the next section, usually the dominant or the relative major.

Figure 19.2

Bach: Invention no. 4 in D Minor, BWV 775, mm. 7–10.

6. On completion of the sequence or sequences, the new key is most often established, and a short passage prepares for the cadence. Measures 15 and 16 of Invention no. 4 (Figure 19.3) introduce derived material in the upper voice while sequence B is coming to completion in the lower voice. The cadence in the relative major (F major) is reached in measures 17 to 18. This completes section 1.

Figure 19.3

Bach: Invention no. 4 in D Minor, BWV 775, mm. 15–18.

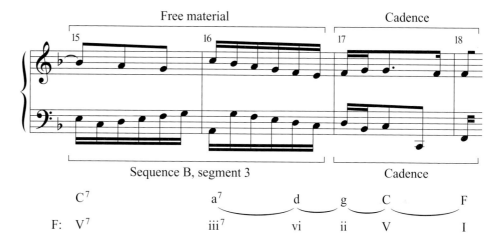

Most inventions are partitioned into subdivisions known as *sections*. Each section concludes with an authentic cadence, thereby making the *sectional form* evident. Bach's inventions are in either two or three sections, and Invention no. 4 (Figure 19.4) contains three sections. For inventions with three sections, the following keys typically occur:

Section	Key(s)
1	Tonic modulating to dominant or relative major
2	Begins in dominant or relative major but features other closely related keys
3	Begins in a closely related key but quickly modulates to reestablish a tonic key

The first sections of inventions are generally more rigidly organized than those that follow. In Invention no. 4, section 2 begins (in F major) with an accompanied motive that is immediately sequenced (sequence C). Note that in sequence C only the lower voice is sequenced. Section 2 has no fewer than three sets of sequences and very little free material. The perfect authentic cadence in measures 37 to 38 signals the end of section 2.

Not all inventions have three sections. However, Invention no. 4 employs section 3 to return the invention to the tonic key (m. 44) and to prepare for the final cadence. This section is organized in a similar manner to that of section 2 but contains only one sequence. Note that the motive and countermotive in measures 44 to 45 are an exact duplicate of measures 5 to 6. The key scheme is an important factor in determining the form of Bach's two-part inventions.

Figure 19.4

Bach: Invention no. 4 in D Minor from *Fifteen Two-Part Inventions*, BWV 775. ♩

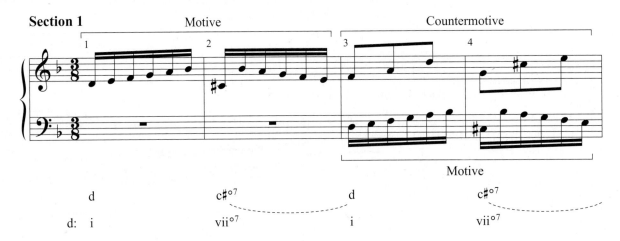

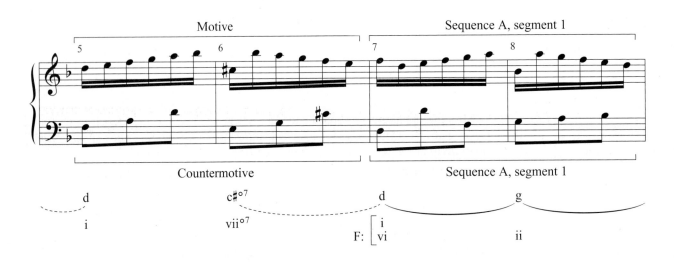

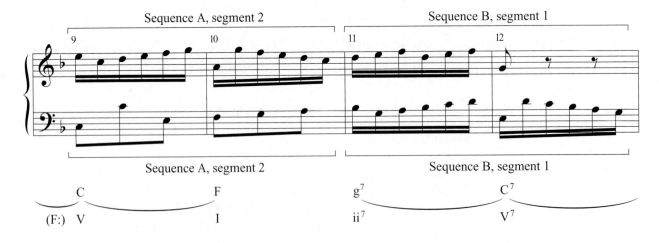

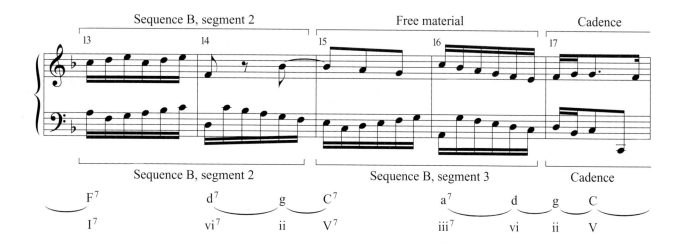

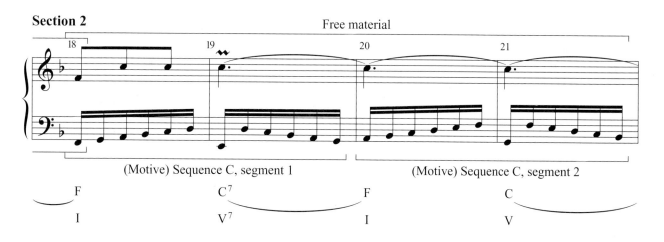

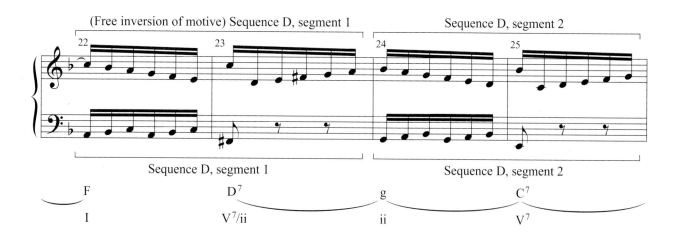

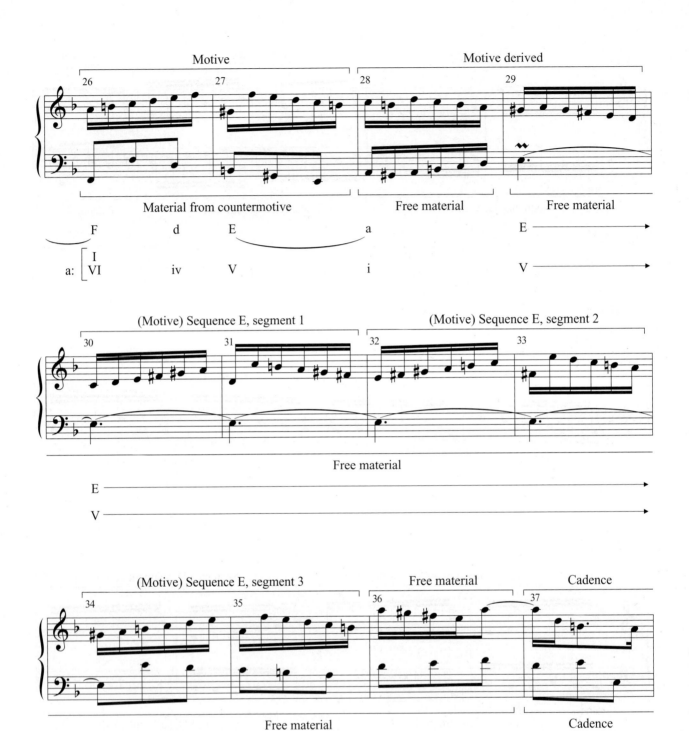

History

Both eighteenth-century counterpoint and sixteenth-century polyphony are considered by many musicians to be among the most distinctively pure and noble of all musical styles. The seeds for the development of eighteenth-century counterpoint reside in sixteenth-century polyphony, and although the two are quite different in many ways, a number of similarities exist. The following chart enumerates the analogous and disparate elements of two-voice writing in both sixteenth- and eighteenth-century writing.

Sixteenth-Century Polyphony	Eighteenth-Century Counterpoint
Similarities	
Successive parallel 5ths, octaves, and unisons are avoided.	Same as in sixteenth century.
Consonances consist of P8ths, P5ths, P1s, M3rds, m3rds, M6ths, and m6ths.	Same consonances as in sixteenth century.
Dissonances are M2nds, m2nds, P4ths, M7ths, m7ths, as well as all diminished and augmented intervals.	Same dissonances as in sixteenth century.
Differences	
Modal (church modes).	Tonal (key oriented).
Vertical sonority based on intervals above the lowest-sounding voice; not constituted as functional harmony.	Based on functional harmony.
Dissonance regulated metrically according to beats and portions thereof.	Dissonance still regulated but not as strictly organized metrically.
Dissonant tones restricted to passing tone, suspension, portamento, nota cambiata, and an occasional neighboring tone.	Nonharmonic devices extend to passing tone, neighboring tone, suspension, anticipation, appoggiatura, escape tone, changing tone, and pedal tone.
Melodic sequences rare.	Melodic sequences an intrinsic part of the style.
Rhythmic figures seldom repeated immediately in the same voice.	Rhythms frequently repeated in the same voice.
No bar lines in original manuscripts.	Bar lines used in original manuscripts.

Applications

Writing Two-Voice Counterpoint

The soprano and bass voices of a four-voice chorale provide a good example of two-voice counterpoint, so you will find the general style quite familiar. However, from the analysis of Invention no. 4, you will remember that the harmony does not change every beat, as so often occurs in chorales. Also, in the chorales, which are most often in quadruple or triple meter, the beat is rarely divided any further than two eighth notes. Instrumental two-voice writing of this period tends to be more florid and less predictable in regard to *harmonic rhythm*. Invention no. 4 maintains a fairly steady harmonic rhythm of one chord per measure, but in no. 10 the harmonic rhythm is quite variable.

To ensure a smooth transition from chorales to instrumental two-voice writing, some guidance is offered to help you avoid common pitfalls.

Harmonic Progression

No instrumental two-voice writing will be successful without a clearly defined basis in functional harmony. Before you begin to write counterpoint, plan the cadences and other chord progressions carefully, making sure they include a sufficient number of circle progressions to provide the necessary forward motion.

Acceptable chord progressions:

I V^6 I^6 ii^6 V   I

Unacceptable chord progressions (no circle progressions and no cadence):

I ii^6 vi iii^6 vi   I

Parallel Perfect Intervals

As in chorale writing, parallel perfect, as well as unequal 5ths, octaves, and unisons, are to be avoided. In two-voice writing you must be even more vigilant concerning these parallels because both voices are exposed (no inner voices). In harmony that sometimes changes only once per measure, it is very easy to overlook such parallels. Some situations to avoid regarding parallels are the following:

1. Direct parallel perfect intervals are not acceptable (Figure 19.5a).
2. Strong accents with intervening counterpoint often suggest parallel perfect intervals and should be avoided (Figure 19.5b).
3. Nonharmonic tones cannot be used to avoid parallel perfect intervals (Figure 19.5c).
4. Even perfect-to-diminished or diminished-to-perfect 5ths are prohibited in two-voice writing (Figure 19.5d).

Figure 19.5

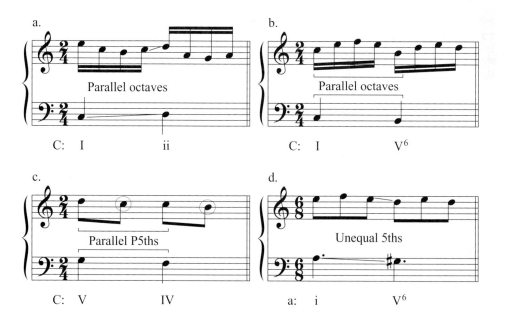

Hidden 5ths and *hidden octaves* (also known as direct 5ths and octaves) occur when the two voices move in similar motion to form a P5th or P8th. Hidden 5ths and octaves are to be avoided when both voices skip to the perfect interval but are permissible if the upper voice moves by step (see Figure 19.6).

Figure 19.6

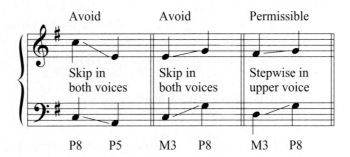

Avoid   Avoid   Permissible

Skip in both voices   Skip in both voices   Stepwise in upper voice

P8   P5   M3   P8   M3   P8

Nonharmonic Tones

With a few exceptions, the nonharmonic tones available in chorale harmonizations are also found in two-voice counterpoint.

Nonharmonic tones to be included in two-voice counterpoint:

Unaccented passing tones
Unaccented neighboring tones
Anticipations (at cadences)
Changing tones
Retardations (sparingly)
Accented passing tones
Accented neighboring tones
7–6, 4–3, and 2–3 suspension
Pedal tones (sparingly)

Nonharmonic tones to avoid in two-voice counterpoint:

The 2–1 and 9–8 suspensions
The appoggiatura

Doublings

As in chorale harmonizations, avoid doubling the 7th scale degree and altered tones.

Harmonic Intervals

Of the harmonic intervals available in two-voice writing, 3rds and 6ths (both major and minor) occur with great frequency. Perfect octaves, 5ths, and unisons, on the other hand, are used sparingly because of their lack of sonority. In the Bach Invention no. 4 (Figure 19.4), harmonic 3rds and 6ths outnumber perfect intervals by nearly 10 to 1. Except for cadence points, try to relegate P8ths, P5ths, and P1s to weak beats or weak portions of beats.

Restrictions on Parallel 3rds and 6ths

Too many successive 3rds or 6ths tend to negate independence of line. For assignments in this chapter, avoid writing more than four successive 3rds or 6ths. Figure 19.7 shows an upper-voice melody with two different bass lines.

Figure 19.7

Avoid too many successive 3rds.

3 3 3 3 3 3 3 3 3 3 3 3

A: IV   ii

The same passage by Bach:

Bach: Gigue from English Suite no. 1 in A Major, BWV 806, m. 38.

A: IV   ii

| Melodic Intervals to Avoid | Avoid melodic augmented 4ths, diminished 5ths, and augmented 2nds, unless the intervals outline the prevailing harmony. |

General Suggestions

Although not strict rules, the following are some considerations you should keep in mind while writing.

Melodic Contour

When you are writing, think of the melodic line (especially the upper voice) that extends for an entire section. Try to give your line a definite shape (often a single ascent and descent) that leads logically to the cadence.

Rhythm

There are no specific rules concerning rhythm, but it is not good practice to introduce sudden changes in both voices at the same time. Writing a two-voice counterpoint with sixteenth-note motion in all measures and then suddenly changing to half- and quarter-note values in both voices is a blatant example of what not to do. Usually the two melodic lines exchange rhythmic activity.

Analysis

When you finish a two-voice counterpoint assignment, analyze it immediately. Circle and name nonharmonic tones, indicate the harmonic rhythm, and provide a Roman numeral analysis. If you find your counterpoint impossible to analyze, you will know there are problems with it.

Play Your Assignment

Either play your assignment or get another class member to play it for you. Otherwise, unless you have unusually good tonal memory, you will not know what you have written. Playing your assignment as you write it will provide insights enabling you to improve its quality. Computer notation programs with MIDI output can be a great help if your keyboard skills are not well developed.

Fresh Ideas

If you get stuck and are unable to proceed, listen to or play parts of either of the two-part inventions presented in this chapter. Often, playing two-voice counterpoint by Bach will bring forth ideas.

Summary

The two-part inventions by J. S. Bach reflect the stylistic practices typical of eighteenth-century counterpoint. Like the polyphony of the sixteenth century, the inventions include extensive imitation between the voices. In contrast to the sixteenth-century style, the inventions are based on the functional harmony of tonality rather than modality.

Each invention begins with a short melodic figure known as the motive, which is immediately followed by a contrasting figure called the countermotive. The melodic, rhythmic, and harmonic ideas presented in the beginning of the invention recur throughout the work.

Following the initial motive and countermotive presentations, sequences are used to facilitate modulation to a closely related key (usually the dominant or the relative major). This modulation leads typically to a cadence ending the first formal section.

The two-part inventions are divided into either two or three formal sections. Series of sequences usually appear in both second and third sections. Each section of an invention typically ends with an authentic cadence.

| Practice | Become familiar with J. S. Bach's two-part inventions through aural analysis. All the *Fifteen Two-Part Inventions,* BWV 772–786, are suitable for aural assessment and present multiple opportunities for various types of analysis. Listen to both live performances and recordings of these works to hear the elements of the contrapuntal style. With each listening, attempt to identify one or more of the following: |

1. the motive
2. the countermotive
3. imitation
4. sequences
5. cadences
6. sections
7. tonal centers

After you have made an aural analysis of an invention, check a published score to see if your appraisals reflect the analytical style presented in this chapter. Scores for the two-part inventions are readily available online and at your local library.

Assignment 19.1   Following is two-part Invention no. 8 in F Major by J. S. Bach. Using the model analysis of Invention no. 4 (Figure 19.4) as a guide, prepare the same kind of analysis for Invention no. 8.

Bach: Invention no. 8 in F Major from *Fifteen Two-Part Inventions*, BWV 779. ♪

Assignment 19.2

The following composition contains errors, all of which are violations of guidelines given in this chapter. Find each error and enter it in the table that follows.

Suggested Procedure:

1. Analyze the harmonic intervals in each exercise.
    a. Look for adjacent repetitions of the numbers 1, 5, and 8. Recurrences of these numbers can alert you to unstylistic parallels.
    b. Observe the type of melodic motion used to approach the numbers 5 and 8. Similar motion to these intervals produces hidden 5ths and hidden octaves.
    c. Study the intervals occurring on beat 1 of each measure. Be sure the intervals fit within the context of this compositional style.
    d. Check for excessive use of same intervals and perfect intervals in succession.
2. Examine the dissonant intervals in your analysis to see if they correspond with the nonharmonic tone types appropriate to the composition style.
3. Determine the leading tone of the composition. Scrutinize each presentation of the leading tone to see if it has been doubled vertically in an unstylistic manner.
4. Analyze the melodic intervals in each individual voice. Check for melodic augmented 2nds, augmented 4ths, and diminished 5ths.

Error at letter(s)   **Describe error**

———— ————————————————————————————————————

———— ————————————————————————————————————

———— ————————————————————————————————————

———— ————————————————————————————————————

———— ————————————————————————————————————

———— ————————————————————————————————————

———— ————————————————————————————————————

Assignment 19.3   Each of the examples is the lower voice of a two-voice contrapuntal composition. Copy the given bass line on a separate sheet of score paper and compose an upper voice for each.

In number 1 the harmonic rhythm and chord symbols are given, but in numbers 2, 3, and 4 you must figure out the harmony and harmonic rhythm yourself.

Do not change the given bass line.

Numbers 1 and 2:
a. Write a melody composed mostly of quarter-note values.
b. Write a melody composed mostly of eighth-note values.
c. Write a melody composed of whatever note values you consider appropriate.

Number 3:
a. Write a melody composed mostly of dotted quarter notes.
b. Write a melody containing a mixture of quarter- and eighth-note values.
c. Write a melody containing whatever note values you consider appropriate.

Number 4:
a. Write a melody containing a mixture of half and whole notes.
b. Write a melody containing whatever note values you consider to be appropriate for this particular bass line.

Assignment 19.4   Each of the examples is the upper voice of a two-voice counterpoint composition. Copy the given upper line on a separate sheet of score paper and compose a lower voice for each.

Before you start writing, determine the harmony and harmonic rhythm you intend to follow.

Do not change the given notes.

Numbers 1 and 2:
a. Compose a bass line made up of half-, quarter-, and eighth-note values.
b. Compose a bass line using whatever values you consider appropriate.

Numbers 3, 4, and 5:
a. Compose a bass line made up of quarter- and eighth-note values.
b. Compose a bass line using whatever values you consider appropriate.

Assignment 19.5   Write a two-part invention.

1. Your instructor will tell you whether to write an entire invention or only a section.
2. Use one of the motives provided or make up your own.

Motive no. 1

Motive no. 2

Motive no. 3

3. Before you start to put your invention together, test out several countermotives. Make sure your countermotive is different enough from the motive to be easily identified yet simple enough to avoid problems later. Also, try out your countermotive both above and below the motive, because there will be many times in the invention when the voices may be reversed. Any P5ths (consonant) in the original counterpoint will become P4ths (dissonant) in the inverted version. If you treat P5ths in the original counterpoint as if they were dissonant, the inversion will not be a problem.
4. Use the following form, one of the two-part inventions printed in this text, or another invention supplied by your instructor as a model.

Section	Number of measures	Content
First section	2	Motive alone in upper voice.
	2	Motive in lower voice with countermotive above.
	2–3	Sequence (derived from motive or countermotive) of two or three segments that do not modulate.
	2–3	Sequence (derived from motive or countermotive) that modulates to the dominant or relative major.
	1	Dominant preparation of the new key.
Second section	2	Motive alone in lower voice and in the new key.
	2	Motive in upper voice accompanied by countermotive in the lower voice (new key).
	2	Sequence (derived from motive or countermotive) of two or three segments leading to a third key.
	2	Motive in third key accompanied by countermotive.
	2–3	Sequence (derived from motive or countermotive) of two or three segments leading back to original key.
	1	Dominant preparation of the original key.
Third section	2	Motive accompanied by countermotive in original key.
	2–4	Material derived from either motive or countermotive ending in a deceptive cadence in the original key.
	2–4	Material derived from either motive or countermotive ending in an authentic cadence in the original key.
	26–33 total measures	

5. Arrange the invention for two instruments and perform it in class.

CHAPTER 20

The Fugue

Important Concepts

A *fugue* is a contrapuntal composition in two or more voices built on a *subject* (short melody) that is stated in all voices and repeated throughout the composition. In addition to the broad general contrapuntal design, certain formal characteristics are well established.

Exposition

The first section is called the *exposition,* which is the most fully structured part of the fugue. The exposition serves to introduce the primary melodic materials of the fugue, as well as the supporting contrapuntal elements. In the exposition, the individual voices make their entrances, one at a time, to reveal these thematic elements.

Subject

The basis of the entire fugue is the subject. Subjects are short melodies that can range anywhere from two notes to eight measures in length, but most subjects are one to three measures long. The fugue opens with the subject alone (unaccompanied).

Answer

When the subject is completed, it is imitated in another voice, usually at the P5th above or P4th below. This imitation is known as the *answer.*

If the answer is a literal (exact) imitation of the subject, it is called a *real answer.* If the answer is slightly modified, it is a *tonal answer.* Tonal answers occur for a variety of reasons, but two basic reasons are to create a strong tonic–dominant relationship in the exposition and to take care of situations where the subject modulates. A strong tonic–dominant relationship at the beginning of the subject is often answered as dominant–tonic in the answer (Figure 20.1).

Figure 20.1

Bach: Fugue no. 8 in D-sharp Minor from *The Well-Tempered Clavier,* Book I, BWV 853, mm. 1–3.

A subject that modulates usually takes a tonal answer to prevent the fugue from spiraling out of the closely related key range. Figure 20.2a shows a *modulating subject.* If a real answer were used, it would modulate to a key that is outside the orbit of closely related keys (Figure 20.2b). Instead, Bach modifies the end of the answer to return to the tonic key (Figure 20.2c).

Figure 20.2

Bach: Organ Fugue in C Minor, BWV 574, mm. 1–4.

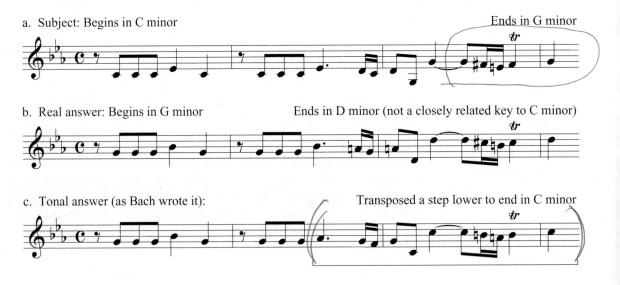

Countersubject

A *countersubject* is the continuation of counterpoint in the voice that began with the subject (see Figure 20.10, mm. 3–4). The countersubject occurs as counterpoint against the answer—not the subject. This is a typical beginning of a fugue:

Soprano voice:		Answer
Alto voice:	Subject	**Countersubject**

Occasionally a second countersubject is introduced, usually in the exposition.

Invertible Counterpoint

Because a countersubject might be used both above and below an answer, composers of the period constructed countersubjects that are *invertible*. These invertible countersubjects were devised to avoid unstylistic dissonances that can occur when a countersubject appears in a different voice. In *inversion at the octave*, all harmonic P5ths require special treatment because when inverted, the P5th becomes a P4th—a dissonance in this style. To find out if a countersubject is invertible, play the first entrance of the answer and countersubject but place the upper voice an octave or two lower. If the P4ths produced by the inversion are properly treated as dissonances, then the countersubject is invertible. Figure 20.3 shows an example of a countersubject that is in invertible counterpoint.

Figure 20.3

Bach: Fugue no. 2 in C Minor from *The Well-Tempered Clavier,* Book I, BWV 847, mm. 7–8.

Bach: Fugue no. 2 in C Minor from *The Well-Tempered Clavier,* Book I, BWV 847, mm. 20–21.

Link

Sometimes a fugue subject ends on a pitch that does not connect conveniently to the countersubject. To make the junction smooth, composers added some extra notes known as a *link*. Links are quite short, occasionally only a few notes. Not all fugues contain a link.

Tenor voice:			Answer
Bass voice:	Subject	**Link**	Countersubject

Bridge

A *bridge* is a short passage at the end of the first entrance of the answer and the beginning of the second entrance of the subject. Its purpose is to modulate back to the tonic key (subject) from the answer (which is in the dominant key). Not all fugues include a bridge.

Soprano:				Subject
Alto:		Answer	**Bridge**	Countersubject
Bass:	Subject	Countersubject	**Bridge**	Free material

Although the design of the exposition differs from fugue to fugue, one simple pattern is shown here:

Soprano	Subject	Countersubject	Free material	Free material
Alto		Answer	Countersubject	Free material
Tenor			Subject	Countersubject
Bass				Answer

Exposition Alternatives

Possible alternative designs are as follows:

1. The order of entrances may be subject–answer–answer–subject.
2. Voices may be introduced in almost any order, such as tenor–alto–soprano–bass, and the number of voices in a fugue varies. A large number contain only three voices.
3. The countersubject does not always appear three times as shown in the chart, and some fugues contain more than one countersubject.
4. Both links and bridges have been omitted from the chart in the interest of simplicity.

Episodes and Entries

The second section of the fugue consists of a series of *episodes* and *entries*. This section is sometimes referred to as the development of the fugue.

Characteristics of an Episode

1. There are no complete statements of subject or answer in any voice during an episode.
2. Episodes frequently contain sequences.
3. Episodes are usually short (a few beats to four measures).

Characteristics of an Entry

1. There are one or more complete statements of subject and/or answer in an entry.
2. If there are multiple statements, they are linked together, occurring more or less continuously, sometimes looking very much like complete expositions.

As you can see from this description, the most important distinction between an episode and an entry is the presence of the subject or answer in entries.

Purpose of Episodes

1. To lead smoothly from one entry of the subject to another.
2. To effect modulations to new keys. A typical second section of a fugue might appear as follows:

End of exposition:	Episode	Subject/answer	Episode	Subject/answer (etc.)
Keys: F major	Modulation	D minor	Modulation	G minor (etc.)

The introduction of keys beyond tonic and dominant occurs in almost all second sections. Almost any of the closely related keys is likely to appear. Measures 17 and 18 of Fugue no. 2 in C Minor, printed in its entirety in Figure 20.10, contain a typical episode (Figure 20.4).

Figure 20.4

Bach: Fugue no. 2 in C Minor from *The Well-Tempered Clavier,* Book I, BWV 847, mm. 17–20.

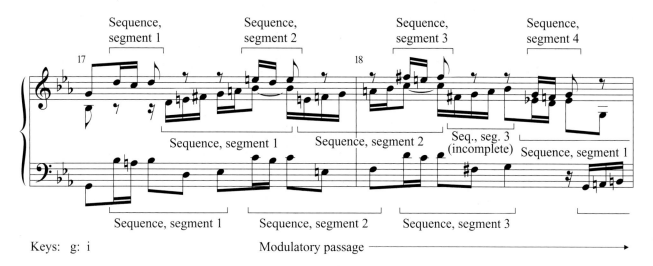

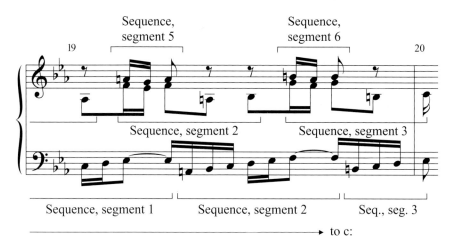

Variants of Subjects and Answers in an Entry	Subjects and answers are treated in a less structured manner after the exposition, as discussed in the following variants.
Stretto	*Stretto* is the overlapping of subjects or answers. That is, a subject enters in one voice and, before it is completed, another subject enters in a different voice (Figure 20.5).

Figure 20.5

Bach: Fugue no. 1 in C Major from *The Well-Tempered Clavier,* Book I, BWV 846, mm. 21–23.

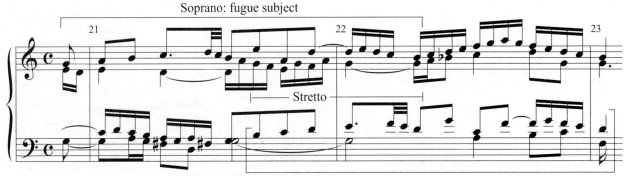

Augmentation

Augmentation in eighteenth-century fugal writing refers to the doubling or tripling of note values. If a certain subject consisted entirely of quarter-note values, that subject might occur later with half-note values. Figure 20.6 shows the fugue subject (alto voice) and its augmentation (bass voice).

Figure 20.6

Bach: Fugue no. 8 in D-sharp Minor from *The Well-Tempered Clavier,* Book I, BWV 853, mm. 62–66.

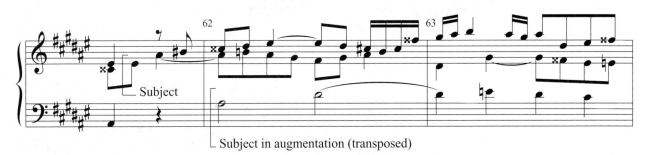

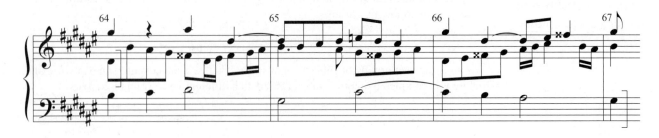

Diminution

Diminution is the reverse of augmentation—note values are reduced. Figure 20.7 shows four statements of a fugue subject in diminution. Notice the two examples of stretto, one in measure 27 and one in measures 28 to 29.

Figure 20.7

Bach: Fugue no. 9 in E Major from *The Well-Tempered Clavier,* Book II, BWV 878, mm. 1–2.

Bach: Fugue no. 9 in E Major from *The Well-Tempered Clavier,* Book II, BWV 878, mm. 27–29.

Retrograde

If a melody is played backward, it is called a *retrograde* (also *cancrizan*—from "crab"). This contrapuntal device is more often found in canons than in fugues. Figure 20.8, an example of a retrograde canon (a melody played forward and backward at the same time), is from Bach's *Musical Offering.* The first four measures of the solution are included on page 466.

Figure 20.8

Bach: Retrograde Canon from *Musikalisches Opfer* (Musical Offering), BWV 1079.

Solution (first four measures only)

Melodic Inversion

This is a device, occurring more often in canons than in fugues, that reverses the direction of the melody. Thus, upward motion becomes downward, and downward becomes upward. Figure 20.9, an excerpt from the *Clavier-Übung*, illustrates melodic inversion. The interval-by-interval change of direction (upper voice) produces a change of mode (F major to F minor).

Figure 20.9

Bach: Duet no. 2 in F Major from *Clavier-Übung,* Part III, BWV 803, mm. 1–4, 74–77.

Theme

Same theme in inversion (treble clef)

Final Part of a Fugue

Near the end of the fugue is a return to the tonic key and usually a restatement of the subject. This section is sometimes referred to as the recapitulation of the fugue. A fugue often closes with a short section called a *coda,* which emphasizes the tonic key.

History

Unquestionably, the most famous of Bach's works for the clavier is the set of preludes and fugues titled *The Well-Tempered Clavier* (completed circa 1742). *Clavier* is a broad term meaning "keyboard," so these compositions were written to be played on any keyboard instrument, except the organ. At the time of Bach (1685–1750), such instruments included the clavichord, the popular harpsichord, and possibly an occasional pianoforte (piano), invented in 1709. Today, because of large concert halls and the ubiquitous piano, *The Well-Tempered Clavier* is very often performed on that instrument. Both the harpsichord and the clavichord can muster only a fraction of the volume possible on a piano.

The complete work is divided into two sections: Book I and Book II. Each book contains a prelude and fugue in each of the 12 possible major and minor keys—a total of 24 preludes and fugues in each book.

Bach's purpose in preparing the work was, in part, to demonstrate the flexibility of a tuning system approaching equal temperament, which at the time was considered experimental. Gradually, the new system gained a measure of acceptance over the more limited mean-tone system (see volume 1), although universal endorsement did not take place until the nineteenth century.

Applications

The following fugue from *The Well-Tempered Clavier* is analyzed according to the descriptions made earlier in this chapter (Figure 20.10).

Figure 20.10

Bach: Fugue no. 2 in C Minor from *The Well-Tempered Clavier,* Book I, BWV 847.

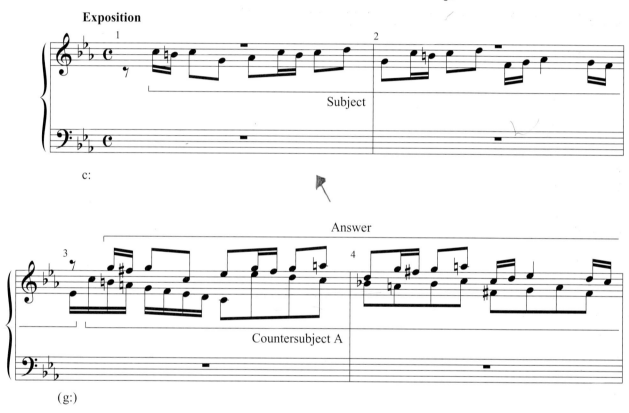

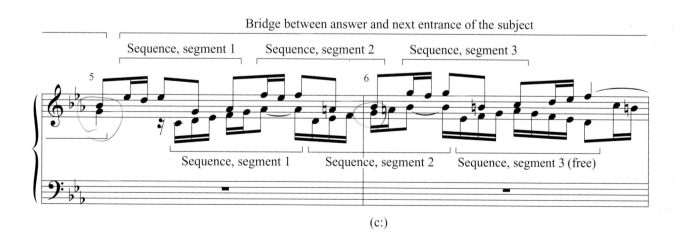

Countersubject A

Countersubject B

Subject

End of exposition | Episodes and entries

Episode 1   Sequence, segment 1   Sequence, segment 2

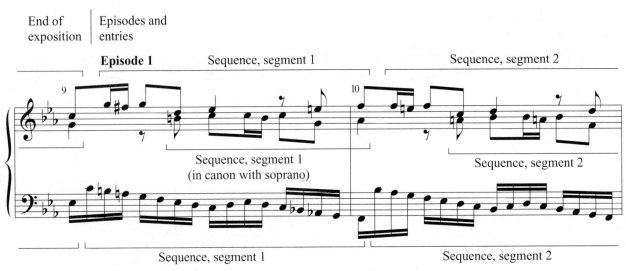

Sequence, segment 1 (in canon with soprano)   Sequence, segment 2

Sequence, segment 1   Sequence, segment 2

Modulating (to E♭:)

Entry 1   Subject

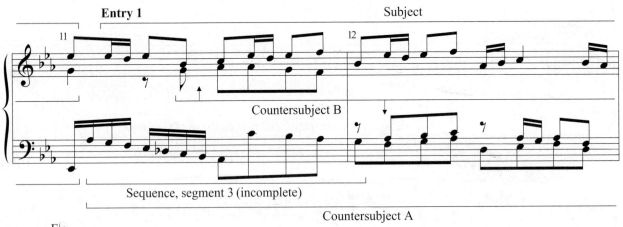

Countersubject B

Sequence, segment 3 (incomplete)

Countersubject A

E♭:

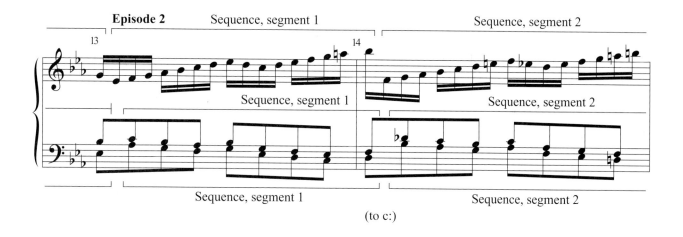

Episode 2

Sequence, segment 1 — Sequence, segment 2

Sequence, segment 1 — Sequence, segment 2

Sequence, segment 1 — Sequence, segment 2

(to c:)

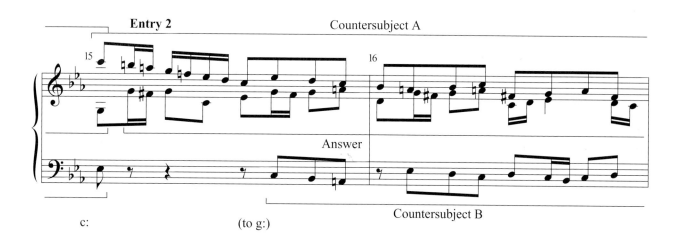

Entry 2 — Countersubject A

Answer

Countersubject B

c: — (to g:)

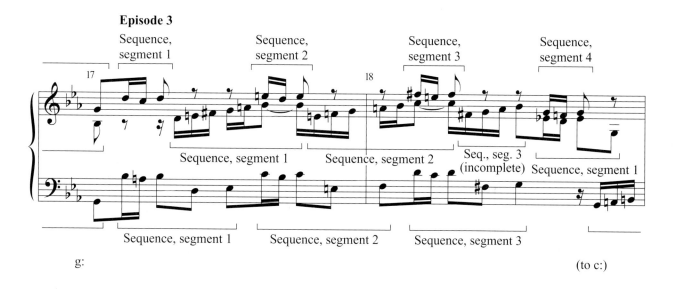

Episode 3

Sequence, segment 1 — Sequence, segment 2 — Sequence, segment 3 — Sequence, segment 4

Sequence, segment 1 — Sequence, segment 2 — Seq., seg. 3 (incomplete) — Sequence, segment 1

Sequence, segment 1 — Sequence, segment 2 — Sequence, segment 3

g: — (to c:)

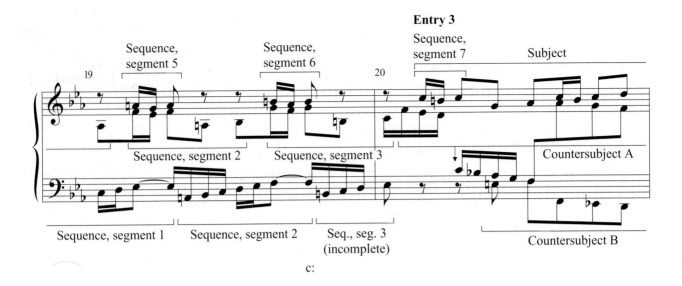

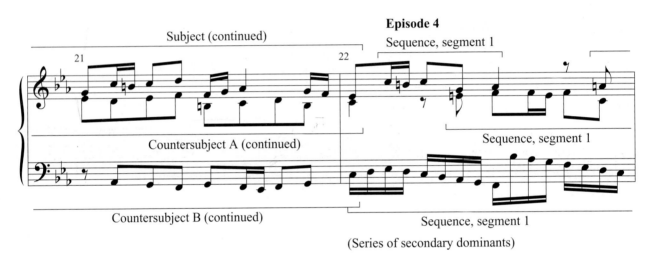

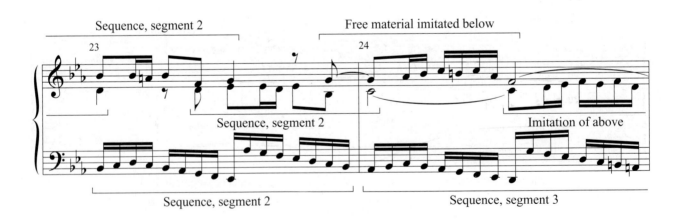

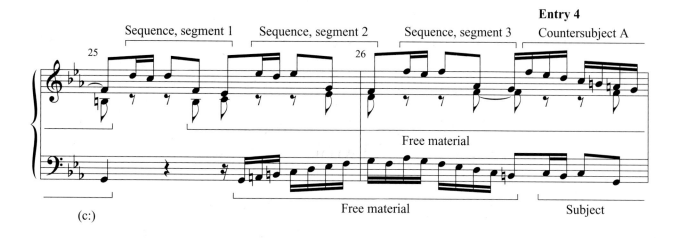

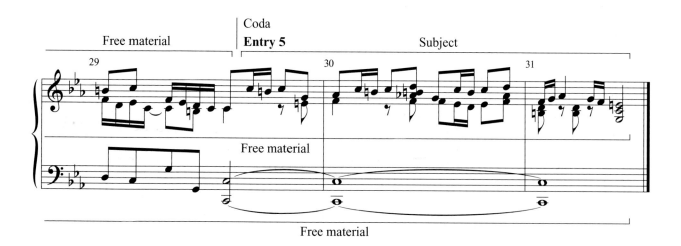

CHAPTER 20   The Fugue   **471**

Form

The following outline diagram illustrates the form of Fugue no. 2 in C Minor:

Exposition ---|

                                                        Bridge---------------|

Upper voice:		Answer in G minor	Sequence (sub.)	Countersubject A
Middle voice:	Subject in C minor	Countersubject A	Sequence (CS A inv.)	Countersubject B
Lower voice:				Subject in C minor
Measures:	1 2	3 4	5 6	7 8

Episodes and entries---

	Episode 1	Entry 1	Episode 2	Entry 2
Upper voice:	Sequence (sub.)	Sub. in E-flat major	Seq. (mm.10–11 inv.)	Countersubject A
Middle voice:	Sequence (sub.)	Countersubject B	Sequence (CS B)	Answer in G minor
Lower voice:	Sequence (free)	Countersubject A	Sequence (CS B)	Countersubject B
Measures:	9 10	11 12	13 14	15 16

Episodes and entries---

	Episode 3	Entry 3	Episode 4
Upper voice:	Sequence (sub.)	Subject in C minor	Sequence (sub.)
Middle voice:	Sequence (from sub.)	Countersubject A	Sequence (sub.)
Lower voice:	Sequence (sub.)	Countersubject B	Sequence (see mm. 9–10)
Measures:	17 18 19	20 21	22 23 24

Episodes and entries------------------------------------- **Coda**-------------------|

	Entry 4	Eps. 5	Entry 5
Upper voice:	Countersubject A	Free mat.	Subject in C minor
Middle voice:	Countersubject B	Free mat.	Chordal expansion
Lower voice:	Subject in C minor	Free mat.	Tonic pedal point
Measures:	25 26 27 28	29 30	31

Subject	The subject, stated in the first two measures, is the basis of the entire composition (Figure 20.11).

Figure 20.11

The subject

Answer	The answer, derived from the subject, is tonal rather than real. The subject and answer are placed together in Figure 20.12 to show the slight alteration of the answer.

Figure 20.12

Countersubject	This fugue has two countersubjects that play principal roles, accompanying either the subject or the answer throughout (Figure 20.13).

Figure 20.13

Countersubject A

Countersubject B

Episodes	The fugue includes five episodes. The episodes contain no complete subjects or answers, but all are based on fragments or motives therefrom. Sequences abound in episodes:

Episode Measures	Sequences	Modulating
9–11	Yes	C minor to E-flat major
13–14	Yes	E-flat major to C minor
17–20	Yes	G minor to C minor
22–26	Yes	No
28–29	No	No

Melodic Inversion

The melody in the lowest voice (mm. 9–10) appears again in the upper voice (mm. 13–14) in melodic inversion (Figure 20.14).

Figure 20.14

This bass voice appears in measures 9 and 10

This soprano voice is the above bass voice in melodic inversion

Miscellaneous Imitation

In addition to the imitation that is a part of the formal design of the fugue are a number of imitations in the episodes. One example is in measures 9 and 10, where the imitation is in sequences (Figure 20.15).

Figure 20.15

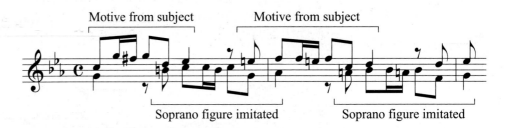

Motive from subject   Motive from subject

Soprano figure imitated   Soprano figure imitated

Summary

The fugue is a contrapuntal composition of two or more voices based on a short melody called the subject. Fugues open with an unaccompanied statement of the subject, followed by individual entrances of the other voices in imitation. When the imitation occurs a P5th above or P4th below the subject, the statement is called the answer. Answers are either real (an exact transposition) or tonal (slightly modified). After a subject has been stated, the same voice often continues as a countersubject.

The formal divisions of fugues are closely aligned with the subject. The first section, the exposition, serves to introduce the primary melodic materials. Following the exposition, alternating sections of episodes and entries serve to develop ideas presented in the exposition. Although the episodes typically do not include full statements of the subject, entries often have multiple statements. A variety of compositional techniques, including stretto, augmentation, diminution, retrograde, and melodic inversion, appear in the entries. Fugues often conclude with a recapitulation of the primary materials.

Practice

J. S. Bach's *The Well-Tempered Clavier,* BWV 846–893, includes 48 fugues in 24 keys appropriate for aural assessment. Listen to as many of these fugues as possible, and identify the subject, answer, and countersubject statements in each fugue. When you are familiar with each fugue's subject, attempt to determine the exposition, episode, and entry sections.

Assignment 20.1

Ten fugue subjects follow. Determine whether each should have a real or a tonal answer, and write the type of answer in the blank provided. Remember that tonal answers are usually given to subjects that

a. Begin on the dominant tone
b. Begin on the tonic and move to the dominant immediately
c. Modulate

1. B.

2.

3.

4.

5.

6.

7.

8.

9.

10.

The two E's
are Episodes and
Entries

1. Select one of the subjects that requires a real answer and write a countersubject. Remember that the countersubject accompanies the answer, not the subject.
2. With this same subject, write a fugue exposition. Use the Bach fugue analyzed in this chapter as a general guide. Remember, however, that different subjects require different treatment, so do not expect to handle your exposition exactly as Bach did.
3. When the exposition is completed, write the remainder of the fugue.
4. Perform the fugue in class. Ask the class members to identify the subject and countersubject, the type of answer, the episodes and entries of the fugue, and other compositional devices that might be present.

Assignment 20.2   This is the sixteenth fugue in the first book of *The Well-Tempered Clavier* by J. S. Bach.

1. Make a complete analysis of the fugue following the same procedures as applied to Fugue no. 2 earlier in this chapter.
2. Arrange the fugue for four instruments and perform it in class.

Bach: Fugue no. 16 in G Minor from *The Well-Tempered Clavier,* Book I, BWV 861.

Chromatic Harmony

This section continues the investigation of chromatic harmony, including harmony that borrows chords from both major and minor modes as well as chords of more distant origin (the Neapolitan 6th and the augmented 6th chords). These harmonic materials were developed during the baroque period and become more common in the classical and romantic periods.

Macro Analysis

Macro analysis is, in many respects, no different from the harmonic analysis found in most music theory textbooks. All tonal music from the beginning of the baroque to the middle of the romantic period contains a preponderance of circle-of-fifth progressions. An example of the circle flow is shown on the next page (circle progressions are shown by the use of slurs). Macro analysis emphasizes the forward movement of a composition through studying and diagnosing the circle patterns. In this example, as is typical of music of this period, every chord is either the beginning or the ending of a circle progression.

To prepare a macro analysis, do the following:

1. Extract the roots of chords and place the chord symbol below the staves. In macro analysis, the chord symbol reflects both the root and the quality of the chord (see volume 1 and Appendix B).

2. Place slurs wherever a circle progression is found. A circle progression occurs between chords whose roots are in a descending 5th or an ascending 4th relationship. In the example on the next page, the first circle progression occurs between $E\flat^7$ and $A\flat$ in measure 9. The opening progression, $A\flat$ to $E\flat^7$ (mm. 8–9), is not a circle progression because the roots of these two chords are an ascending 5th or a descending 4th apart.

3. Place dotted slurs between diminished triads or diminished 7th chords whose roots resolve up a half step. Examples: $b°$ to C, $b^{ø7}$ to C, $b°$ to c, $b°^7$ to c, or $b°^7$ to C. Remember that vii°, vii°7, and vii^{ø7} are considered weaker dominants, thus the dotted slur.

4. Sometimes you can show circle relationships (with a slur) where the chords are not adjacent. The $E\flat$ (m. 13) and the $A\flat^7$ (m. 16) connected by a slur emphasizes that a strong, although not adjacent, relationship exists between the two chords. This helps to indicate the musical inclination toward the target chord in measure 17. A target chord occurs at the end of a circle series. Often, a longer, uninterrupted circle series creates greater tension and produces a stronger target than a shorter series simply by virtue of its length. Nevertheless, circle series that complete a phrase or are otherwise in prominent positions within the phrase also create strong targets whether the circle series is long or short.

5. When making a macro analysis, ignore the second inversion triads that usually occur inside the circle progression (especially I_4^6). Triads in second inversion seldom take part in functional harmony, as may be observed in the following progression: ii^6 (I_4^6) V.

Schubert: *Moment Musical,* op. 94, no. 2, D. 780, mm. 9–17. ♪

What important information was discovered from this macro analysis? The entire excerpt moves from the E♭⁷ in measure 9 toward the ultimate target, D♭, in measure 17. The macro analysis shows how the E♭ to A♭ circle progression continues from measure 9 to 13, then moves quickly in measure 15 to 17 to the target, D♭. The same chord (D♭) occurs in measure 15 but is approached by a diminished 7th chord.

By studying the intricacies of circle patterns, you will more easily recognize compositional types. This will become more apparent in future chapters. For a summary listing of the macro analysis symbols, see Appendix H.

CHAPTER 21

Borrowed Chords

Topics	In Major Keys: ii°⁶, ii°⁷, iv, ♭VI, vii°⁷	In Minor Keys: I (Picardy 3rd)	Modal Mixture

Important Concepts

Borrowed Chords in Major Keys

Borrowed chords are chords borrowed from a parallel major or minor key. Another term often used is *modal mixture*.

Because the parallel minor key with its three scale forms provides a rich variety of triad and 7th chord colors, selections from this assortment are often borrowed for use in major keys. Although a large number of chords in the minor keys are available, the five borrowed chords in Figure 21.1 have received by far the greatest utilization by composers.

Figure 21.1

Five diatonic chords in D major

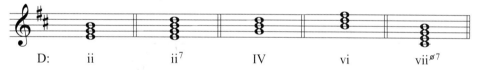

Same chords borrowed from parallel minor

The chords in Figure 21.1 are borrowed from the parallel minor, which accounts for the alterations. Notice that B, the sixth scale degree in D major, is lowered to B♭ in each of the borrowed chords. This lowered sixth scale degree is a distinctive characteristic of borrowed chords in major keys and can be used to identify chords from the parallel mode.

Common Positions

Although borrowed chords may occur in any position, certain positions are most commonly associated with each of the chords. The table that follows on page 482 lists the common positions for the borrowed chords in major keys.

481

Chord	Most Common	Fairly Common
ii°	ii°6	—
ii∅7	ii∅65	ii∅7, ii∅43
iv	iv	iv6
♭VI	♭VI	—
vii°7	vii°65	vii°43, vii°42

Progression
All borrowed chords progress in the same manner as the diatonic chords they replace, except for the ♭VI, which progresses to V or V^7.

Purpose
Borrowed chords are almost universally used as color chords: that is, they are employed to provide variety through the use of contrasting scale forms. Figure 21.2 from the song cycle *Die Winterreise* (Winter's Journey), in F minor, contains two color chords—a borrowed ii°6 and a borrowed iv.

Figure 21.2

Schubert: "Das Wirtshaus" ("The Inn") from *Die Winterreise* (Winter's Journey), op. 89, no. 21, D. 911, mm. 8–9. ♩

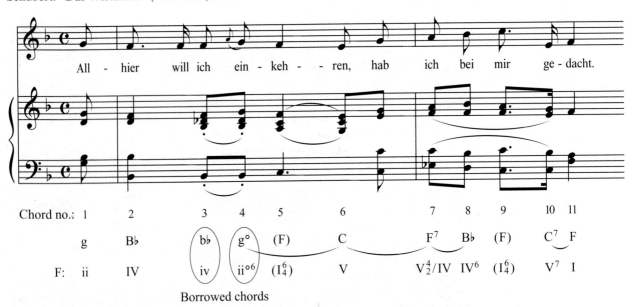

In Figure 21.2, borrowed chords occur at chord numbers 3 and 4. Play the piano part (the two lower staves) of the example twice, once as written and once ignoring the D-flats in both chords 3 and 4. Although the composition would sound acceptable without the accidentals, the addition of the borrowed chords gives the example a unique effect. The effects generated by borrowed chords are often referred to as "color" effects. Can you name at least two chords in Figure 21.2 that are not part of circle progressions (neither the beginning nor the ending of a circle progression)? In performing this work, would it be proper to emphasize (play louder) the D-flats in chords 3 and 4? Does your answer agree with that of your instructor?

Figure 21.3, "Wanderers Nachtlied," illustrates a vii°43 and a ii∅65 borrowed from B♭ minor.

Figure 21.3

Schubert: "Wanderers Nachtlied" ("Wanderers' Night Song") II, op. 96, no. 3, D. 768, mm. 4–6.

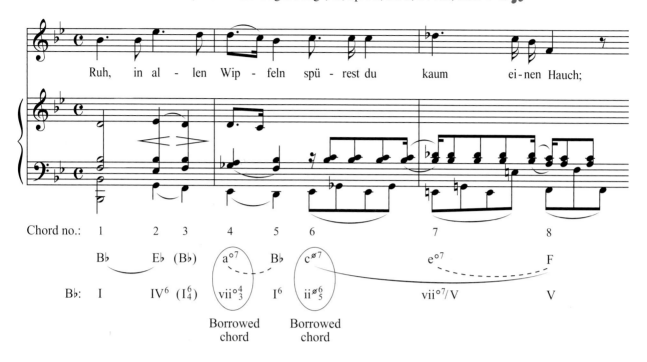

As with other examples of borrowed chords, the borrowed vii°7 and borrowed ii⌀7 in Figure 21.3 have no influence on the circle progressions (B♭ to E♭, a°7 to B♭, and e°7 to F). They are maintained throughout, but the delicate changes in mode generate interesting musical effects not available in major or minor systems alone. Play this example, first with the G-flats (as written) and a second time with G-naturals. Do you like Schubert's choice of borrowed chords? Note that the leading-tone 7th chord (vii°⁴₃) still resolves to the tonic and that the borrowed ii⌀⁶₅ still moves to the dominant at the end of the excerpt.

Figure 21.4, an excerpt from Bach's "Vater unser im Himmelreich," contains a ♭VI borrowed from F minor.

Figure 21.4

Bach: "Vater unser im Himmelreich" ("Our Father in Heaven"), BWV 90.5, m. 9–10.

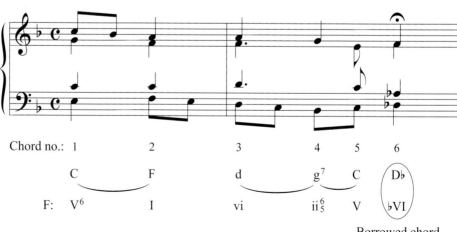

The final chord (no. 6) in Figure 21.4 is a cadence ending with a borrowed chord. Can you name the cadence type at numbers 5 and 6? Notice also that circle progressions dominate the example and are missing only at the very last progression (C to D♭). Play the example first as written, then with an F major triad substituting for the D♭ chord at the cadence (thus creating an authentic cadence).

Figure 21.5 illustrates the tonic chord (I) borrowed from the parallel major.

Figure 21.5

Picardy 3rd:

e: I

Bach: "Jesu, meine Freude" ("Jesus, My Joy"), BWV 81.7, mm. 12–13.

Chord no.: 1   2   3   4   5   6   7

              e   a   e   F♯⁷   B   E

e: i   i⁶   iv⁶   i   V⁶₅/V   V   I

                                                       Picardy 3rd

The *Picardy 3rd* (chord no. 7) that ends Figure 21.5 is a pattern that dates back to the Renaissance period, where cadences ending with minor triads were not considered strong enough and had to be changed to major.

The final chord, the Picardy 3rd of this excerpt, is by no means a requirement. Play the example, first as written and then without the G-sharp (play G-natural). Most students agree that using the Picardy 3rd is indeed an interesting artistic gesture, but it is by no means a necessity.

Chord no. 5 (F♯⁷) is a secondary dominant. How would you change the fifth chord from a secondary dominant to a diatonic 7th chord?

History

Mixing of major and minor modes developed in the baroque period and was considered a part of the general style. Borrowed chords are found often in the music of the baroque period (Figure 21.6).

Figure 21.6

Bach: Prelude no. 1 in C Major from *The Well-Tempered Clavier,* Book I, BWV 846, mm. 13–15.

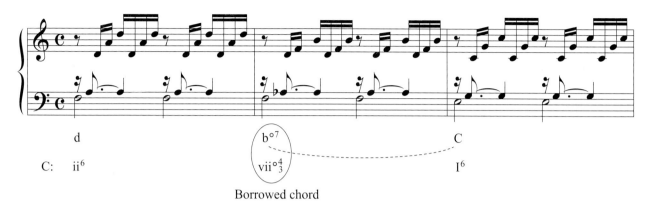

Borrowed chord

Composers in the classical period also used borrowed chords. Their frequency and use is little changed from that of the baroque. Notice the similar borrowed chord use (vii°$_3^4$) in Figures 21.6 and 21.7. In both examples, the borrowed chords resolve to I^6 with the leading tone resolving up a m2 and the chord seventh resolving down a step.

Figure 21.7

Mozart: Sonata in D Major, K. 576, II: Adagio, mm. 13–16.

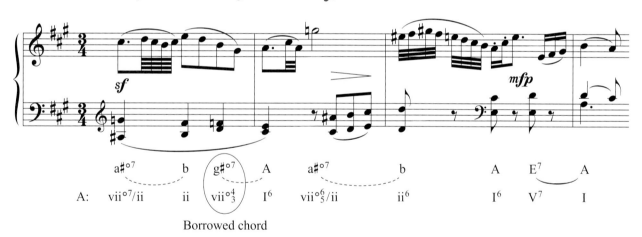

Borrowed chord

The romantic and post-romantic period saw a freer use of borrowed chords, including a chromatic approach and departure. The excerpt in Figure 21.8, by Hugo Wolf (1860–1903), shows the typical vi–ii–V circle progression embellished with two incidences of the borrowed ii^{ø7}. The chromatic fluctuation between the diatonic and borrowed versions of the chord (ii$_5^6$ and ii^{ø7}) creates prolonged tension before movement to the dominant.

Figure 21.8

Wolf: "Wiegenlied" ("Cradle Song"), mm. 26–30.

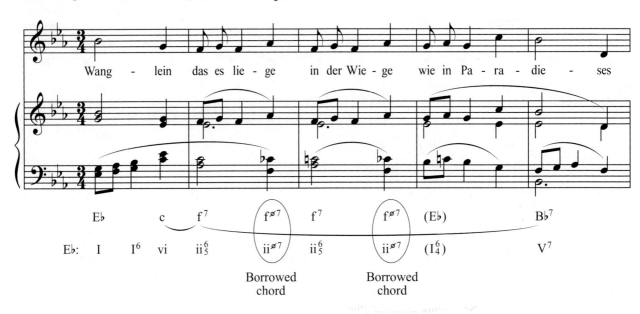

Applications

Borrowed chords may be used as substitutes for diatonic chords and, with few exceptions, follow the general principles employed for the same chords when unaltered.

Voice Leading

A few guidelines, which you already know, will make the writing of borrowed chords easy. Do not double either of the notes that create a tritone. It is generally best not to double an altered note. Usually the best note to double in any situation is the first, fourth, or fifth scale degree.

Here are some guidelines for writing and analyzing the five most common borrowed chords (from the minor) in major keys.

The $ii^{\circ 6}$ Chord

The $ii^{\circ 6}$ chord is usually found in first inversion because it is a diminished triad. Double the bass note of the $ii^{\circ 6}$ chord (not part of the tritone). Move the bass voice upward by step, and move the upper three voices in contrary motion to the bass when moving to V or V^7. See Figures 21.2 and 21.9 for examples.

Figure 21.9

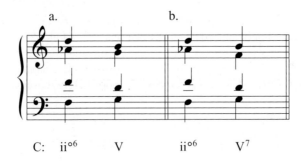

The ii^{ø6}₅ Chord

In the ii$^{ø6}_{5}$ chord, all four factors (root, 3rd, 5th, and 7th) are usually present. Otherwise, the recommendations for ii°6 apply for ii$^{ø6}_{5}$ as well. Move the bass voice upward by step, and the upper three voices in contrary motion to the bass when moving to V or V^7. See Figures 21.3 and 21.10.

Figure 21.10

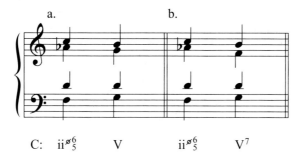

C: ii$^{ø6}_{5}$ V   ii$^{ø6}_{5}$ V^7

The iv Chord

The iv chord follows the preceding general principles. In root position, double the bass. When progressing to V or V^7, move the bass voice up a step and the upper three voices in contrary motion to the bass. See Figure 21.2 for an example. This chord contains no tritone. See Figure 21.11 for other examples.

Figure 21.11

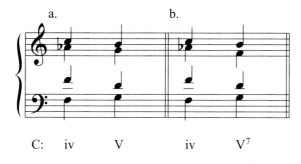

C: iv   V   iv   V^7

The ♭VI Chord

Double the tonic (the 3rd of triad and first scale degree) of the ♭VI chord. Move the bass voice downward and at least two of the upper voices upward. As usual, parallel unisons, 5ths, and octaves are avoided. See Figures 21.4 and 21.12 for examples.

Figure 21.12

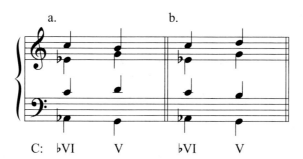

C: ♭VI   V   ♭VI   V

The vii°⁷ Chord

The diminished 7th chord appears with all four factors. The chord is usually in root position, but other positions may appear from time to time. The diminished 7th chord contains two tritones, but often only one can be resolved. In root position, move the bass voice up to tonic and the upper three voices downward in contrary motion. See Figures 21.3 and 21.13.

Figure 21.13

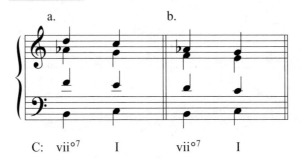

C: vii°⁷   I   vii°⁷   I

The Picardy 3rd

This is the major tonic (I) in a minor key. The Picardy 3rd chord is customarily in root position at the ending of a composition or a large musical section. Double the bass (root) of I. See Figure 21.5 for an example.

Summary

Chords borrowed from the parallel major or minor key are known as borrowed chords. This blending of major and minor is often referred to as modal mixture. Although any chord can be borrowed from the parallel key, only six borrowed chords occur frequently in music literature (in major keys, ii°⁶, ii∅⁷, iv, ♭VI, and vii°⁷; in minor keys, I). Figure 21.14 provides a summary of these chords and their resolutions in their most common positions.

Figure 21.14

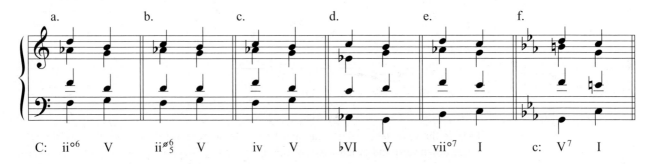

C: ii°⁶   V   ii∅⁶₅   V   iv   V   ♭VI   V   vii°⁷   I   c: V⁷   I

Practice

Knowing the differences between diatonic chords and borrowed chords is critical to your understanding of modal mixture. As you begin learning borrowed chords, first make sure you can write the diatonic counterparts accurately. Then, alter the diatonic version to become a borrowed chord (Figure 21.15). Complete your practice by playing and singing the notes of both types of chords.

Figure 21.15

C: ii   ii°   ii⁷   ii∅⁷   IV   iv   vi   ♭VI   vii∅⁷   vii°⁷   c: i   I

Assignment 21.1   Spell the requested borrowed chords in the keys indicated.

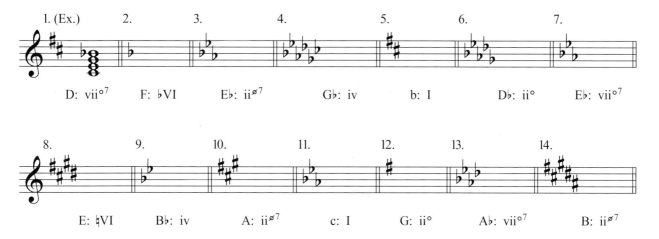

1. (Ex.)   2.   3.   4.   5.   6.   7.

D: vii°⁷   F: ♭VI   E♭: ii⌀⁷   G♭: iv   b: I   D♭: ii°   E♭: vii°⁷

8.   9.   10.   11.   12.   13.   14.

E: ♮VI   B♭: iv   A: ii⌀⁷   c: I   G: ii°   A♭: vii°⁷   B: ii⌀⁷

Assignment 21.2   The Roman numerals in the following exercises represent borrowed chords. For each measure, do the following:
1. Write each requested chord in four-part harmony on the staves provided.
2. Write the chord that most conventionally follows the chord you wrote in step 1.
3. Analyze both chords.

The example illustrates the correct procedure.

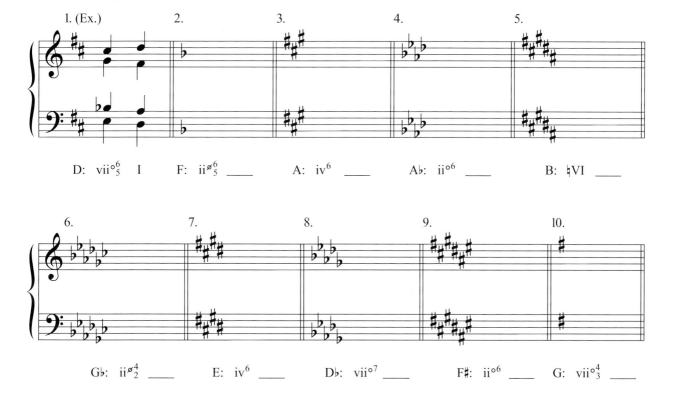

1. (Ex.)   2.   3.   4.   5.

D: vii°⁶₅ I   F: ii⌀⁶₅ ____   A: iv⁶ ____   A♭: ii°⁶ ____   B: ♮VI ____

6.   7.   8.   9.   10.

G♭: ii⌀⁴₂ ____   E: iv⁶ ____   D♭: vii°⁷ ____   F♯: ii°⁶ ____   G: vii°⁴₃ ____

Assignment 21.3

Following are four-part phrases with alto and tenor voices omitted.

As a keyboard assignment:

If your instructor requests you to do so, play each chorale phrase on the piano, adding the alto and tenor voices according to the figured-bass symbols. If you have difficulty with this assignment, try the following suggestions:

1. Play each chord in simple position (all voices within one octave and with the left hand). Listen to the sound and try to remember the particular quality of each chord.
2. When you have the sounds well in mind, play the two outer voices alone.
3. Start adding the alto and tenor. Play the soprano, alto, and tenor with the right hand and put your fifth finger on the key representing the soprano voice.
4. Place your third finger on the next factor down and your thumb on the lowest right-hand factor. Do not leave out any factors in the right hand.
5. Check to see if this position causes a voice-leading error. If not, then proceed to the next chord and repeat the procedure.

As a written assignment:

1. Add alto and tenor voices according to the figured-bass symbols.
2. Provide a complete harmonic analysis.

1.

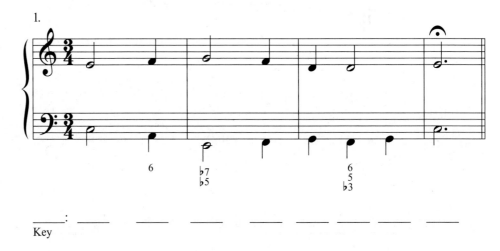

Key

2.

Key

3.

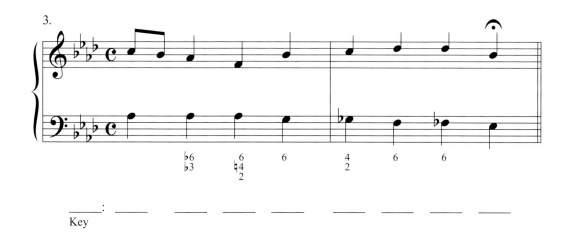

4.

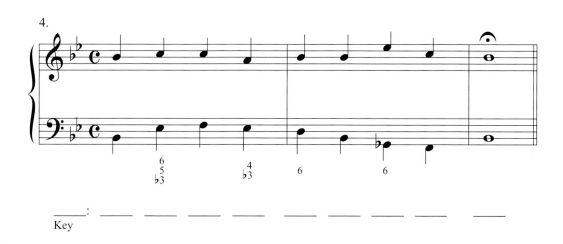

5.

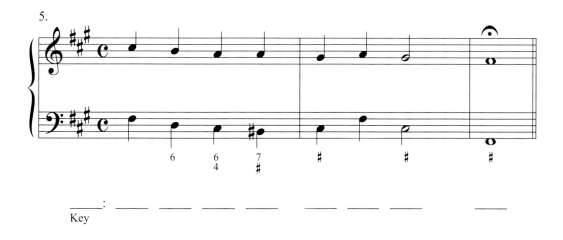

Assignment 21.4   Each exercise is a figured-bass voice.

As a keyboard assignment:

1. Play each exercise, adding the soprano, alto, and tenor voices.
2. Become familiar with the chords first, then work to obtain an interesting soprano voice line, perhaps with an ascent and a descent.
3. Look at the soprano melody lines in Assignment 21.3 for ideas.
4. If you have other difficulties with this assignment, use the procedures described in Assignment 21.3 and adapt them.

As a written assignment:

1. On a separate sheet of paper write out each figured-bass line, leaving a staff above for the soprano and alto.
2. If you have difficulty with this assignment, write the letter names of each chord factor under the figured-bass symbols. This will help you fashion a better soprano melody line.
3. When you have decided on a suitable soprano melody line, write it on the staff and fill in the alto and tenor accordingly.
4. To help in writing the soprano melody, observe the soprano voices in Assignment 21.3. Each is a traditional chorale melody and will give you an idea of the style.

Assignment 21.5

Following is a complete chorale harmonization by Bach. It contains several chromatic chords and includes modulation.

1. A fermata marks the end of each phrase.
2. Sing the chorale in class and have a class member direct the performance.
3. Make a complete harmonic analysis of the chorale, including circling and labeling each nonharmonic tone.
4. Discuss the borrowed chords, as well as the secondary dominant and leading-tone chords appearing in the chorale. Which diatonic chords have been altered to result in the chromatic chords? Do all the chromatic chords resolve as expected?

Bach: "Herzliebster Jesu, was hast du verbrochen" ("Dearest Jesus, How Hast Thou Transgressed"), BWV 245.

Assignment 21.6

Following is a complete chorale melody.

1. Harmonize the melody on a separate sheet of score paper.
2. Use a harmonic rhythm of one chord per quarter note.
3. Write out all possible harmonies as described in previous chapters, then select a suitable harmonization and write the block chords beneath the melody tones. Be sure to include at least two or three borrowed chords.
4. Convert the block chords to four-part harmony with special emphasis on an interesting bass line.
5. Add appropriate nonharmonic tones.
6. Perform the compositions in class using a student quartet, each singing one of the four parts (soprano, alto, tenor, and bass).

Bach: "Wo Gott zum Haus nicht gibt sein Gunst" ("If God Does Not Give His Blessings"), BWV 438.

Assignment 21.7

Write a composition of approximately 16 to 24 measures in length.

1. Plan the composition in three-part form.
2. Use four-measure phrases.
3. Plot the harmonic progressions first in block chords.
4. Add an appropriate melody.
5. Convert the block chords to the idiomatic style of the medium you choose. As an example, if you write for a group of stringed instruments, arrange the harmony to accommodate the peculiarities of the instruments involved.
6. Be sure to include at least three or four borrowed chords. Remember that borrowed chords can generally substitute for their diatonic counterparts.

CHAPTER 22

Neapolitan 6th Chords

Topic

Neapolitan 6th: N^6

Important Concepts

The *Neapolitan 6th* chord is a major triad on the lowered second scale degree of a major or minor scale (Figure 22.1).

Figure 22.1

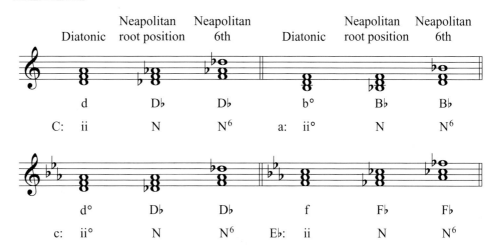

Diatonic | Neapolitan root position | Neapolitan 6th | Diatonic | Neapolitan root position | Neapolitan 6th

d | D♭ | D♭ | b° | B♭ | B♭

C: ii | N | N^6 | a: ii° | N | N^6

d° | D♭ | D♭ | f | F♭ | F♭

c: ii° | N | N^6 | E♭: ii | N | N^6

Characteristics

The Neapolitan 6th chord produces a distinctive and colorful effect resulting from the chromatic modification of the supertonic chord. Although it is common practice to use N^6 as the analysis symbol for the Neapolitan 6th, ♭II^6 also appears as a representation for the chord.

Position

The Neapolitan usually appears in first inversion—thus the name Neapolitan "sixth."

Name

The meaning of the name Neapolitan is unknown, but some believe that it is a reference to the "Neapolitan" school of eighteenth-century opera composers.

Mode

The Neapolitan is found far more often in minor than in major keys.

Progression

The Neapolitan progresses most often to the dominant chord. Although this progression may be delayed or interrupted by other pre-dominant chords, ultimately the resolution is to V.

Figure 22.2 shows a typical use of the Neapolitan. The Neapolitan is an altered ii chord, so the N^6–V–I is an altered circle progression (A♭–D–g). Perform Figure 22.2 if you have a pianist and singer, or play the chords in the accompaniment. Then play the same example again, changing the A-flat in chord number 3 to an A-natural. You can then get the full effect of the Neapolitan chord. No doubt you have heard many Neapolitan chords without realizing it.

Figure 22.2

Schubert: "Der Müller und der Bach" ("The Miller and the Brook") from *Die schöne Müllerin* (The Miller's Beautiful Daughter), op. 25, no. 19, D. 795, mm. 22–27. ♪

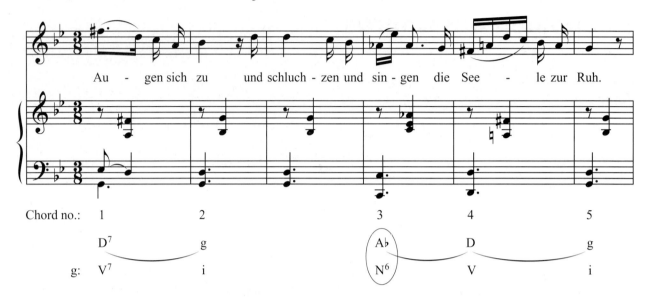

Figure 22.3 is an excerpt from the familiar "Moonlight" sonata by Beethoven. First play the excerpt as written, then change the D-naturals in chord 3 to D-sharps. Notice the similar effect to that of Figure 22.2.

Figure 22.3

Beethoven: Sonata in C-sharp Minor ("Moonlight"), op. 27, no. 2, I: Adagio sostenuto, mm. 49–51. ♪

In Figure 22.4 you see how several chords can each point toward the dominant chord (chord 3). Play the example as printed, then play only chords 1 and 3 (leaving out g♯°7). Because both chords (1 and 2) resolve naturally to the dominant (V), they are called pre-dominant effects. Later you will see larger and more complex pre-dominant sections.

Figure 22.4

Mozart: Fantasia in D Minor, K. 397, mm. 8–9.

Chord no.: 1   2   3

d: N⁶   vii°⁷/V   V

Some Exceptional Uses of the Neapolitan

Although the Neapolitan is usually found in minor keys and in first inversion, it sometimes appears in a number of other places.

1. A Neapolitan may, on occasion, be included in a passage consisting of nonfunctional harmony. During the classical period the nonfunctional harmony often contained a series of first-inversion triads in parallel motion (Figure 22.6).
2. The Neapolitan may sometimes be found in root position (Figures 22.7 and 22.8).
3. The Neapolitan, especially in the romantic period, may be preceded by V^7/N or vii°⁶/N, thus the N becomes a tonicized chord (Figure 22.8).
4. The Neapolitan is occasionally found in the major mode (Figure 22.9).
5. Somewhat rare is a Neapolitan chord that also contains a 7th factor.

History

The Neapolitan 6th first appeared in the baroque period and was treated very conservatively. Most often the N^6 was placed near a cadence point and was considered a substitute for the diatonic ii⁶ or ii°⁶ (Figure 22.5).

Figure 22.5

Bach: Evangelist's recitativo from the *St. Matthew Passion*, BWV 244, no. 68, mm. 1–3.

Des-glei-chen schmä-he-ten ihn auch die   Mör-der, die mit ihm ge-kreu-zi-get war-en.

G   f#°⁷   Db   G   c

c: V⁶   vii°⁷/V   N⁶   V   i

In the classical period, nontraditional examples surface occasionally. Figure 22.6, from a piano sonata by Haydn, shows a series of nonfunctional first-inversion triads that descend in parallel motion. The N⁶ is one of the chords in the series and takes part in the stepwise downward movement.

Figure 22.6

Haydn: Sonata in E Minor, Hob. XVI:34, I: Presto, mm. 114–117. ♪

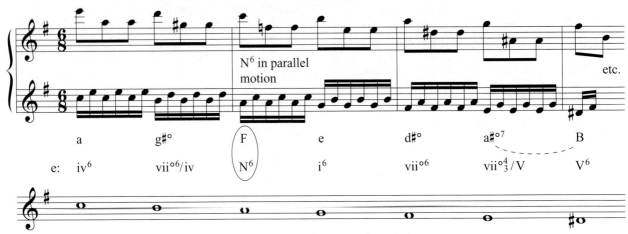

Descending bass line—nonfunctional parallel first-inversion triads

The use of the N⁶ continued throughout the romantic period and treatment broadened considerably. Figure 22.7 shows the Neapolitan in root position, with considerable parallel voice leading, and a final tonic chord that leaves some doubt about its actual function as a tonic. Most listeners hear the N as a passing chord: i^6–N–V^7/iv.

Figure 22.7

Schubert: "Der Doppelgänger" ("The Double") from *Schwanengesang* (Swan Song), D. 957, no. 13, mm. 56–63. ♪

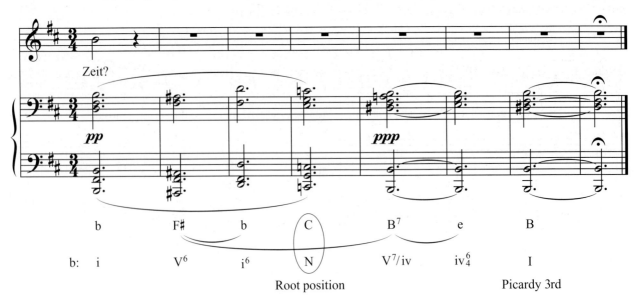

Figure 22.8 illustrates the Neapolitan tonicized by a secondary leading tone. The tonicized chord appears in first inversion following an earlier presentation of the Neapolitan in root position.

Figure 22.8

Chopin: Prelude in G-sharp Minor, op. 28, no. 12, mm. 70–73.

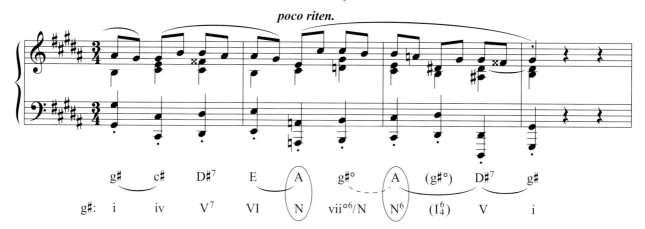

Because the N6 is primarily a device of the baroque, classical, and romantic periods, its presence in the post-romantic and impressionistic period is rare. However, the composers of this transitional period occasionally returned to the idiom of the romantic period. The example in Figure 22.9 by Amy Beach, written in 1904, reveals a Neapolitan 6th with nearly traditional treatment.

Figure 22.9

Beach: *Variations on Balkan Themes,* op. 60, Variation VI, mm. 19–22.

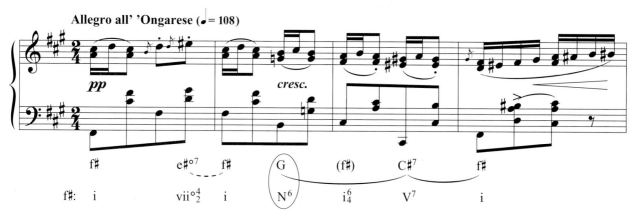

Applications	The Neapolitan 6th may be used as a chromatic substitute for its diatonic counterpart, ii. Well-established voice-leading principles avoid same-voice chromatic alterations between the N^6 and its subsequent resolution to the dominant. The following guidelines are provided to assist you with writing the N^6 chord and its resolution.

Voice Leading

Doubled Note

Double the bass note (third of the chord) whenever possible.

Motion to V

When moving from the N^6 to V, you can usually move the upper voices (soprano, alto, and tenor) down in contrary motion to the bass to the nearest chord tones of V. Note the unique melodic diminished 3rd in the soprano voice, considered a desirable trait by composers (Figure 22.10a).

Motion to V^7

In the progression N^6 to V^7 you can also move two voices downward, but the remaining voice may be kept as a common tone. This motion will result in a doubled root and omitted fifth in V^7 (Figure 22.10b). Avoid chromatic voice leading (D♭ to D, for example) in any voice when leaving N^6 (Figure 22.10c).

Tonic $^6_4$

When the N^6 proceeds to I^6_4 or i^6_4, watch out for parallel 5ths. Turn them upside down—into parallel 4ths (Figures 22.10d and 22.10e).

Figure 22.10

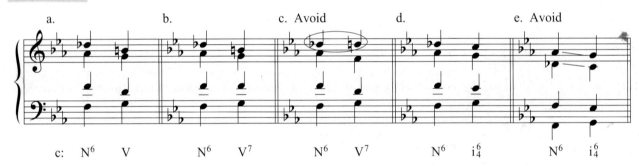

Summary

The Neapolitan 6th is a chromatic chord built on the lowered second scale degree (♭II^6). It usually appears in first inversion but can occur in other positions. Although the N^6 appears frequently in minor keys, numerous examples of major key N^6 chords exist. The N^6 is a pre-dominant chord that resolves either directly or indirectly to the dominant.

Practice

You will probably find the Neapolitan 6th chord fairly easy to write. It is a simple major triad positioned a mere minor 2nd above tonic. What you may forget, though, is that the N^6 occurs most often in first inversion.

Using a piano or keyboard, travel around the circle of fifths by playing the tonic of each key center, followed by a major triad positioned a m2 above the tonic. Immediately invert the chord by revoicing the N^6 with the third in the bass. Sing the notes of this simple position N^6 from bottom to top (third, fifth, root).

When you are proficient at spelling and singing the N^6, expand your practice to include the resolution progressions (N^6–V–i and N^6–V–I).

Assignment 22.1   Each triad in four-part harmony given below is the V chord in a minor key.

1. Determine the key and write it in the blank beneath the staves.
2. Write the key signature on the grand staff at the beginning of each exercise.
3. Determine the Neapolitan 6th chord in this key and write it in four-part harmony so that it leads smoothly to the V triad.
4. Place the analysis in the blanks beneath each chord.

1. (Ex.)   2.   3.   4.

g : N⁶   V   C : N⁶   V   g♯ : N⁶   V   f♯ : N⁶   V
Key   Key   Key   Key

5.   6.   7.   8.

b : N⁶   V   f : N⁶   V   d : N⁶   V   c♭m : N⁶   V
Key   Key   Key   Key

Assignment 22.2   The soprano and bass voices for four-part chorale phrases are given on the next page.

As a keyboard assignment:

1. If your instructor requests you to do so, play each chorale phrase on the piano, adding the alto and tenor voices according to the figured-bass symbols.
2. If this proves too difficult, play each chord in simple position (all voices within one octave and with the left hand).
3. When you are familiar with the sound of each progression, begin working with both hands, fitting the upper voices into their range.

As a written assignment:

1. Add the tenor and alto voices according to the figured-bass symbols.
2. Provide a complete harmonic analysis.

Assignment 22.3 Each exercise consists of a figured-bass voice.

As a keyboard assignment:

1. Play each exercise, adding soprano, alto, and tenor voices.
2. Become familiar with the chords first, then work to obtain an interesting voice line, perhaps with an ascent and a descent.
3. If your instructor concurs, use keyboard voicing—three upper voices with the right hand and the bass with the left.

As a written assignment:

1. On a separate sheet of paper write out each figured bass, leaving a staff above for the soprano and alto.
2. Complete the remaining three upper voices according to the figuration supplied.
3. Observe part-writing practices cited in this chapter.
4. To help in writing the soprano melody, observe the soprano voices in Assignment 22.2. Each is a traditional chorale melody and will give you an idea of the style.

Assignment 22.4

Each exercise is similar to a music illustration in this chapter.

1. Add the macro analysis and Roman numerals using the illustrations as a guide.
2. Write a short excerpt (25 to 100 words) for each exercise, summarizing the analysis or explaining a portion of the analysis that cannot be explained otherwise. Use the analyzed illustrations in this chapter as a guide.

1. Chopin: Valse in B Minor, op. 69, no. 2, mm. 142–145.

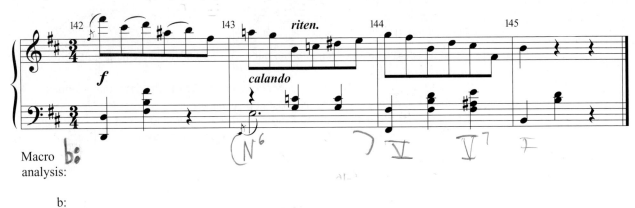

Macro
analysis:

b:

2. Chopin: Scherzo in C-sharp Minor, op. 39, no. 3, mm. 634–637.

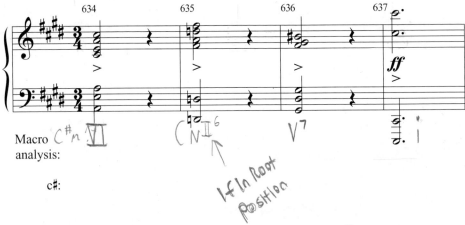

Macro
analysis:

c#:

3. Chopin: Valse in C-sharp Minor, op. 64, no. 2, mm. 189–192.

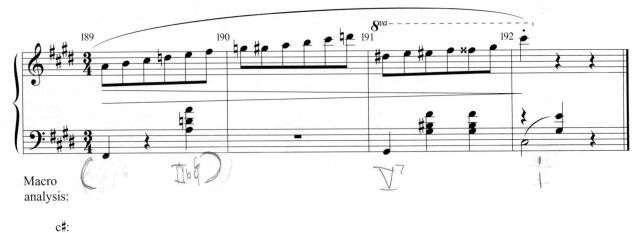

Macro
analysis:

c#:

4. Beethoven: Bagatelle in A Minor, op. 119, no. 9, mm. 17–20.

Macro
analysis:

a:

5. Chopin: Mazurka in A Minor, op. 7, no. 2, mm. 11–16.

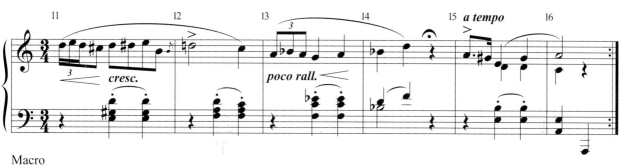

Macro
analysis:

a:

6. Haydn: Sonata in D Major, Hob. XVI:37, II: Largo e sostenuto, mm. 15–19.

Macro
analysis:

d:

7. Mozart: Sonata in F Major, K. 280, II: Adagio, mm. 43–46.

Macro
analysis:

f:

Assignment 22.5   For the following composition:

1. Make a complete analysis (macro or Roman numeral).
2. Discuss the following:
   a. The use of Neapolitan 6th chords
   b. The overall form of the composition
   c. Cadence formulae
   d. Harmonic rhythm

Maria Theresia von Paradis: *Sicilienne.*

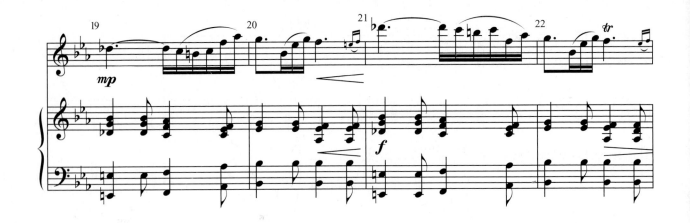

CHAPTER 23

Augmented 6th Chords

Italian 6th: It⁶   French 6th: Fr⁶   German 6th: Gr⁶

Important Concepts

Augmented 6th chords are chords that have been altered to include the interval of an augmented 6th. Their sound is unique and so different from the diatonic chords that they are given special analysis symbols: It⁶, Fr⁶, and Gr⁶.

Figure 23.1

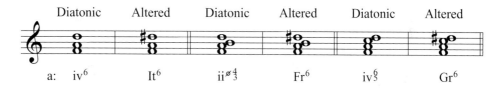

Three Types

Figure 23.2 shows the three types of augmented 6th chords. The geographic names are traditional, and their origin is unknown.

Italian 6th: M3rd + Aug. 6th (total of three different notes)

French 6th: M3rd + Aug. 4th + Aug. 6th (total of four different notes)

German 6th: M3rd + Perf. 5th + Aug. 6th (total of four different notes).

Figure 23.2

The augmented 6th chords have three notes in common (Figure 23.3).

Figure 23.3

Whole notes = notes in common

a: It^6 Fr^6 Gr^6

Bass Note Location   The bass note (or lowest-sounding tone) is usually a major 3rd below the tonic in both major and minor keys (Figure 23.4).

Fourth Scale Degree   The fourth scale degree is raised in all three types of augmented 6th chords (Figure 23.4).

Figure 23.4

Tonic   Raised 4th scale degree

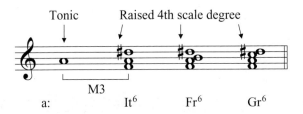

M3

a: It^6 Fr^6 Gr^6

Progression   The most common progressions from an augmented 6th chord are shown in Figure 23.5.

The Italian 6th resolves to V directly or through i$_4^6$.
The French 6th resolves to V directly or through i$_4^6$.
The German 6th must resolve to V through i$_4^6$.

Figure 23.5

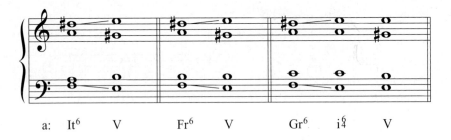

a: It^6 V   Fr^6 V   Gr^6 i$_4^6$ V

Note that the German 6th is often followed by i$_4^6$ to avoid parallel fifths. The augmented 6th expands out to an octave in all three chord types.

Figure 23.6 shows the German 6th chord in a musical context.

Figure 23.6

Schumann: "Ich kann's nicht fassen" ("I Cannot Comprehend") from *Frauenlieben und Leben* (A Woman's Life and Loves), op. 42, no. 3, mm. 48–52.

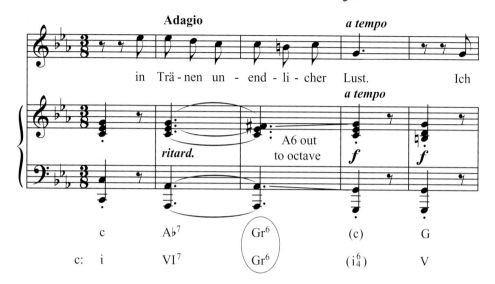

Notice the standard voice leading in Figure 23.6:

1. The augmented 6th (A♭–F♯) resolves to an octave.
2. The Gr^6 resolves to the dominant (through the i$_4^6$ in this case).
3. The bass note (A♭) in the Gr^6 is a major 3rd below the tonic (C).

(The parallel octaves in the bass are not intended as independent voices but are merely a way to make the bass voice more prominent.)

Figure 23.7 shows a French 6th chord in a march by John Phillip Sousa.

Figure 23.7

Sousa: *The Free Lance March*, mm. 29–32.

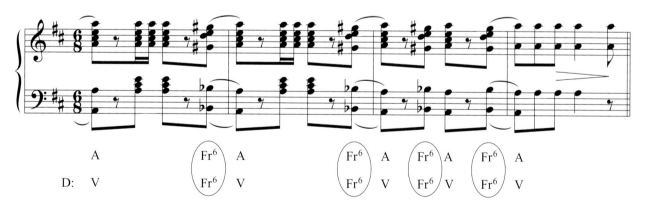

The Fr^6 is repeated four times in this short excerpt. Notice how the three principles of resolution previously described are observed each time.

Figure 23.8 shows an Italian 6th chord in another march by Sousa.

Figure 23.8

Sousa: *The Liberty Bell March*, mm. 81–84. ♩

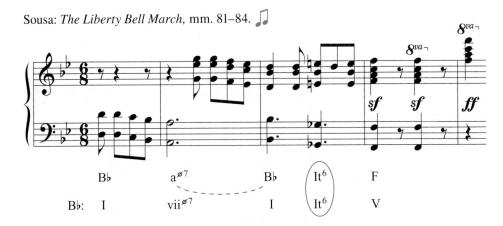

Again, notice how the three principles are observed in the resolution of the It⁶ in Figure 23.8. It should be obvious from these examples that the three types of augmented 6th chords are treated in much the same way.

Figure 23.9 is a highly chromatic example from a Haydn symphony. Functional harmony is suspended through measures 81 and 82, and the music is organized around a descending chromatic bass line (G, G♭, F, E, E♭, D, D♭). Nevertheless, when the German 6th chord is reached at the end of the passage, it resolves in the normal way.

Figure 23.9

Haydn: Symphony no. 97 in C Major, II: Adagio ma non troppo, mm. 81–84. ♩

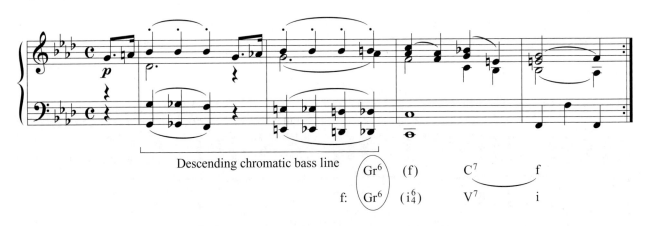

The harmonic thrust of the preceding passage is to prepare for the dominant. Such passages are often called pre-dominant sections.

Exceptions

Although by far the largest number of augmented 6th chords occur as described, some exceptions should be noted, as follows:

Added Notes

In some cases an augmented 6th chord may include added notes.

Different Position

Occasionally, augmented 6th chords occur in positions other than those listed. Traditionally the chord maintains its name (augmented 6th) even when the augmented 6th is inverted to a diminished 3rd (Figure 23.10).

| Bass Note on Other Scale Degrees | In rare instances the bass note of any augmented 6th chord may be a scale degree other than the customary major 3rd below tonic (Figure 23.10). |

Bass Note on Other Scale Degrees

In rare instances the bass note of any augmented 6th chord may be a scale degree other than the customary major 3rd below tonic (Figure 23.10).

Augmented 6th Interval Inverted

Sometimes the augmented 6th interval is inverted, thus creating a diminished 3rd (Figure 23.10).

Irregular Resolution

There are times when the resolution of an augmented 6th chord may not follow standard progression. Nonetheless, this type of unexpected progression frequently signals a delayed resolution (Figure 23.10).

Figure 23.10

Chopin: Ballade no. 2, op. 38, mm. 184–185. ♫

Augmented 6th chords on various scale degrees

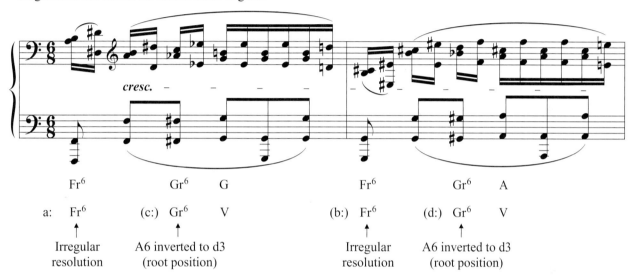

History

Treatment of the augmented 6th chords in the baroque period was conservative. Figure 23.11 is from a toccata by Domenico Zipoli (1688–1726), a contemporary of Bach. Notice how the i$_4^6$ is used to avoid parallel 5ths.

Figure 23.11

Zipoli: Toccata from *Sonate d'Intavolatura per Organo e Cimbalo*, mm 1–4. ♫

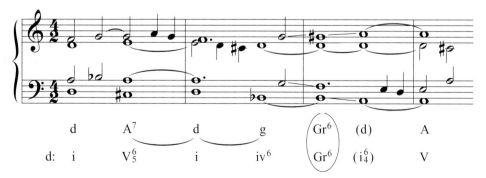

In the classical period, the augmented 6th chords were used much more frequently. Figure 23.12 shows the Fr^6 used in the standard way.

Figure 23.12

Mozart: "Das Veilchen" ("The Violet"), K. 476, mm. 39–42.

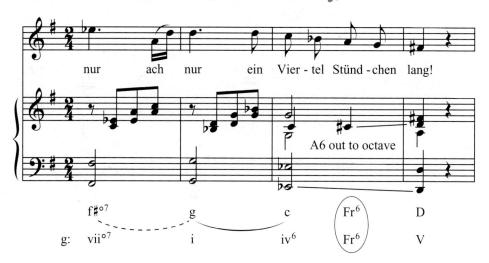

The use of augmented 6th chords reached their zenith during the romantic period, and handling of the chords became freer and more unpredictable. Figure 23.13 contains an augmented 6th chord in a different position, with the augmented 6th interval inverted into a diminished 3rd.

Figure 23.13

Chopin: Prelude in G Minor, op. 28, no. 22, mm. 36–41.

Although a number of examples of chords bear the augmented sound in the post-romantic and impressionistic period, few would be considered true augmented 6th chords. In Figure 23.14, a German 6th chord progresses directly to the tonic, destroying the characteristic sound of the augmented 6th resolution to an octave.

Figure 23.14

Ravel: Sonatine, I: Modéré, mm. 81–84.

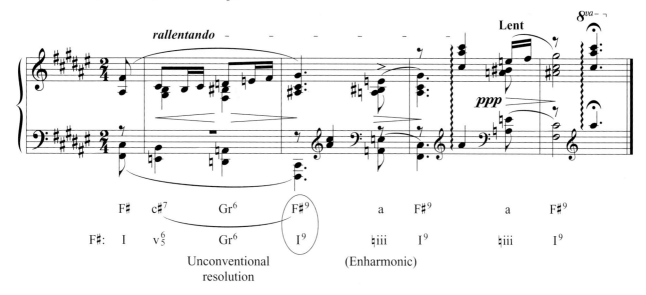

Augmented 6th chords occur throughout popular music, but especially in ragtime. Scott Joplin, one of the better-known composers of ragtime, often used these chords in his compositions (Figure 23.15). Note again the string of pre-dominant chords—ii⁶, Gr⁶, and I⁶₄.

Figure 23.15

Joplin: *Binks' Waltz,* mm. 95–100.

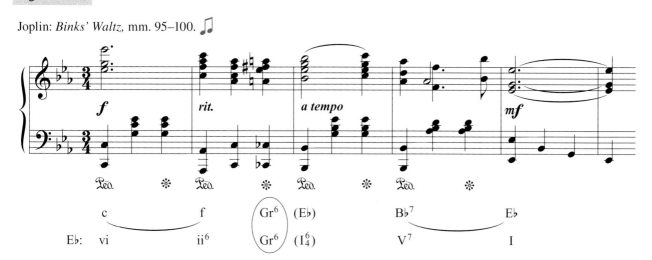

The following descriptions serve as general guidelines for writing augmented 6th chords.

Voice Leading

Although the three chords in this category share the common element of the augmented 6th, individual consideration is required with regard to doubling and voice leading.

Doubling

Neither of the two notes forming the augmented 6th interval is ever doubled. In the Italian 6th, double the tonic scale degree (the 3rd above the bass note).

Resolution

The augmented 6th chords are normally resolved using the following three principles:

The Italian 6th resolves to V directly or through i_4^6.
The French 6th resolves to V directly or through i_4^6.
The German 6th must resolve to V through i_4^6.

Figure 23.16 illustrates the resolution of the It^6 and the Fr^6 directly to V, as well as through i_4^6 before progressing to V. The bass note of the augmented 6th chord resolves down a half step—either to the root of V or the fifth of i_4^6.

Tonic $\frac{6}{4}$

The progression from augmented 6th chords to i_4^6 is only a partial resolution. The final resolution occurs when V is reached.

Figure 23.16

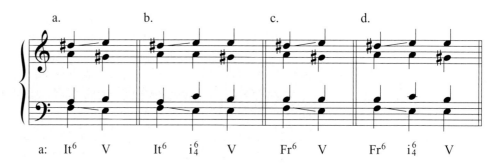

a: It^6 V It^6 i_4^6 V Fr^6 V Fr^6 i_4^6 V

Parallel 5ths

To avoid parallel 5ths, the Gr^6 proceeds to i_4^6 or I_4^6 instead of V. Figure 23.17a shows the parallel 5ths that result if the Gr^6 is resolved directly to the dominant. The preferred resolution through the i_4^6 is shown in Figure 23.17b.

Figure 23.17

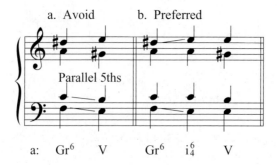

a: Gr^6 V Gr^6 i_4^6 V

The Gr⁶ chord has two spellings. In major keys, the pitch a P5 above the bass note is sometimes respelled as a doubly augmented 4th (AA4):

Spelling of Gr⁶ in C minor: A♭ C E♭ F♯.

Spelling of Gr⁶ in C major: A♭ C D♯ F♯.

In major keys the normal spelling of the Gr⁶ (Figure 23.18a) results in an undesirable chromaticism (C♮–C♯). In these cases composers spelled the Gr⁶ enharmonically to achieve a more normal voice leading (B♯–C♯), as shown in Figure 23.18b.

Figure 23.18

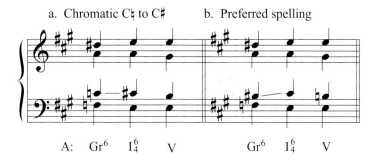

a. Chromatic C♮ to C♯   b. Preferred spelling

A: Gr⁶   I$^6_4$ V   Gr⁶   I$^6_4$ V

Summary

The Italian 6th, French 6th, and German 6th chords have been altered to include the interval of an augmented 6th. These chords have three notes in common: the tonic, a bass note a major 3rd below the tonic, and the raised fourth scale degree. Only the It⁶ is limited to these three notes. The Fr⁶ and the Gr⁶ also include a fourth note (the Fr⁶ has an A4 above the bass; the Gr⁶ has a P5 above the bass).

Standard voice-leading practice dictates that the augmented 6th in all three chords resolve outward in contrary motion to the octave. Although the It⁶ and the Fr⁶ can resolve to V directly or through i$^6_4$, the Gr⁶ must resolve through i$^6_4$ before progressing to V (or parallel 5ths will occur). To avoid undesirable chromaticism in major keys, some composers spelled the Gr⁶ enharmonically.

Occasionally, augmented 6th chords are varied. They may include added notes or appear in an irregular position. They may be positioned on an unexpected scale degree or have an unexpected resolution. Although such exceptions do occur, they are not the norm.

Figure 23.19 provides a summary of these three chords in their most common positions with their expected resolutions.

Figure 23.19

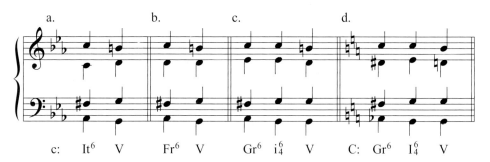

a.   b.   c.   d.

c: It⁶   V   Fr⁶   V   Gr⁶   i$^6_4$ V   C: Gr⁶   I$^6_4$ V

All the chords presented thus far in volumes 1 and 2 are easily considered in simple root position. The quality of the triad or seventh chord is evident when the thirds are stacked in the uncomplicated organization of root position. With the augmented 6th chords, this process becomes complicated by the augmented 6th interval present in all three chords. If you reorganize the It^6, Fr^6, or Gr^6 into root position, the augmented 6th becomes a diminished 3rd. Because of this phenomenon, you may find it helpful initially to build augmented 6th chords in the following manner:

Step 1: Write the tonic note on the staff.

Step 2: Write the interval of a major 3rd below the tonic.

Step 3: Above the lowest note (the note that is a major 3rd below the tonic), write the interval of an augmented 6th.

Step 4: Combine the three notes.

If you follow these steps, the end result will be an It^6 chord (Figure 23.20).

Figure 23.20

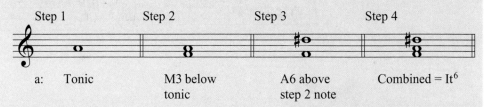

Step 1	Step 2	Step 3	Step 4
a: Tonic	M3 below tonic	A6 above step 2 note	Combined = It^6

When you are able to write the It^6, the process of creating the Fr^6 and Gr^6 is fairly straightforward. For the Fr^6, add an A4 above the lowest sounding note. For the Gr^6, add a P5 (Figure 23.21).

Figure 23.21

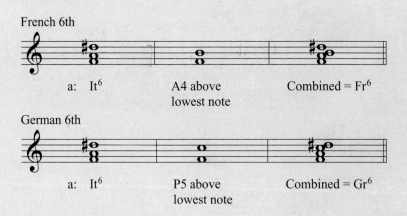

French 6th

a: It^6 A4 above lowest note   Combined = Fr^6

German 6th

a: It^6 P5 above lowest note   Combined = Gr^6

Assignment 23.1

1. Write the requested chord in simple position on the staff.
2. Name the key. Each given tone is the bass note of the augmented 6th chord and is a major 3rd below the tonic of a minor key.
3. The example illustrates the correct procedure.

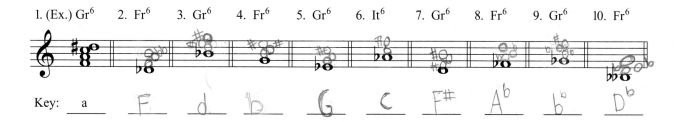

1. (Ex.) Gr⁶   2. Fr⁶   3. Gr⁶   4. Fr⁶   5. Gr⁶   6. It⁶   7. Gr⁶   8. Fr⁶   9. Gr⁶   10. Fr⁶

Key: a   F   d   b   G   C   F#   Ab   b   Db

Assignment 23.2

In each exercise, an augmented 6th chord in four-part harmony is given.

1. Write the most conventional resolution in four-part harmony.
2. In the blank provided, name the key. The bass tone of each given augmented 6th chord is a major 3rd below the tonic of the key.
3. Analyze both chords (the given chord and its resolution).

The example illustrates correct procedure.

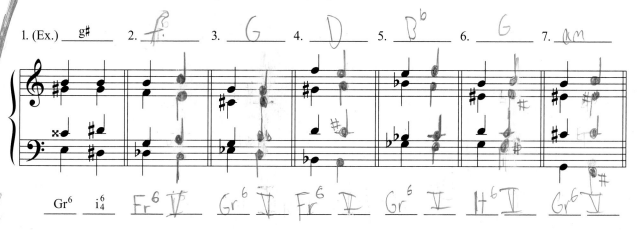

1. (Ex.) g#   2. f#   3. G   4. D   5. Bb   6. G   7. am

Gr⁶ i⁶₄   Fr⁶ V   Gr⁶ I   Fr⁶ I   Gr⁶ I   It⁶ I   Gr⁶ V

Assignment 23.3

The following examples are taken from four-part chorale phrases.

As a keyboard assignment:

1. Play each chorale phrase on the piano, adding the alto and tenor voice according to the figured-bass symbols.
2. If you have difficulty with this assignment, play each chord in simple position (all voices within one octave and with the left hand).
3. When you are familiar with the sound of each example, begin working with both hands, fitting the upper voices into their proper range.

As a written assignment:

1. Add the alto and tenor voices according to the figured-bass symbols.
2. Provide a complete harmonic analysis.

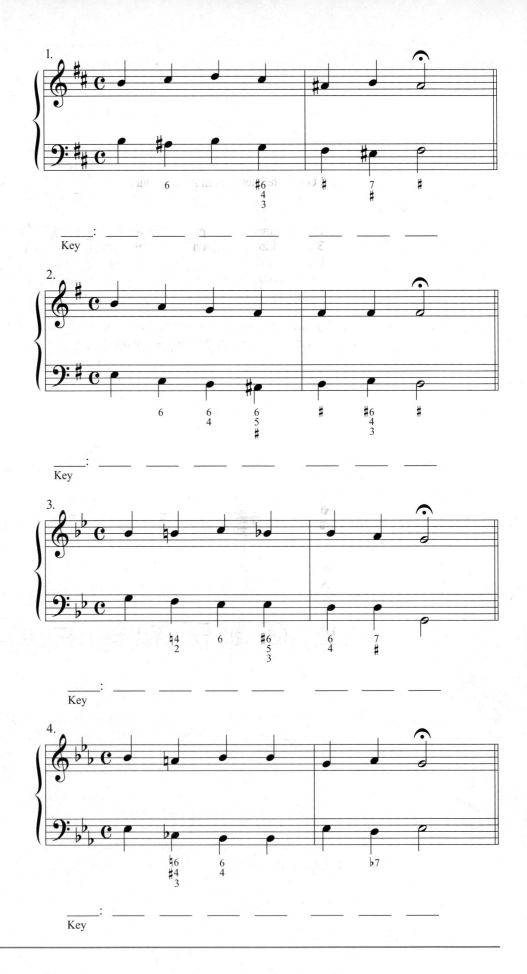

1.

Key _____ : _____ _____ _____ _____ _____ _____

2.

Key _____ : _____ _____ _____ _____ _____

3.

Key _____ : _____ _____ _____ _____ _____

4.

Key _____ : _____ _____ _____ _____ _____

Assignment 23.4

The following phrases are figured-bass lines.

As a keyboard assignment:

1. Play each figured bass, adding soprano, alto, and tenor according to the figured-bass symbols.
2. If you have difficulty, become familiar with the chords first, then work on a good soprano melody.
3. Look at the melodies in Assignment 23.3 for ideas.

As a written assignment:

1. On a separate sheet of paper, copy out the bass notes and figuration.
2. Be sure to include an additional staff for the soprano and alto voices.
3. If you have difficulty with this assignment, write out the pitches in simple position (one above the other without regard for voicing). With this procedure you will be better able to fashion a desirable melody.
4. When you think you have an acceptable soprano melody, fill in the inner voices (alto and tenor).
5. When you are finished, provide a complete analysis.

Assignment 23.5   Each excerpt is similar to the music analyzed in this chapter.

1. Add a macro analysis and a Roman numeral analysis using the illustrations as a guide.
2. Write a short essay (50 to 100 words) for each excerpt, summarizing the analysis. Use the descriptions in the chapter as a guide.

1. Joplin: *The Cascades,* mm. 38–41.

2. Tom Turpin: *The St. Louis Rag,* mm. 66–68.

3. Joplin: *The Chrysanthemum,* mm. 17–20.

Macro
analysis:

Bb:

4. Mozart: Sonata in F Major, K. 332, III, mm. 61–65.

Macro
analysis:

    C:

5. Mozart: Sonata in D Major, K. 284, III: Variation VII, mm. 2–5.

Macro
analysis:

    d:

6. Mozart: Sonata in D Major, K. 284, III: Variation XII, mm. 26–29.

Macro
analysis:

    D:

Assignment 23.6   The excerpts that follow contain augmented 6th chords. Provide a complete harmonic analysis of each excerpt and discuss the following:

1. How many instances of augmented 6th chords did you find in the excerpts?
2. How many chords in the excerpts are part (either beginning or end) of a circle progression?
3. Name all chords (other than augmented 6th chords and triads in second inversion) that are not part of a circle progression.

1. Beethoven: Sonata in F Minor, op. 2, no. 1, I, mm. 139–152.

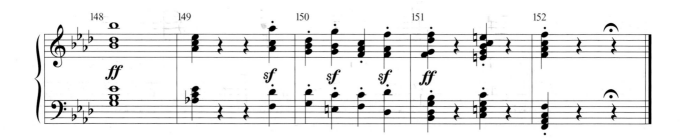

2. Beethoven: Thirty-two Variations, WoO 80, Variation XXX.

3. Beethoven: Sonata in C Minor ("*Pathétique*"), op. 13, no. 8, III, mm. 41–51.

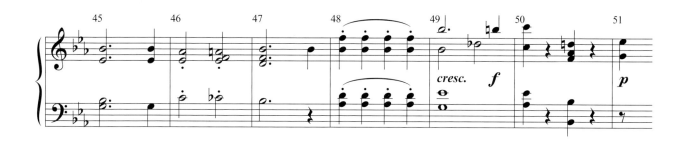

4. Tchaikovsky: Piano Concerto no. 1 in B-flat Minor, op. 23, II, mm. 13–20.

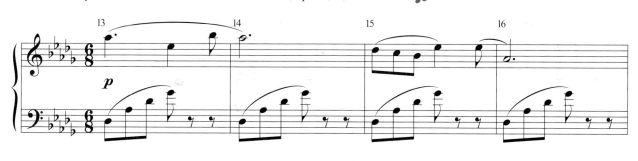

5. Tchaikovsky: Mazurka from *Album for the Young,* op. 39, no. 10, mm. 35–52.

The Classical Period

Many of our best-known composers lived during the classical period (1750–1825). Haydn, Mozart, and Beethoven all lived in this artistically rich period. The balance shifted even more than in the baroque period in favor of instrumental music, although operas continued to be written. Chamber music, orchestral music, and other instrumental works gained ascendancy. The sonata and the symphony developed during the classical period, and the string quartet took the place of the older trio sonata. The pianoforte (our modern piano), invented in 1709 by Christofori, became a popular household instrument. In the classical period the orchestral literature grew in size and importance, and the orchestra itself acquired more color and flexibility. Clarinets became permanent fixtures in the orchestra, along with flutes, oboes, and bassoons.

In the following section we examine representative movements from classical sonatas. Most of these movements are in one of three forms: theme and variation, sonata, and rondo. The classical theme and variation developed out of instrumental variations by sixteenth- and seventeenth-century composers such as Antonio de Cabezón, William Byrd, and Girolamo Frescobaldi, whereas the sonata form has historical precedents in the rounded binary forms of the baroque dance suite. The classical rondo developed from the French rondeau of Jean-Baptiste Lully, Jean-Philippe Rameau, and François Couperin. These forms, which were perfected in the classical period, became the most prominent forms of the romantic period and have persisted into the twenty-first century.

CHAPTER 24

Variation Technique

Topics	Variation	Theme and Variation	Change of Harmony
	Continuous Variation	Embellished Melodic Line	Change of Tempo
	Ground Bass	Unique Rhythmic Figure	Extended Pitch Range
	Basso Ostinato	Change of Meter	Harmonic Motive
	Chaconne	Change of Mode	Repeated Motive
	Passacaglia	Alberti Bass Figure	Change of Voice

Important Concepts

Variation is the transformation of a musical idea using a variety of modification techniques. A musical idea can be a melody, bass line, chord progression, phrase structure, or combination of these elements. Changes often include alterations, developments, and embellishments to an assortment of musical materials. The musical idea is usually presented first, and then followed by variation treatment of elements, such as the melody, harmony, rhythm, meter, mode, texture, and expression markings.

In Figure 24.1 the musical idea is a melody that is then decorated with neighboring tones.

Figure 24.1

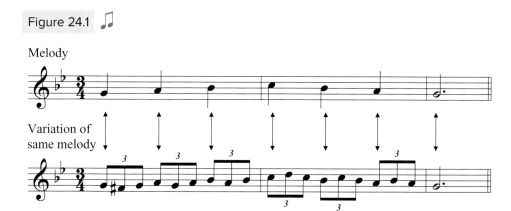

Two types of variations are widely recognized, *continuous variations* and *theme and variations.*

Continuous Variation

Continuous variation is a technique based on the uninterrupted flow of a repeated bass line, repeated harmonic progression, repeated rhythmic pattern, or various combinations of the three. The composer weaves new musical materials around the repeated pattern.

One of the most common types of continuous variation employs a *ground bass*—also called *basso ostinato.* The ground bass (the primary musical idea) usually consists of a short melody of four to eight measures that is generally maintained in the lowest voice and is repeated throughout the composition. The terms *chaconne* and *passacaglia* refer to specific types of continuous variation compositions. Although the two terms were used interchangeably in the seventeenth century, passacaglia was often associated with a repeated ground bass and chaconne with a repeated harmonic progression. The composition by André Raison (1654–1719) in Figure 24.2 predates the better-known passacaglia by Bach.

Figure 24.2

Raison: Passacaille in G Minor from *Messe du Deuxième Ton* (Mass of the Second Tone), mm. 1–18. ♪

1st statement of ground bass (basso ostinato)

2nd statement of ground bass (basso ostinato)

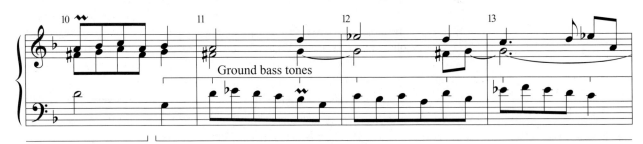

3rd statement of ground bass (basso ostinato)

4th statement of ground bass (basso ostinato)

The ground bass in Figure 24.2 is four measures long. Above the bass, the composer has created a two-voiced contrapuntal texture. Notice that the upper lines are different for each statement of the ground bass. As is typical with most continuous variation compositions, there is little if any pause between the statements of the ground.

Statements one and two of the ground bass are the same, but statements three and four include rhythmic changes (see Figure 24.3). Furthermore, the third statement of the ground bass has been decorated with nonharmonic tones in eighth notes. Despite these changes to the bass melody, the original tones are present.

Figure 24.3

1st and 2nd statements of ground bass (mm. 3–6 and 7–10)

3rd statement of ground bass (mm. 11–14)

4th statement of ground bass (mm. 15–18)

Theme and Variation

Theme and variation describes a composition where a theme is stated first and then followed by a series of variations. Each variation is complete within itself and is usually followed by a short pause.

Figures 24.4 to 24.11 illustrate some of the more frequent techniques of variation. The theme chosen is the first phrase of "God Save the King," better known in the United States as "America." Most of the illustrations are excerpted from Beethoven's set of variations (1803). Beethoven employed the entire melody, but for purposes of space conservation, only the first phrase is shown here. Figure 24.4 is the first phrase of the theme.

Figure 24.4

Beethoven: Seven Variations on "God Save the King," WoO 78, Theme, mm. 1–6.

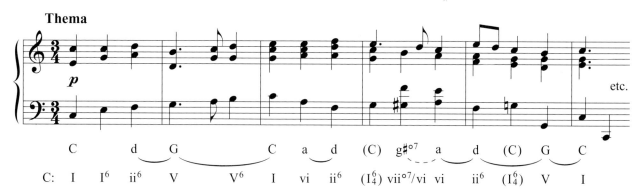

Embellished Melodic Line	One of the most common techniques is to decorate the theme with additional notes. In Figure 24.5 the original melody notes are present but highly embellished. A change of meter also occurs.

Figure 24.5

Beethoven: Seven Variations on "God Save the King," WoO 78, Variation VII, mm. 1–6. ♩♪

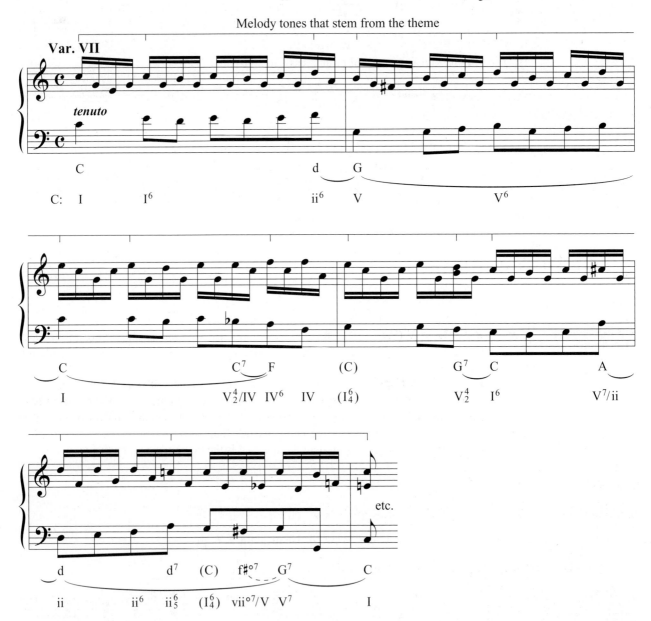

Unique Rhythmic Figure	In Variation VI (Figure 24.6), Beethoven introduces a short rhythmic figure (dotted 8th–16th) not present in the original. The figure is heard 14 times in this short excerpt.
Change of Meter	Whereas the original theme ("America") is in $\frac{3}{4}$ meter, Variation VI is in $\frac{4}{4}$.
Embellished Melodic Line	As in Variation VII (Figure 24.5), the melody in Variation VI is also embellished.

Figure 24.6

Beethoven: Seven Variations on "God Save the King," WoO 78, Variation VI, mm. 1–6.

Change of Mode In Variation V (Figure 24.7) there is a change of mode to the parallel minor (C major to C minor).

Alberti Bass Figure In Variation V (Figure 24.7) an Alberti bass has been added. Although the original theme is in block chords, the chords of Variation V are arpeggiated in an ascending Alberti bass pattern. As with many of the variations in this set, an embellished melodic line is also included.

Figure 24.7

Beethoven: Seven Variations on "God Save the King," WoO 78, Variation V, mm. 1–6.

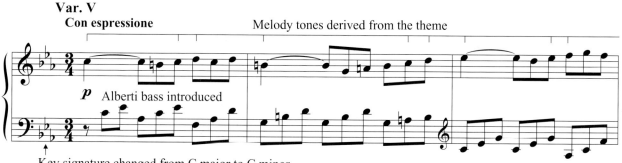

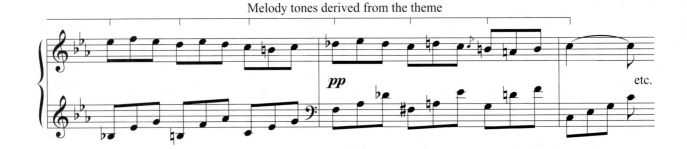

Melody tones derived from the theme

Change of Harmony   In Variation VII (Figure 24.8) the variation begins in a different key (D minor), and the harmony is considerably more complex. The melody itself is couched in the key of F major, but the harmonization in D minor establishes an added variation dimension.

Change of Tempo   Variation VII also demonstrates another variation technique—change of tempo. The new tempo, Adagio, contributes to contrast between this variation and the theme.

Figure 24.8

Beethoven: Seven Variations on "God Save the King," WoO 78, Variation VII (transition to coda), mm. 26–31. ♪

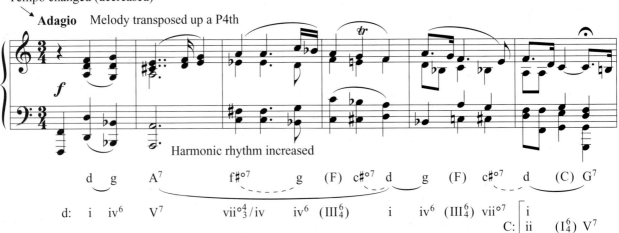

Extended Pitch Range   In Variation IV (Figure 24.9) the range of the melody is extended to cover three octaves, whereas the original melody occupies the range of a diminished 5th.

Harmonic Motive   A repeated harmonic motive also occurs in Variation IV. The motive is considered to be harmonic because the emphasis centers on the series of dominant 7th chords and their respective resolutions. Notice how each major-minor seventh chord in measures 1, 2, and 3 resolves as expected. This harmonic pattern takes on the characteristic of a motive because of the series of repetitions.

Figure 24.9

Beethoven: Seven Variations on "God Save the King," WoO 78, Variation IV, mm. 1–6.

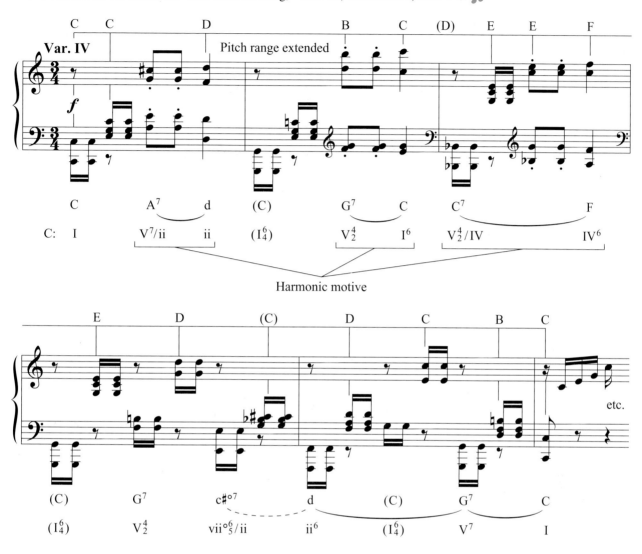

Repeated Motive

In Figure 24.10 (not by Beethoven), a motive from the original melody is used as the basis for a variation. Note the imitation between the two melodic lines.

Figure 24.10

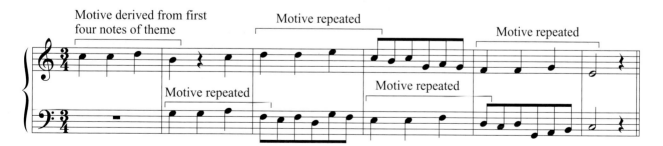

Change of Voice

In Figure 24.11 (also not by Beethoven), the melody is found in the lower voice instead of the upper voice.

Figure 24.11

Theme placed in another voice

Melody placed in bass clef

History

Both continuous variations and theme and variations find their immediate roots in the sixteenth century. Continuous variations (also known as *basso ostinato*) were employed in English music of the late sixteenth century, and the formal aspects were maintained through the baroque, classical, and romantic periods nearly intact. The *Fitzwilliam Virginal Book* (about 1619) contains a number of continuous variations by William Byrd, John Bull, and Giles Farnaby.

Compositions known as theme and variations have their roots in sixteenth-century Italy and Spain, originating in dance forms such as the *passamezzo* and the *romanesca*. Almost all the important composers of the baroque, classical, and romantic periods wrote compositions using theme and variation techniques.

Summary

The following variation techniques have been illustrated in this chapter. These are only a few of the many techniques available to composers, but they represent the more common procedures.

Embellished melodic line	Change of harmony
Unique rhythmic figure	Change of tempo
Change of meter	Extended pitch range
Change of mode	Use of harmonic motive
Change of key	Use of a repeated melodic motive
Use of an Alberti bass figure	Change of voice

Practice

Locate a copy of the *Fitzwilliam Virginal Book* at your music library or on the internet, and look over the compositions, noting all works in continuous variation form. Study the examples you find and determine where the recurring sections occur. Note the methods used to vary each statement of the main musical statement.

Also look in your school library or online for examples of theme and variations. These are usually identified either in the title of the work or in the title of the movement in the case of multimovement works. Sonatas from the classical period are a good place to begin your search. Note the variation techniques employed for each variation.

Listen to live performances or recordings of the compositions you identify as variations. Do an aural assessment of both variation types.

Assignment 24.1   The following chaconne is an example of continuous variation.

1. Make a complete harmonic analysis of the composition. Circle nonharmonic tones and label them by type.
2. On the score, indicate where each statement of the recurring harmonic progression begins and ends.
3. On a separate sheet of paper, identify the relationship between the inital statement of the recurring harmonic progression and each variation. Describe any techniques you find interesting.

Fischer: Chaconne in A Minor from the *Musicalischer Parnassus, Melpomene Suite.*

Assignment 24.2   Write a composition in continuous variation form.

1. Select an ostinato of four measures.
2. Plan the composition so that the ostinato is repeated eight times.
3. Sketch ideas for each new ostinato repetition.
4. Plan a perfect authentic cadence at the end of the eighth repetition.
5. Make the earlier variations on the ostinato simpler and of thinner texture.
6. Plan a gradual crescendo from the third or fourth repetition of the ostinato to the final (eighth) repetition, creating a climax with thick texture and increased dynamics.
7. If you have difficulty composing an ostinato theme of your own, you may use one of these:

Assignment 24.3

This assignment includes the complete theme and 14 excerpts from Beethoven's 24 variations on Righini's theme "Venni Amore."

On a separate sheet, indicate in detail the technique or techniques used in each variation. Some variations contain more than one technique and may include types not listed in this chapter. Describe in your own words any different or combined techniques you find that are interesting.

Beethoven: Twenty-four Variations on "Venni Amore," by Righini, WoO 65.

Var. II

Var. IV

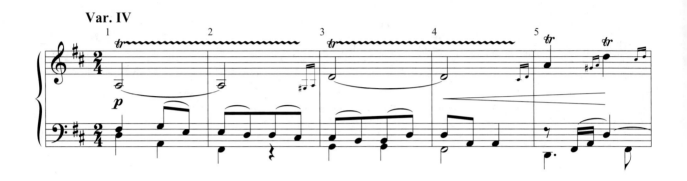

Var. V

Var. XI

Var. XII

Var. XIII

Var. XVI

Var. XIX

Var. XX

Var. XXI

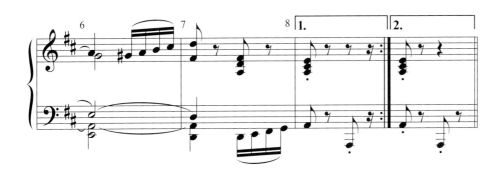

Var. XXIV
Allegro

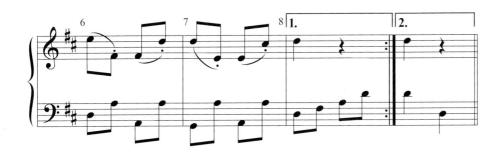

Assignment 24.4   This theme is the basis for a composition in theme and variation form.

1. Using the theme, write a set of five variations using the following techniques:
   a. Embellished melodic line
   b. Introduction of an Alberti bass figure
   c. Theme placed in another voice
   d. Change of meter
   e. Change of mode

2. Write your composition for any medium you want as long as it can be performed in class.

Russian Folk Song.

Assignment 24.5   Compose a set of five variations on a theme of your choosing. You may select a well-known theme (like "Pop Goes the Weasel") or the theme from a popular song, or you may make up your own theme.

As a diversion, play only the variations (omit the statement of the theme) in class and let class members guess the theme title.

CHAPTER 25

Sonata Form

Important Concepts

Sonata form is one of the larger structures in tonal music. The name denotes a composition or movement with three major sections identified as the *exposition,* the *development,* and the *recapitulation.* The term *sonata form* distinguishes the form of a single movement from the term *sonata,* which generally refers to all movements of a multimovement composition.

General Pattern

The outline of the form as shown in the following table is simply a point of departure. Few actual examples adhere rigidly to this structure. As each section of sonata form is discussed in detail, the alternatives and deviations from the norm are noted.

Section	Key
Exposition	
Theme 1, or theme group 1	Tonic
Transition	Tonic to dominant, or tonic to relative major (in minor keys)
Theme 2, or theme group 2	Dominant, or relative major (in minor keys)
Theme 3 (optional)	Dominant, or relative major (in minor keys)
Codetta (optional)	Dominant, or relative major (in minor keys)
Development	
No standard design, but one or more themes are developed	Various keys—usually more than one
Recapitulation	
Theme 1, or theme group 1	Tonic
Transition	Tonic (no modulation or return to tonic)
Theme 2, or theme group 2	Tonic
Theme 3, or theme group 3	Tonic
Coda (optional)	Tonic

The first movement from Haydn's Sonata in G Major, Hob. XVI:G1, is analyzed and discussed, section by section (Figures 25.1–25.6), to illustrate the parts of sonata form.

Exposition

The *exposition* states the material on which the entire movement is based. In this example the exposition is the first 28 measures of the work (Figures 25.1–25.3).

First Theme or Theme Group

The *first theme* of the sonata, in the key of G major, is stated in the first 12 measures (Figure 25.1). The purpose of the first theme is to provide stability and a frame of reference for the following sections. In the Haydn sonata, the tonic key is emphasized by tonic prolongation and dominant–tonic repetitions but gives way to modulation at the cadence.

Sometimes in larger sonatas, several melodies are presented in this first section. In such cases, they are referred to as a *theme group*.

Figure 25.1

Haydn: Sonata in G Major, Hob. XVI:G1, I, mm. 1–12.

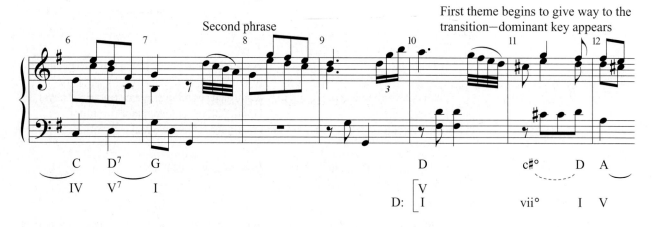

Transition

The *transition* (mm. 13–16) creates a smooth connection between the first and second themes (Figure 25.2). Although a transition can include the modulation from the tonic key to the new key, the transition in the Haydn sonata reinforces the key of D major that appeared at the end of the first theme.

Transitions may contain only first theme material, only second theme material, combinations of these materials, or material unrelated to either theme.

Figure 25.2

Haydn: Sonata in G Major, Hob. XVI:G1, I, mm. 13–16.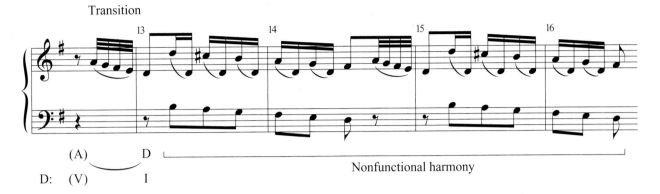

Second Theme or Theme Group

The *second theme* of sonata form generally tends to be more lyrical than the first theme. In Figure 25.3, the second theme (mm. 17–28) contrasts with the first theme and is in the dominant key. In movements in minor keys, the second theme is often in the relative major key. In some early sonatas, the second theme is a restatement of the first theme in the dominant key. These sonata form movements with only one theme are known as *monothematic*.

Figure 25.3

Haydn: Sonata in G Major, Hob. XVI:G1, I, mm. 17–28.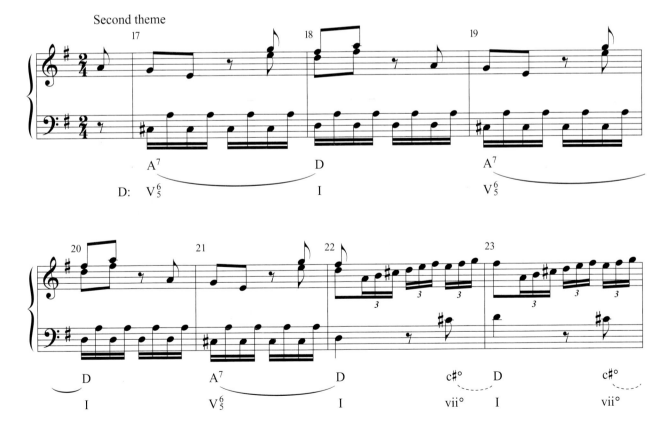

Third Theme (Closing Theme)

Some sonata form movements, particularly those of extended length, have a *third theme*. This theme is often called a *closing theme*; it is usually in the same key as the second but has a character that distinguishes it as a separate unit.

Codetta

A *codetta* (small coda) often completes the exposition. A codetta has the general characteristics of an extended cadence. In this case, a cadential extension serves to complete the exposition (Figure 25.3).

Development

The *development* consists of measures 29 to 53 (Figure 25.4). Development sections include motivic manipulation of the themes from the exposition. Several keys not found in the exposition appear. In the Haydn sonata, the development contains the first and second themes from the exposition, and the keys of C major, D major, and E minor are visited briefly. No standardized organization exists for developments, but most divide into identifiable subsections, distinguished by the thematic material.

Figure 25.4

Haydn: Sonata in G Major, Hob. XVI:G1, I, mm. 29–53.

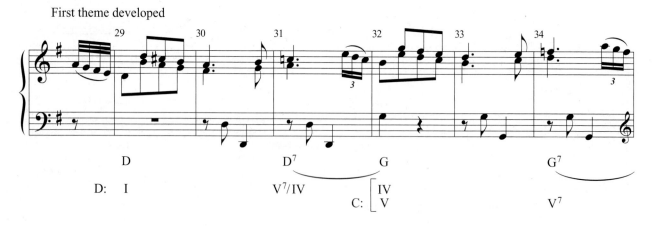

Second theme developed

Retransition

The *retransition* is a passage at the end of the development that anticipates the recapitulation by combining fragments of the first theme and by modulating to the tonic key. The return to the original key is often accompanied by a dominant prolongation that signals the impending arrival of the tonic. In the Haydn sonata, the retransition consists of measures 54 to 57 (Figure 25.5).

Figure 25.5

Haydn: Sonata in G Major, Hob. XVI:G1, I, mm. 54–57. ♪

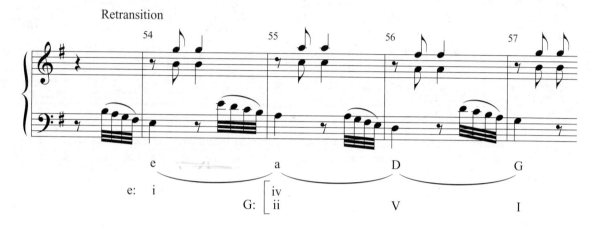

Recapitulation

The *recapitulation* is the balance of the sonata form. In some ways the recapitulation is quite similar to the exposition, but the original key of the composition is used for all themes. Transitions are often shorter than in the exposition because there is no need to modulate. In the Haydn sonata, the recapitulation occurs from measure 58 to the end (Figure 25.6).

Coda

A *coda,* if present, is similar to, but larger than, the codetta that ended the exposition. In the case of the Haydn sonata, the movement ends in a similar manner to the exposition with a cadential extension concluding the movement (Figure 25.6)

Figure 25.6

Haydn: Sonata in G Major, Hob. XVI:G1, I, mm. 58–80. ♪

Transition begins

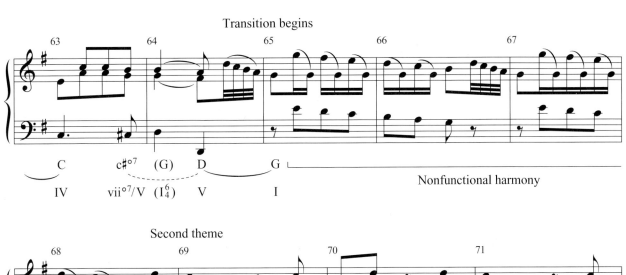

Nonfunctional harmony

Second theme

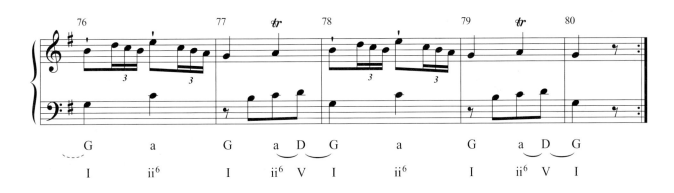

Although the term *sonata* was used in a variety of ways prior to 1750, this chapter addresses the form as it emerged in the mid-eighteenth century.

Sonata form developed from rounded binary form, in which the exposition was part 1 and the development–recapitulation was part 2. The process of maturation was slow, and although the binary form of the baroque period (1600–1750) contained all the necessary ingredients for sonata form, the actual culmination did not take place until the mid-eighteenth century. The form was perfected and received wide acceptance during the classical period, which saw its most concentrated application.

Application

The Mozart sonata movement in Figure 25.7 is given a complete analysis for purposes of illustration. A harmonic analysis (both macro analysis and traditional analysis) and a sectional analysis are placed directly on the score. Arrows appearing with the harmonic analysis indicate the continuation of an existing harmony. The circled numbers mark phrase beginnings, and their endings are shown by two vertical lines (‖). A discussion of important features of the work and a summary can be found on pages 565 to 567.

Of Mozart's nineteen piano sonatas, this is the seventh and may have been written in Salzburg in 1777 before the outset of a tour that included Munich, Augsburg, and Mannheim. Mozart composed the work at the age of 21, but it was not published until five years later in 1782.

Figure 25.7

Mozart: Sonata in C Major, K. 309, I. ♩♪

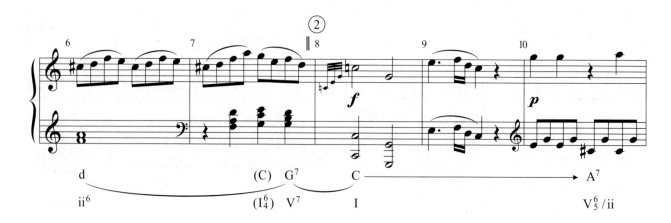

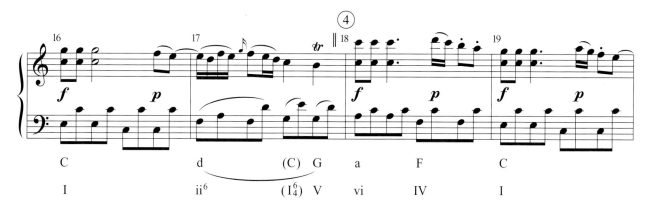

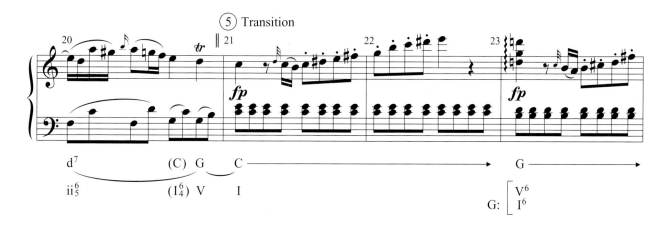

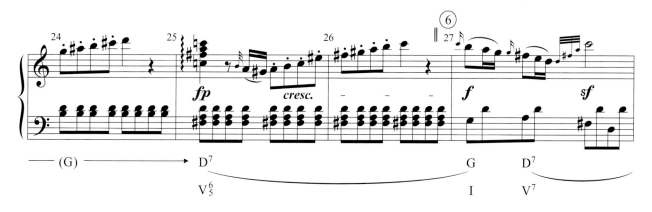

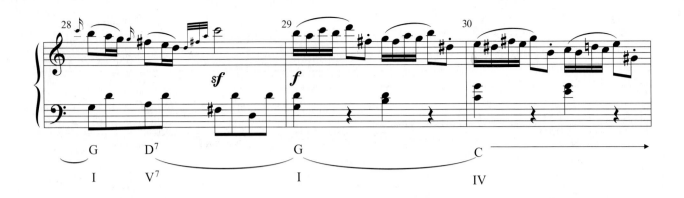

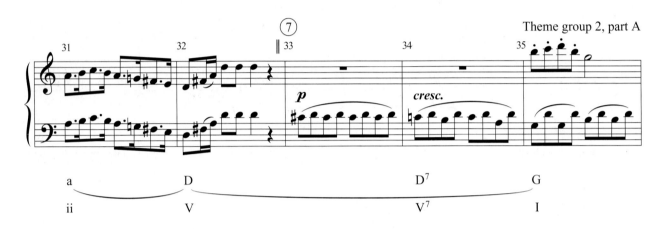

Theme group 2, part A

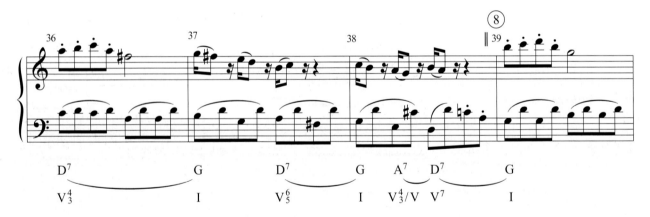

Theme group 2, part B

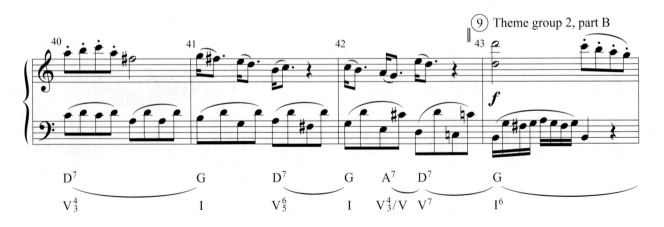

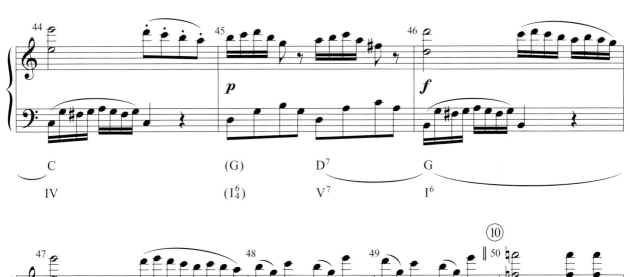

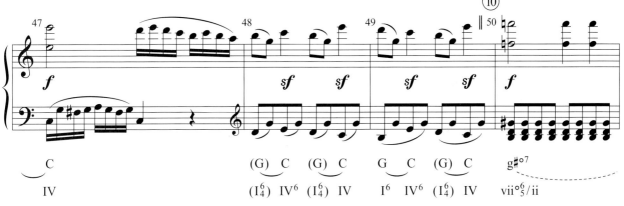

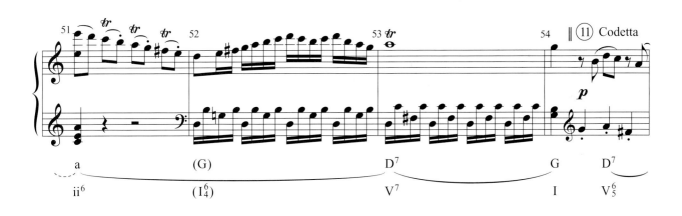

Development

⑫ (From theme group 1, part A)

g ⟶

g: iv ⟶

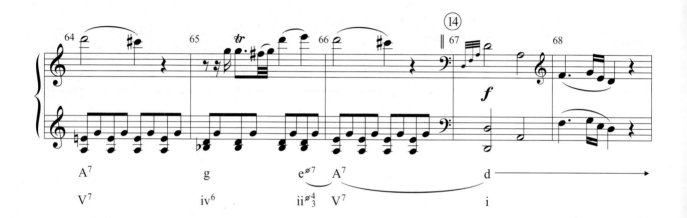

A⁷   g   e^{ø7}   A⁷   d ⟶

V⁷   iv⁶   ii^{ø4/3}   V⁷   i

— (d) ⟶ b^{ø7}   E⁷   d   b^{ø7}   E⁷

a: iv⁶   ii^{ø4/3}   V⁷   iv⁶   ii^{ø4/3}   V⁷

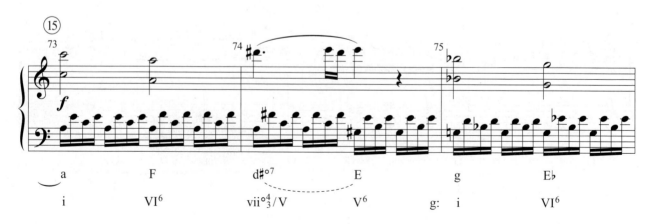

a   F   d♯^{o7}   E   g   E♭

i   VI⁶   vii^{o4/3}/V   V⁶   g: i   VI⁶

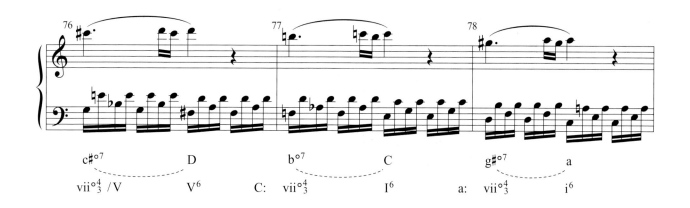

$$c\#^{\circ 7} \qquad\qquad D \qquad\qquad b^{\circ 7} \qquad\qquad C \qquad\qquad g\#^{\circ 7} \qquad\qquad a$$
$$\text{vii}^{\circ 4}_{3}/V \qquad V^{6} \qquad C: \text{vii}^{\circ 4}_{3} \qquad I^{6} \qquad a: \text{vii}^{\circ 4}_{3} \qquad i^{6}$$

⑯ (From codetta)

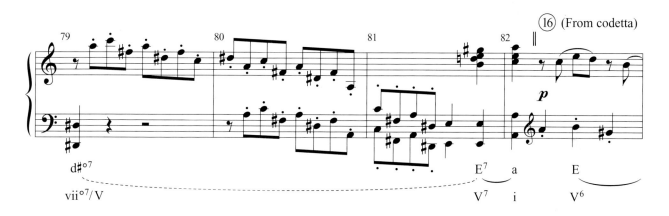

$$d\#^{\circ 7} \qquad\qquad\qquad\qquad\qquad\qquad\qquad\qquad E^{7} \quad a \qquad E$$
$$\text{vii}^{\circ 7}/V \qquad\qquad\qquad\qquad\qquad\qquad\qquad\qquad V^{7} \quad i \qquad V^{6}$$

⑰ (From theme group 1, part A)

$$a \quad F \quad b^{\circ} \quad E \quad a \qquad b^{\circ} \quad g\#^{\circ} \quad a \quad F \quad b^{\circ} \quad E \qquad a$$
$$i \quad VI \quad \text{ii}^{\circ 6} \quad V \quad i \qquad \text{ii}^{\circ} \quad \text{vii}^{\circ} \quad i \quad VI \quad \text{ii}^{\circ 6} \quad V \qquad i$$

⑱

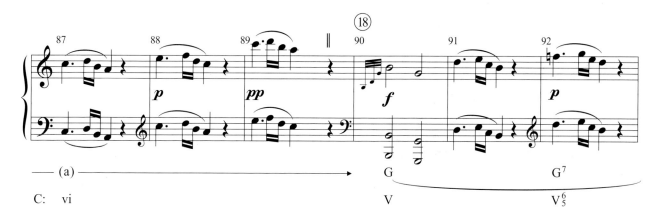

$$(a) \qquad\qquad\qquad\qquad\qquad\qquad\qquad\qquad\qquad G \qquad\qquad\qquad G^{7}$$
$$C: \text{vi} \qquad\qquad\qquad\qquad\qquad\qquad\qquad\qquad V \qquad\qquad\qquad V^{6}_{5}$$

Recapitulation

(19) Theme group 1, part A

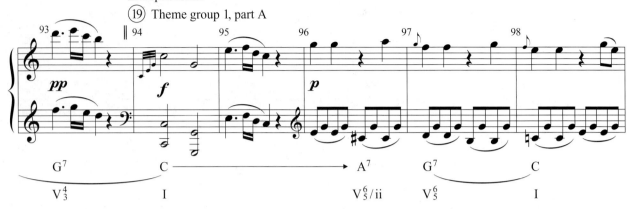

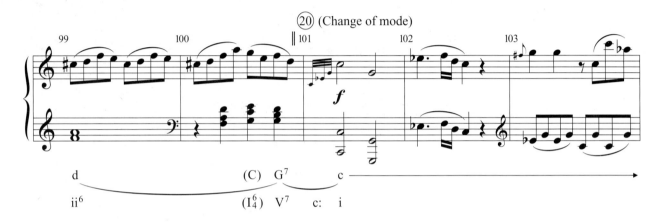

(20) (Change of mode)

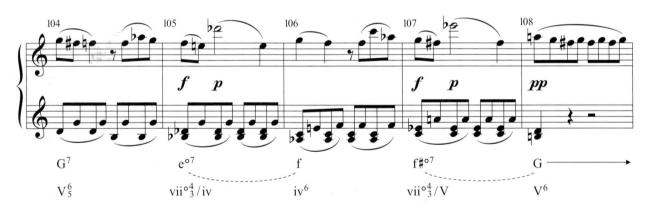

(21) Theme group 1, part B

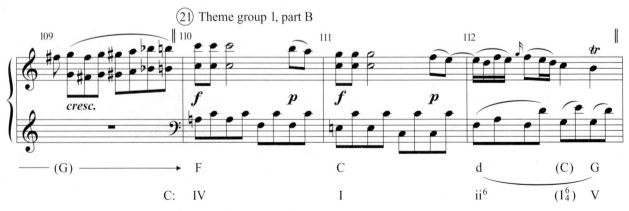

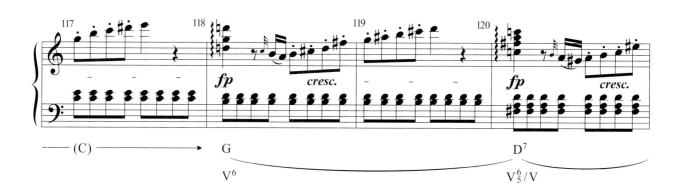

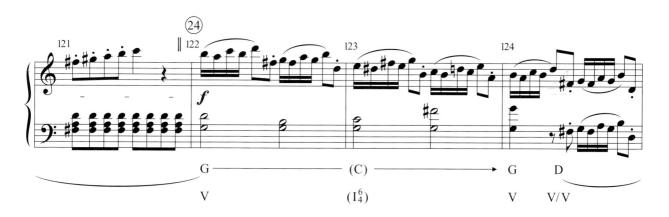

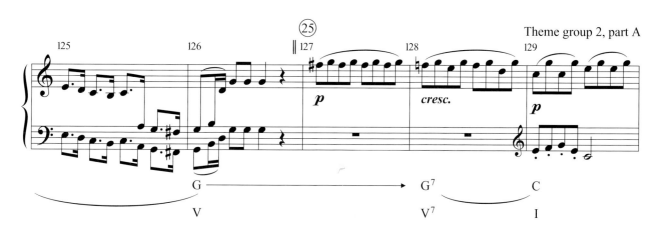

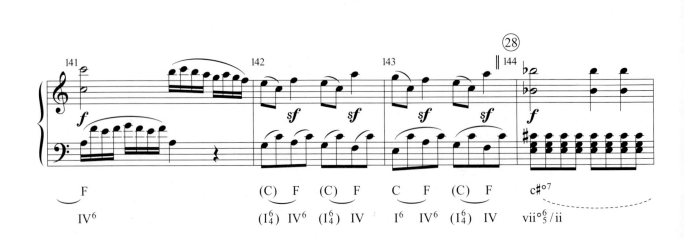

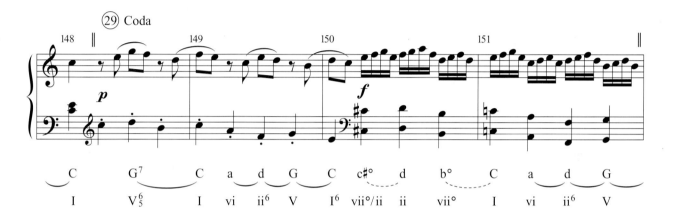

(29) Coda

(30) (From theme group 1, part A)

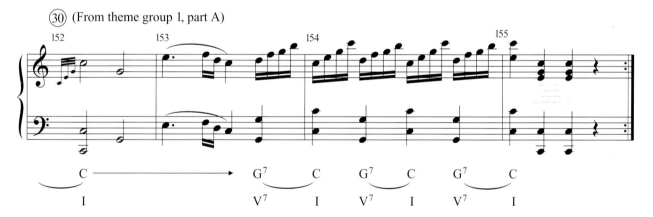

Formal Outline

Section	Phrase	Measures	Key(s)	Remarks
Exposition	1	1–7	C	Theme group 1, part A
	2	8–14	C	Theme group 1, part A, continued
	3	15–17	C	Theme group 1, part B
	4	18–20	C	Theme group 1, part B, continued
	5	21–26	C–G	Transition
	6	27–32	G	Transition, second phrase
	7	33–38	G	Theme group 2, part A (2 measure extension)
	8	39–42	G	Theme group 2, part A, continued
	9	43–49	G	Theme group 2, part B
	10	50–54	G	Theme group 2, part B, continued
	11	54–58	G	Codetta
Development	12	59–62	d	Derived from theme group 1, part A
	13	63–66	d	Derived from theme group 1, part A
	14	67–72	d–a	Derived from theme group 1, part A
	15	73–82	a	Derived from theme group 1, part A
	16	82–85	a	Derived from codetta
	17	86–89	a	Derived from theme group 1, part A
	18	90–93	a–C	Derived from theme group 1, part A
Recapitulation	19	94–100	C	Theme group 1, part A
	20	101–109	C	Theme group 1, part A (change of mode)
	21	110–112	C	Theme group 1, part B
	22	113–115	C	Theme group 1, part B, continued
	23	116–121	C	Transition
	24	122–126	C	Transition, second phrase
	25	127–132	C	Theme group 2, part A
	26	133–136	C	Theme group 2, part A, continued
	27	137–143	C	Theme group 2, part B
	28	144–148	C	Theme group 2, part B, continued
	29	148–151	C	Coda
	30	152–155	C	Coda

| General Comments | This sonata movement is a textbook example of sonata form. The larger sections (exposition, development, recapitulation) are easily discernible. The characteristics that make this movement unique and distinguish it from others are found in the phrase and period relationships. |

| Phrases | Phrases are frequently of odd lengths in comparison with the conventional four-measure phrase. |

Phrases	Phrase Lengths
Phrase 1	7 measures long
Phrase 2	7 measures long
Phrase 3	3 measures long
Phrase 4	3 measures long
Phrase 5	6 measures long
Phrase 6	6 measures long
Phrase 7	6 measures long
Phrase 8	4 measures long

| *Period Construction* | Parallel periods (where the phrases are related one to the other) tend to be of similar, if unconventional, length. Although phrases 7 and 8 appear to differ in length, phrase 7 is a four-measure phrase with an extension in the accompaniment, which does not distort the parallel period relationship. |

Parallel Periods	Phrase Lengths
Phrases 1 and 2	Both phrases 7 measures long
Phrases 3 and 4	Both phrases 3 measures long
Phrases 5 and 6	Both phrases 6 measures long
Phrases 7 and 8	Phrases 6 and 4 measures long

| *Phrase Members* | A number of phrases are composed of dissimilar phrase members, such as those shown in Figure 25.8, taken from the first phrase. |

Figure 25.8

Mozart: Sonata in C Major, K. 309, I, mm. 1–7.

Phrase Overlap (Elision)

Some phrases in this work overlap with the subsequent phrase (Figure 25.9). As an example, phrase 2 begins in measure 8, but the logical conclusion (resolution of the V^7) of phrase 1 is the first beat of phrase 2 (m. 8). For purposes of simplicity, the elision of phrases is not shown in the analysis. Because 16 of the 30 phrases contain elisions, it becomes one of the distinctive features of the work.

Figure 25.9

Mozart: Sonata in C Major, K. 309, I, mm. 7–8.

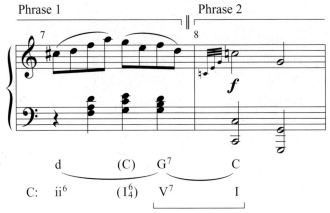

Nonoverlapping Phrases

Only five phrases come to full closure within the four-measure unit. A perfect authentic cadence is reached in each of these phrases:

Phrase	Measures	Remarks
10	50–54	Signals codetta of exposition to follow
11	54–58	End of codetta (and exposition)
15	73–82	Development section
28	144–148	Signals codetta of recapitulation
30	152–155	End of movement

Delayed Resolution

In three instances, the flow of circle progressions is interrupted at the end of the phrase, and completion (tonic) is withheld—seven measures in one instance.

Circle in Phrase	Measures	Tonic Reached in Measure	Tonic Triad Delayed
3	15–17	21	4 measures
20	101–109	116	7 measures
21	110–112	116	4 measures

Phrases 12 and 17 have no harmonic movement and therefore lack a strong harmonic cadence.

Harmony

The basic understructure of the composition, as revealed by the analysis, is uncomplicated. Circle progressions dominate the movement as expected and shape the overall harmonic scheme.

Harmonic Structure

Excluding progressions that depart from tonic (I to vi, I to ii, I to V, etc.), most progressions are part of circle progressions.

Secondary Dominant and Leading-Tone Chords

Most secondary dominant and leading-tone chords resolve as expected. The exception is a V^7/ii in measure 3, where its resolution is elided (omitted from the string of circle progressions—V^7/ii [ii] V^7 I). The progression is repeated again in the recapitulation.

Absence of Altered Chords

Aside from the numerous secondary dominant and secondary leading-tone chords, the movement is free of altered chords (N^6, It^6, Gr^6, and Fr^6).

Closely Related Keys

All modulations (to G major, D minor, and A minor) are closely related to the tonic.

Conclusions

A significant feature of this movement is the elision of phrases. Ending one phrase and beginning another at the same moment gives a listener little time to savor the achieved goal and prepare for the next. Elision gives the movement a dynamic forward motion throughout.

Theme groups are clearly stated, transitions are traditionally constructed, and the harmonic schemes are typical of the period.

Summary

Sonata form, an outgrowth of rounded binary form, has three primary sections: the exposition, the development, and the recapitulation. The movement's primary musical materials are presented in the exposition, manipulated in the development, and restated in the recapitulation.

Practice

Obtain scores and corresponding recordings for any of the piano sonatas by Haydn, Mozart, and Beethoven at your music library or from the internet. As you study the scores, notice that each piano sonata is a multi-movemented composition. Begin listening to each piano sonata while following the score, and attempt to identify which individual movements are in sonata form. First movements of piano sonatas are frequently in sonata form, but sonata form can also appear in other piano sonata movements. If you find it difficult to figure out which movements are in sonata form, look for a mid-movement repeat sign. A repeat sign usually signals the end of an exposition section.

When you are fairly certain you have located a sonata form movement, attempt to identify the large sections of the form (exposition, development, and recapitulation). If you can locate the large sections, attempt to find the subsections. Remember that the tonal centers (keys) will be helpful in identifying the themes. See how many of the following sections, themes, and passages you can identify:

Exposition
    Theme 1, or theme group 1
    Transition
    Theme 2, or theme group 2
    Theme 3 (optional)
    Codetta (optional)

Development
    Themes developed
    Retransition (optional)

Recapitulation
    Theme 1, or theme group 1
    Transition
    Theme 2, or theme group 2
    Theme 3 (optional)
    Coda (optional)

If you find this task too overwhelming, consider choosing one or more of the following movements in sonata form:

Haydn: Sonata in D Major, XVI:37 (I)
Mozart: Sonata in F Major, K. 332 (I)
Beethoven, Sonata in G Major, op. 49, no. 2 (I)

Assignment 25.1

1. Make a complete analysis of this movement using the approach illustrated in this chapter.
2. Invite a student to perform the work in class.
3. Discuss the movement in class, and compare its form with that of the first movement of the Mozart sonata analyzed in this chapter.
4. Invite a member of the piano faculty to the class and ask him or her to discuss performance practices for this particular work.

Beethoven: Sonata in F Minor, op. 2, no. 1, I.

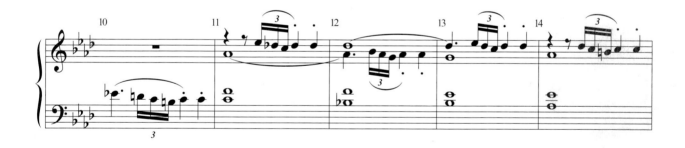

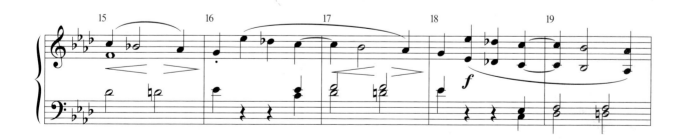

Assignment 25.2

1. Write the exposition of a sonata form.

2. Compose your own first and second theme. (Add a third theme if you want.)

3. Use the first movement of the Beethoven Sonata no. 1 in F minor as a model for the form.

4. Place the first theme in G minor.

5. Place the second theme in B-flat major.

6. The transition will probably provide the greatest difficulty. It may be wise to write the transition after composing the first and second themes. Plot harmonic progressions backward from the beginning of the second theme to ensure that the transition will be smooth and logical.

7. Use the first movement of the Beethoven piano sonata as a guide for form, but write the composition for any instrument or combination of instruments that interests you.

8. Perform your composition in class.

9. Have members of the class identify the various sections of the exposition just by listening.

10. Continue the composition through the development section.

11. Complete the movement by adding the recapitulation.

CHAPTER 26

Rondo Forms

Topics

Refrain	Retransition	Seven-part Rondo
Episode	Three-part Rondo	Sonata Rondo
Transition	Five-part Rondo	

Important Concepts

Rondo form is one of the larger classical forms, consisting of recurring sections called *refrains* interspersed with contrasting sections called *episodes*.

Refrain

The refrain (also known as the rondo theme) is repeated from one to four times during the course of the composition, almost always in the tonic key, and often with variations.

Episode

The episode is inserted between the recurring statements of the refrain. Episodes are typically in contrasting keys. A typical rondo form is as follows:

Sections:	Refrain	Episode 1	Refrain	Episode 2	Refrain
	A	**B**	**A**	**C**	**A**
Keys:	C major	G major	C major	A minor	C major

Transition

A *transition* sometimes connects a refrain to an episode.

A (transition) **B** **A**

Retransition

Often a *retransition* is used to make the return from an episode to the refrain as smooth as possible. A retransition may be included even in instances where a transition is not present.

A (transition) **B** (retransition) **A**

Rondo Types

The following four formal outlines represent the most common types of rondo.

Type	Outline
Three-part rondo	**A B A** (transition and retransition are optional)
	If both the transition and retransition are absent, the three-part rondo is indistinguishable from the three-part form. Three-part form is often found in slow movements from sonatas and symphonies of the classical period.

Type	Outline
Five-part rondo	**A B A C A** (transitions and retransitions are optional)
	The five-part rondo occurs often in slow movements of sonatas, symphonies, and string quartets.
Seven-part rondo	**A B A C A B A** (transitions and retransitions are optional)
	Possibly the most common rondo type; it occurs in the final movement of classical symphonies, string quartets, and solo sonatas.
Sonata rondo	**A B A Development A B A**
	A mixture of sonata and rondo forms. It is like a rondo with the A B C sections and similar to sonata form with the development between the exposition and recapitulation.

General Pattern

The third movement of Mozart's Sonata in C Major, K. 545, is analyzed section-by-section in its entirety to demonstrate an example of a rondo (Figures 26.1–26.6). ♪ Following that presentation is a summary outline of the form.

Refrain 1

The refrain (A) of this rondo form is first presented in measures 1 to 8 (Figure 26.1). Notice that the entire passage is in the key of C major, and nearly all harmonic progressions are circle progressions. The refrain consists of only two phrases, which form a parallel period.

Figure 26.1

Mozart: Sonata in C Major, K. 545, III, mm. 1–8. ♪

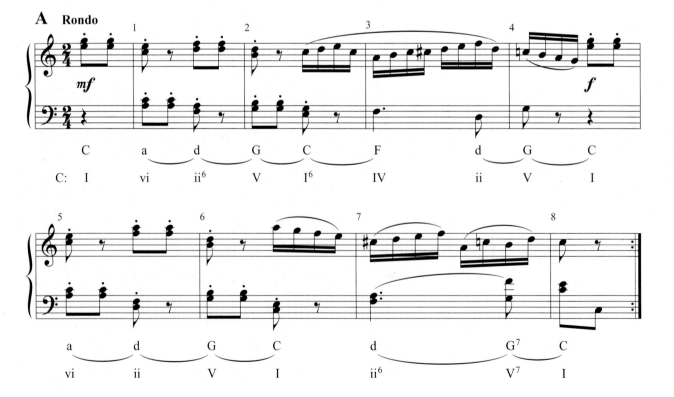

The first episode (B) is in the key of G major, the dominant key. This section (mm. 9–16) contains material that is similar to the A section and closes with a retransition (mm. 17–20). Notice the modulation from G major back to C major, which is an important feature of most retransition sections (Figure 26.2).

Figure 26.2

Mozart: Sonata in C Major, K. 545, III, mm. 9–20.

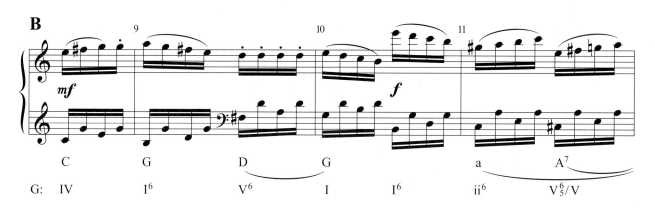

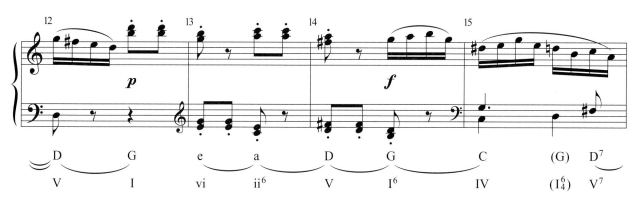

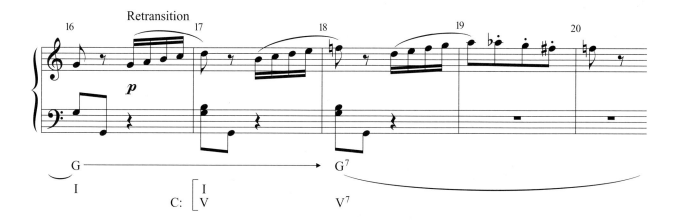

Refrain 2

The refrain (A) returns in measures 21 to 28 unaltered from its first appearance. Like its original presentation, this second statement is in the tonic key of C major (Figure 26.3).

Figure 26.3

Mozart: Sonata in C Major, K. 545, III, mm. 21–28. ♪

Episode 2

The second episode (C) is in the key of A minor, the relative minor key (mm. 29–48). Again, as in the first episode, the melodic materials are similar to those of the refrain. The section closes with a short codetta (mm. 49–52) that functions as a retransition (Figure 26.4).

Figure 26.4

Mozart: Sonata in C Major, K. 545, III, mm. 29–52. ♪

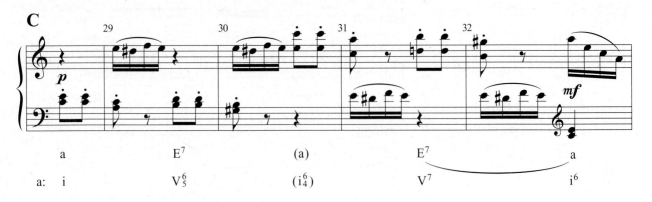

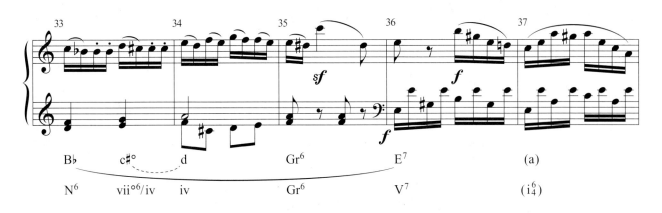

Bb   c#°   d   Gr⁶   E⁷   (a)

N⁶   vii°⁶/iv   iv   Gr⁶   V⁷   (i⁶₄)

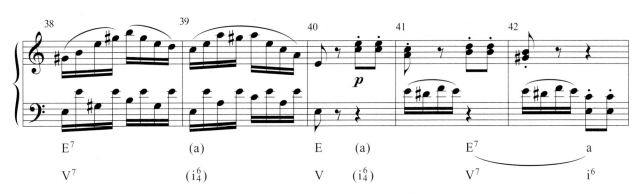

E⁷   (a)   E   (a)   E⁷   a

V⁷   (i⁶₄)   V   (i⁶₄)   V⁷   i⁶

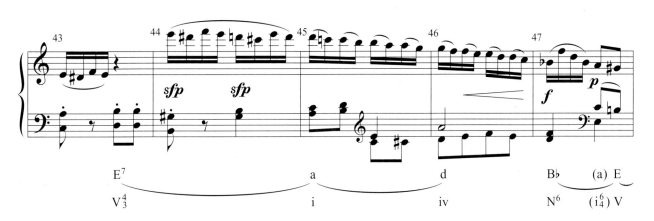

E⁷   a   d   Bb   (a) E

V⁴₃   i   iv   N⁶   (i⁶₄) V

Codetta/retransition

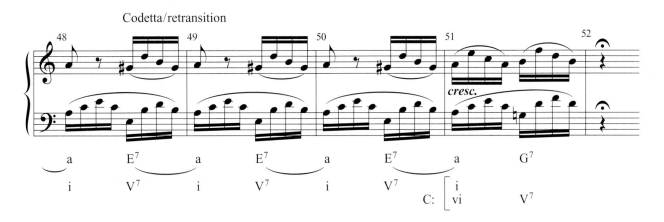

   a   E⁷   a   E⁷   a   E⁷   a   G⁷

   i   V⁷   i   V⁷   i   V⁷   ⌈ i   V⁷
                                                          C: ⌊ vi

Refrain 3

A second return of the refrain (A) in measures 53 to 60 is again unaltered from its first appearance (Figure 26.5). As with the first and second appearances, the refrain is in the original key of C major.

Figure 26.5

Mozart: Sonata in C Major, K. 545, III, mm. 53–60.

Coda

The coda section (mm. 61–73) consists entirely of cadence formulas in the tonic key (Figure 26.6). The melodic materials show some relationship with the codetta that closed the second episode (mm. 48–51).

Figure 26.6

Mozart: Sonata in C Major, K. 545, III, mm. 61–73.

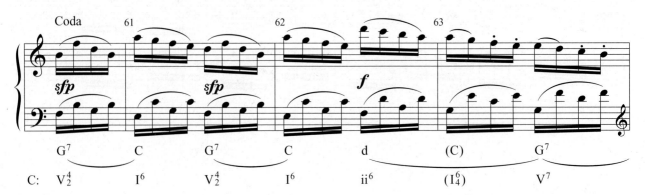

Form

The sonata movement by Mozart in Figures 26.1–26.6 provides a very clear example of five-part rondo form. The three statements of the refrain are exact repetitions of one another, and the two episodes are in contrasting keys (the dominant and the relative minor). Following is a summary outline of the work.

Formal Outline			
Section	**Measures**	**Key(s)**	**Remarks**
Refrain 1 (A)	1–8	C	Parallel period
Episode 1 (B)	9–16	G	Contrasting period
Retransition	17–20	to C	Four-measure phrase based entirely on the G chord
Refrain 2 (A)	21–28	C	Exact restatement of refrain 1
Episode 2 (C)	29–48	a	Three-phrase period with irregular phrase lengths (8, 4, and 8 measures)
Codetta/ retransition	49–52	to C	Cadence repetition in A minor ending with the dominant in C major
Refrain 3 (A)	53–60	C	Exact restatement of refrain 1
Coda	61–73	C	Repeated cadence formulas in the tonic key

Departures from Standard Rondo Form

In no other form is there more latitude for flexibility than in the rondo forms. Among the departures from the so-called ideal structure, transitions and retransitions may often be omitted or enlarged, recurrences of refrains may be diminished or enlarged in length, and particular episodes are sometimes repeated later. The following table shows some of the variants:

Type	Standard Outline	Variant
Three-part rondo	A B A	A B C A
Five-part rondo	A B A C A	A B A B A
Seven-part rondo	A B A C A B A	A B A C B A
Sonata rondo	A B A Development A B A	A B A Development B A

History

The rondo of the classical period developed from the *rondel,* a vocal form of the medieval period (500–1450). The troubadours of Provence (southern France) employed a type of composition with a recurring section, also called *rondeau.* These *rondeaux* (plural) were composed throughout the Renaissance (1450–1600). In the baroque period (1600–1750), Bach used in some of his instrumental suites a similar rondo-like form (again *rondeau*). Other composers of the same period also adopted the form.

The rondo forms discussed in this chapter are those of the classical period (1750–1825), the era that developed and perfected the form. The preclassical form is often called *rondeau.* Its sections were generally shorter and more numerous than those of the classical rondo.

Application

The third or "finale" movement from the Haydn piano sonata in Figure 26.7 provides an example of a typical five-part rondo. The on-score harmonic analysis includes both macro and Roman numeral assessments. Sectional labels include circled numbers to mark phrase beginnings, and two vertical lines (‖) to identify phrase endings. A discussion of important features of the work can be found on pages 590 to 591.

Figure 26.7

Haydn: Sonata in D Major, Hob. XVI/37, III: Finale.

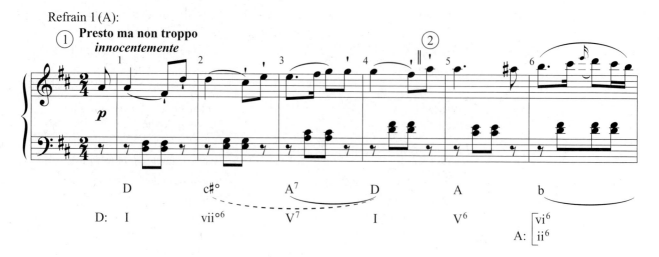

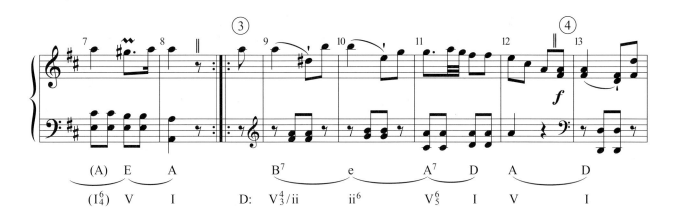

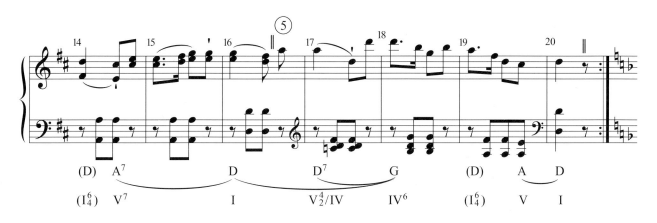

Episode 1 (B):

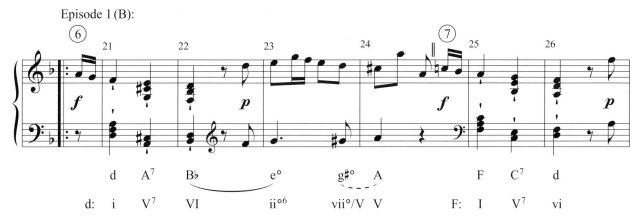

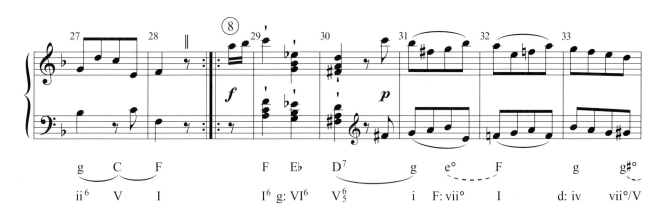

Episode 2 (C):

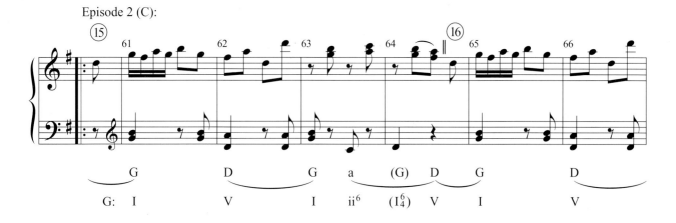

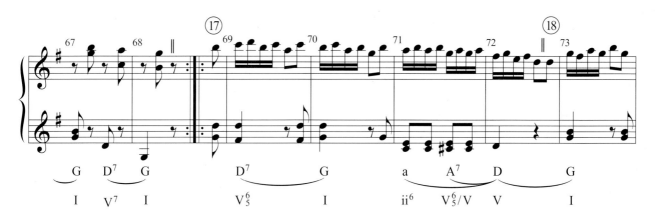

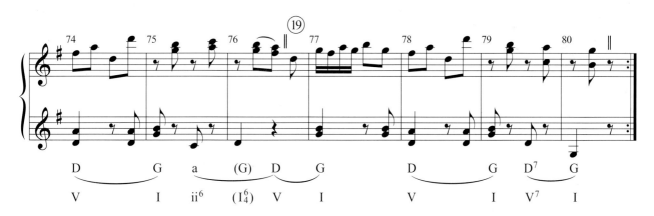

Retransition

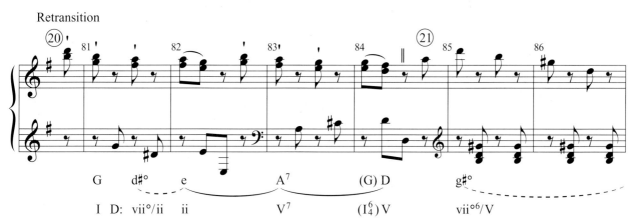

Refrain 3 (A′):

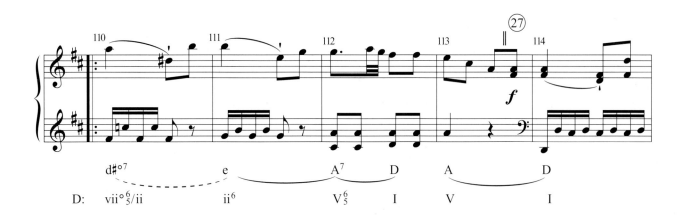

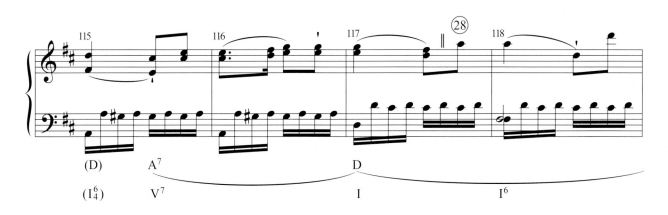

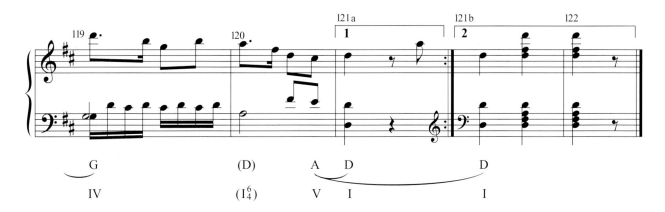

Form

This sonata movement by Haydn is a five-part rondo (A B A C A′). It includes a regularly recurring refrain (A) in D major, a first episode (B) in the parallel key of D minor, and a second episode (C) in the closely related key of G major.

Each section of the rondo is in a small binary or rounded binary (incipient three-part) form of its own. The final refrain (A) statement beginning in measure 94 includes a written out repeat, rather than a repeat sign, to accommodate the Alberti bass accompaniment beginning in measure 102.

This rondo movement departs from many five-part rondos in that transition passages from the refrain sections to the episodes are nonexistent. Furthermore, the first episode (B) does not include a retransition to the second refrain

Formal Outline

Section	Measures	Key(s)	Remarks
Refrain 1 (A)	1–20	D–A–D	Rounded binary
Episode 1 (B)	21–40	d–F–d	Binary
Refrain 2 (A)	41–60	D–A–D	Rounded binary
Episode 2 (C)	61–80	G	Rounded binary
Retransition	81–93	G to D	Dominant prolongation
Refrain 3 (A′)	94–122	D–A–D	Rounded binary

Melodic Materials

Figure 26.8 presents the opening measures from the refrain and the two episodes from this rondo movement. Although several rhythmic figures are reiterated frequently throughout this work, the themes are not based on a recurring melodic motive that is consistently repeated or sequenced. This contrasts with the Mozart Sonata in C Major, K. 545 rondo appearing earlier in this chapter where the melodic materials of the episodes are similar to those of the refrain (Figures 26.1–26.6).

Figure 26.8

Haydn: Sonata in D Major, Hob. XVI/37, III: Finale.

Refrain 1 (A), mm. 1–4.

Episode 1 (B), mm. 21–24.

Episode 2 (C), mm. 61–64.

Of the twenty-eight total phrases, only four depart from the conventional four-measure length. This tendency toward traditional phrase lengths contributes to the straightforward and uncomplicated transparency of the movement.

Phrases	Measures	Phrase Lengths
Phrase 8	29–34	6 measures long
Phrase 9	35–40	6 measures long
Phrase 21	85–93	9 measures long
Phrase 28	118–122	5 measures long

Harmony

Circle progressions flow constantly throughout the movement, reinforcing the tonal centers. Chromatic chords are limited to secondary dominant and leading-tone chords that resolve as expected.

All three refrain sections (A) begin and end in the tonic of the original key (D major) with excursions to the dominant (A major). These digressions to the dominant coincide with the conclusion of the first section of the rounded binary form upon which the refrain (A) is constructed.

The first episode (B) is in the parallel minor (D minor) with a modulation to the relative major (F major) in measures 25–29. The return to D minor from F major (measures 29–35) includes a brief hint of G minor (measures 29–31). The G minor tonality, however, is never quite established and listeners may hear the G minor triad only as a subdominant in D minor. Switching to the parallel minor in the B section permits the inclusion of the only key in the composition (F major) that is not closely related to the original (D major).

The second episode section (C) is entirely in the subdominant (G major) thus creating the need for a retransition (measures 81–93) back to D major and the return of the final refrain (measures 94–122).

Conclusions

A significant feature of this rondo movement is the inclusion of small forms as subsections. Both binary and rounded binary (incipient three-part) forms are clearly identifiable based on the regular phrase structure, key signature changes, harmonic movement, and sectional divisions.

Summary

Rondo forms are recognizable by their recurring refrains alternating in presentation with episodes. The harmonic structure of the classical rondo is built around statements of the refrain in the tonic key, interrupted by episodes in contrasting keys. Transitions and retransitions are optional. Often a rondo-form composition ends with a coda.

The following table outlines the most common types of rondo form:

Type	Outline
Three-part rondo	**A B A**
Five-part rondo	**A B A C A**
Seven-part rondo	**A B A C A B A**
Sonata rondo	**A B A Development A B A**

Find copies of music scores and recordings at your local music library or on the internet for the following composition movements in rondo form:

Three-part rondo:
> Beethoven: Sonata in E-flat Major, op. 7 (II)
> Haydn: Symphony no. 100 in G Major (II)

Five-part rondo:
> Mozart: Sonata in C Minor, K. 457 (II)
> Beethoven: Sonata in C Major, op. 2, no. 3 (II)
> Beethoven: Sonata in C Minor, op. 13 (II)

Seven-part rondo:
> Beethoven: Sonata in A Major, op. 2, no. 2 (IV)
> Beethoven: Sonata in C Minor, op. 13 (III)
> Beethoven: Symphony no. 6, op. 68 in F Major (V)

Sonata rondo:
> Beethoven: Sonata in E-flat Major, op. 27, no. 1 (IV)
> Haydn: Symphony no. 94 in G Major (IV)

Listen to each movement while following the score. Attempt to identify each time the refrain is presented. Next, listen for the episodes. After you have identified the refrains and episodes, attempt to locate transitions, retransitions, and codas.

Assignment 26.1

The following composition is in rondo form.

1. Make a complete harmonic analysis of the movement (macro and Roman numeral).
2. Prepare a formal outline as shown in the examples on pages 583 and 590.
3. Discuss the general characteristics of the movement and compare it with the rondo movements analyzed in this chapter.
4. Look through the macro analysis and find as many patterns as you can that might assist a performer in memorizing the composition.

Haydn: Sonata in C Major, Hob. XVI:35, III.

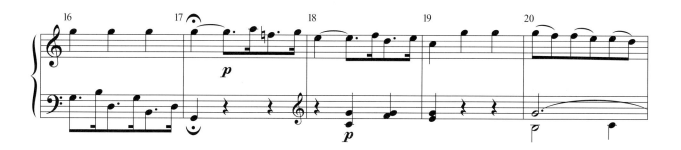

Extended and Chromatic Harmony

The chord vocabulary introduced in the following chapters represents the outer limits of tertian (third-based) harmony. These harmonic devices, which increase the dissonance level and chromaticism of the musical landscape, were much favored by composers in the nineteenth and twentieth centuries for their colorful and dramatic effects. The 9th, 11th, and 13th chords developed as logical extensions of the tertian system by piling additional thirds above the 7th chords. Altered dominants and chromatic mediants represent the triumph of chromaticism over the diatonic system. These harmonic devices will be presented in a four-part chorale setting for the most part, but they usually occur in music that goes beyond this basic texture.

CHAPTER 27

9th, 11th, and 13th Chords

Topics

V^9 $\qquad$ V^{11} $\qquad$ V^{13} $\qquad\qquad$ Nondominant 9th, 11th, and 13th Chords

---

Important Concepts

Extended sonorities known as 9th, 11th, and 13th chords are created by adding additional thirds to chords. These chords include dissonances that could be interpreted as nonharmonic tones; therefore, analyzing a chord as a 9th, 11th, or 13th requires that dissonant factors be given sufficient prominence to be explained as chord tones.

Characteristics

The superposition of thirds results in extended chords with five, six, and seven different pitches. Because these chords contain more than four notes, it is necessary to omit some notes in four-voice writing.

Figure 27.1

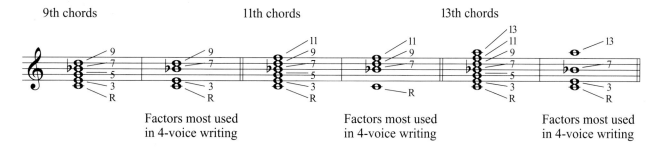

9th chords $\qquad\qquad$ 11th chords $\qquad\qquad$ 13th chords

Factors most used in 4-voice writing $\qquad$ Factors most used in 4-voice writing $\qquad$ Factors most used in 4-voice writing

Position

9th, 11th, and 13th chords tend to lose their identity when inverted, so they are generally found in root position.

Mode

9th, 11th, and 13th chords are found in both major and minor keys. Note that in the major, V^9 and V^{13} contain a major 9th and major 13th, respectively, whereas in the minor mode both are minor intervals. The 11th in V^{11} is unaffected by changes of mode (Figure 27.2).

Figure 27.2

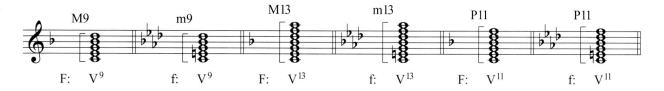

F: V^9 $\qquad$ f: V^9 $\qquad$ F: V^{13} $\qquad$ f: V^{13} $\qquad$ F: V^{11} $\qquad$ f: V^{11}

Most 9th, 11th, and 13th chords of the common-practice period are dominant chords (V^9, V^{11}, V^{13}), although the extended factors can be added to other chords, such as the tonic or subdominant.

Figure 27.3 includes an example of a dominant 9th chord. The V^9 appears in root position and includes the root, 3rd, 7th, and 9th factors (the 5th is missing). Notice how the 9th of the chord (D♭) is positioned as the top note in a rhythmically prominent position that is sustained for a significant duration of time.

Figure 27.3

Chopin: Mazurka in F Minor, op. 63, no. 2, mm. 9–11. ♩

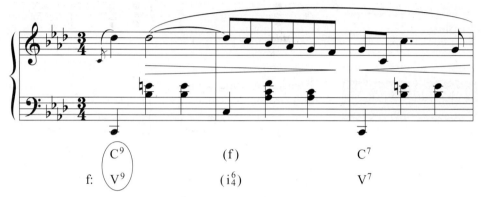

9th chord factors:
root, 3rd, 7th, 9th

The addition of a 9th, 11th, or 13th to chords does not change their function. For example, V^{13} chords still resolve to I or i; ii^9 chords normally progress to the dominant (V). These chords occur frequently in a series of circle progressions.

Figure 27.4 demonstrates the functional use of a dominant 11th chord. The V^{11} is part of a circle progression (ii^7–V^{11}–I) and resolves as expected to the tonic. The 11th chord is composed using the traditional arrangement of chord factors—the root, 7th, 9th, and 11th. The 3rd and 5th have been omitted.

Figure 27.4

Debussy: First Arabesque from *Deux Arabesques*, mm. 44–46. ♩

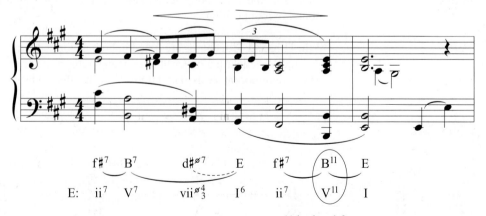

11th chord factors:
root, 7th, 9th, 11th

In Figure 27.5, the dominant 13th chord is restated several times, emphasizing the dominant–tonic relationship. Each presentation of the 13th chord includes the root, 3rd, 7th, and 13th, but the 5th, 9th, and 11th are omitted. Notice that the 13th (A) is the highest sounding factor—a traditional placement for the 13th of a chord.

Figure 27.5

Chopin: Ballade no. 2, op. 38, mm. 43–45 ♩

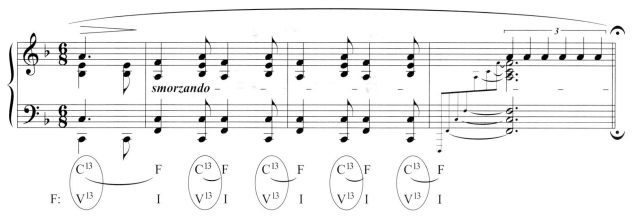

13th chord factors: root, 3rd, 7th, 13th

Secondary Dominants

9th, 11th, and 13th chords also occur as secondary dominants—V^9/V, V^{11}/V, V^{13}/V, $V^9/$ii, $V^{11}/$ii, $V^{13}/$ii, and the like. They resolve in the same manner as their triad and 7th chord counterparts (Figure 27.6).

Figure 27.6

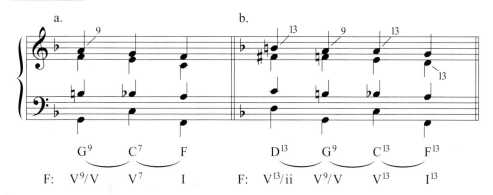

History

In the centuries prior to 1600, the intervals of the 9th and the 11th were established as dissonances and manipulated much in the same manner as other dissonant intervals. In the baroque and classical periods, instances occurred where 9ths, 11ths, and 13ths were given significant rhythmic distinction, but these dissonances usually resolved before the chord changed and were considered triads or 7th chords with nonharmonic tones. True 9th, 11th, or 13th chords were rare in music of the baroque and classical periods.

It was in the romantic period that the 9th, 11th, and 13th chords became common. Figure 27.7 illustrates a V^{13} that proceeds immediately to I. The 13th factor (B) moves down a 3rd to G, the root of the tonic triad.

Figure 27.7

Schumann: "Kleine Studie" ("Short Study") from *Album for the Young*, op. 68, no. 14, mm. 60–64.

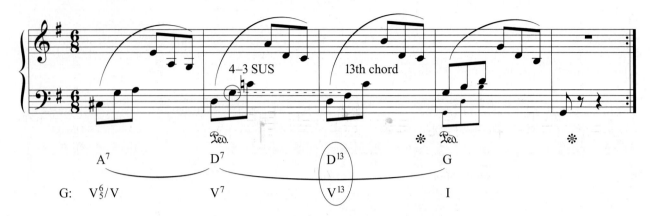

In Figure 27.8, the 9th resolves before a change of harmony but achieves the strength of a true chord factor through its duration (two measures).

Figure 27.8

Wagner: *Tristan und Isolde*, act II, scene 2 (voice part omitted), mm. 610–613.

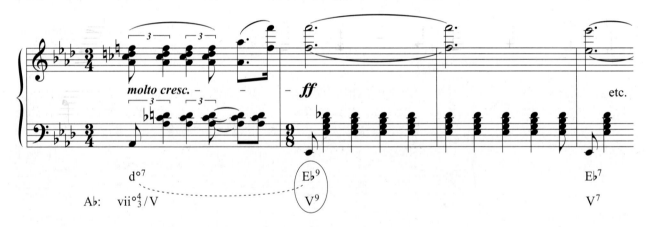

In the period from 1875 to 1920, 9th, 11th, and 13th chords reached their greatest use. The excerpt in Figure 27.9 illustrates the expansion of a supertonic chord to include extended factors (ii^7 ii^9 ii^{11}) in preparation for a cadence with a dominant 11th chord. The 11th (G) of the V^{11} does not resolve downward because it is a common tone with the tonic triad.

Figure 27.9

Ravel: *Valses nobles et sentimentales* (Noble and Sentimental Waltzes), I, mm. 75–80.

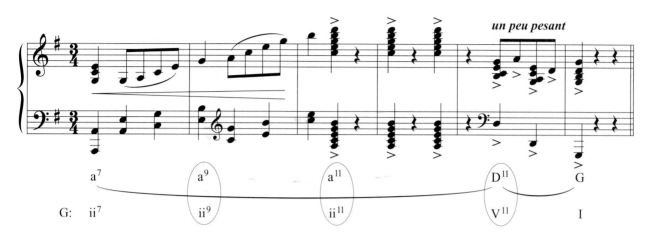

Figure 27.10 is from a composition written in 1901 by Scott Joplin. Although Joplin used most of the harmonic vocabulary of the late romantic period, he used 9th, 11th, and 13th chords somewhat sparingly.

Figure 27.10

Joplin: *The Augustan Club Waltz,* mm. 125–132.

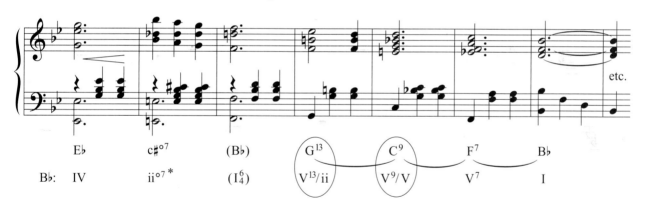

*This chord is discussed in Chapter 30, pp. 641–643.

In later styles of jazz and popular music, the 9th, 11th, and 13th chords became very common. In some styles nearly all chords are 9th, 11th, 13th, or added-tone chords. Figure 27.11, from a song published in 1916, provides an example of a dominant-to-tonic progression with both chords extended to include 9ths. The 9ths in both chords are prolonged and receive emphasis through their voicing in the melody.

Figure 27.11

Hubbell and Golden: "Poor Butterfly," refrain mm. 1–4. ♪

Applications

Voice Leading

The V⁹ Chord

The V¹¹ Chord

The V¹³ Chord

The following set of guidelines refers to the voice-leading practices for chords of the common-practice period. With the 9th, 11th, and 13th chords, doubling is not a primary consideration. Instead, you will want to remember which factors are typically omitted and the manner with which the 9ths, 11ths, and 13ths resolve.

The root, 3rd, 7th, and 9th are the most common factors present in the V^9 chord. Omit the 5th factor. Resolve the 9th and 7th downward to the 5th and 3rd of the tonic triad (Figure 27.12a).

The root, 7th, 9th, and 11th are the most common factors present in the V^{11} chord. Omit the 3rd and 5th factors. The 11th is usually retained as a common tone when V^{11} resolves to I or i (Figure 27.12b).

The root, 3rd, 7th, and 13th are the most common factors present in the V^{13} chord. Omit the 5th, 9th, and 11th factors. The 13th is most often in the soprano and usually resolves a 3rd downward to the tonic factor of I or i (Figure 27.12c). If the tonic following V^{13} is a 9th chord, the 13th of the V^{13} sometimes resolves to the 9th of I^9 (Figure 27.12d).

Figure 27.12

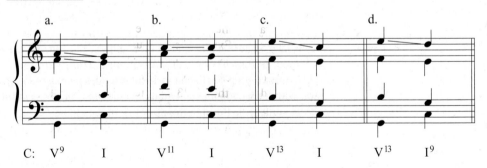

The 9th, 11th, and 13th chords are used extensively in jazz, in the harmonization of popular songs, in instrumental arrangements, and in lead sheets such as those in fake books. For each of these purposes, chord symbols are often employed to indicate the harmony. Although many different chord symbol systems exist, the symbols appearing in the two volumes of this text reflect the symbols presented in *The New Real Book* series (Sher Music Co.). These symbols are adaptations of the recommendations made by Carl Brandt and Clinton Roemer in *Standardized Chord Symbol Notation* (Roevick Music Co., 1976) and are widely used in jazz.

Figure 27.13 lists chord symbols for several of the 9th, 11th, and 13th chords commonly found in jazz and popular music. A more complete listing of chord symbols (including triads, 7th chords, and alternative symbols) is shown in Appendix C.

Figure 27.13

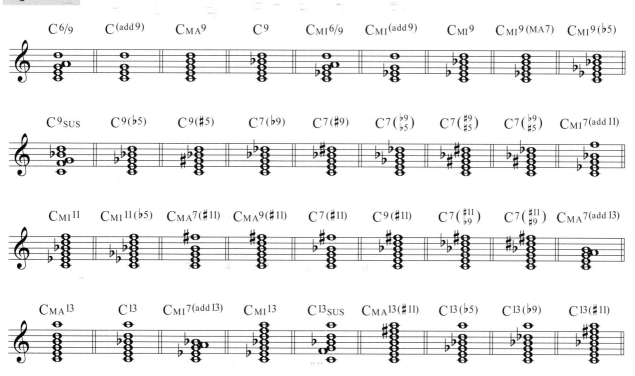

Summary

The stacking of thirds using five, six, and seven different notes results respectively in 9th, 11th, and 13th chords. The byproduct of these extensions is dissonance, which means the dissonant factors must be distinctive enough to function as chord tones (rather than as non-harmonic tones). Extended chords usually appear in root position.

Voice leading in the common-practice style requires the omission of a note or notes for the extended chords. Ninth chords usually have an omitted 5th; 11th chords have an omitted 3rd and 5th; and 13th chords have an omitted 5th, 9th, and 11th. In the common-practice period, they appear most often as dominant function chords and tend to follow the resolutions of their triad equivalents. They also occur frequently as extended secondary dominants.

Ninth, 11th, and 13th chords are extremely common in jazz and popular music. Their notation is commonly represented by popular music symbols.

One of the most distinctive features of the extended chords is their common appearance in root position with the 9th, 11th, or 13th as the highest sounding chord factor. Although these chords can appear on any scale degree, you are encouraged to consider them first as dominant function chords.

Begin by writing a V^7 chord (major-minor) in root position. Using diatonic notes, add a 9th, followed by an 11th, and then a 13th. Play or sing through the chord notes to verify that the chord is written correctly.

After you can spell the diatonic V^9, V^{11}, and V^{13} chords fluently in all major and minor keys, practice extracting the pitches that are usually omitted in four-part voice leading. Notice how the root and the minor 7th of the V^7 chord are included in all three of the extended chords.

Figure 27.14

All chord factors included

Four-note versions

Assignment 27.1　Write the requested 9th, 11th, and 13th chords. If you forget what the popular music chord symbols mean, consult the chart in Appendix I.

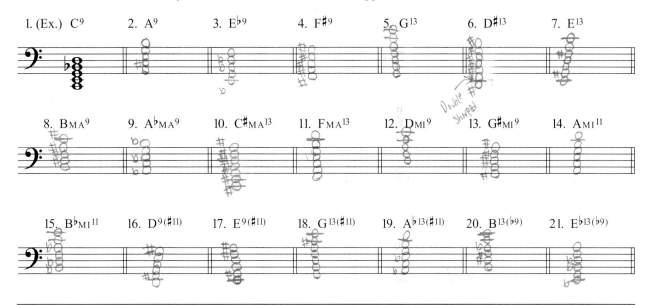

1. (Ex.) C⁹　　2. A⁹　　3. E♭⁹　　4. F♯⁹　　5. G¹³　　6. D♯¹³　　7. E¹³

8. BMA⁹　　9. A♭MA⁹　　10. C♯MA¹³　　11. FMA¹³　　12. DMI⁹　　13. G♯MI⁹　　14. AMI¹¹

15. B♭MI¹¹　　16. D⁹(♯11)　　17. E⁹(♯11)　　18. G¹³(♯11)　　19. A♭¹³(♯11)　　20. B¹³(♭9)　　21. E♭¹³(♭9)

Assignment 27.2　Following are dominant 9th, 11th, and 13th chords in four-part harmony. Both primary and secondary dominants are included in the exercise.

1. Write the most conventional resolution for each chord in four-part harmony.
2. Analyze the given chord and its resolution.

The example illustrates the correct procedure.

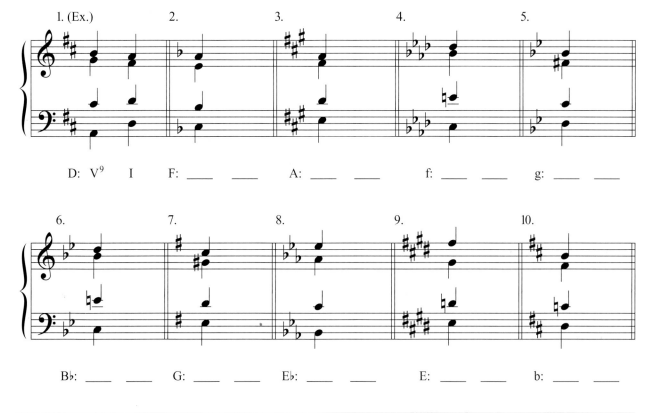

1. (Ex.)　　2.　　3.　　4.　　5.

D: V⁹　I　　F: ____ ____　　A: ____ ____　　f: ____ ____　　g: ____ ____

6.　　7.　　8.　　9.　　10.

B♭: ____ ____　　G: ____ ____　　E♭: ____ ____　　E: ____ ____　　b: ____ ____

Assignment 27.3

Add the alto and tenor to the following phrases and analyze each chord.

1. Follow voice-leading recommendations on page 604.
2. Observe all previous suggestions regarding doubling, spacing, voice order, and voice range.
3. Avoid large skips (skips greater than a P5th).

1.

2.

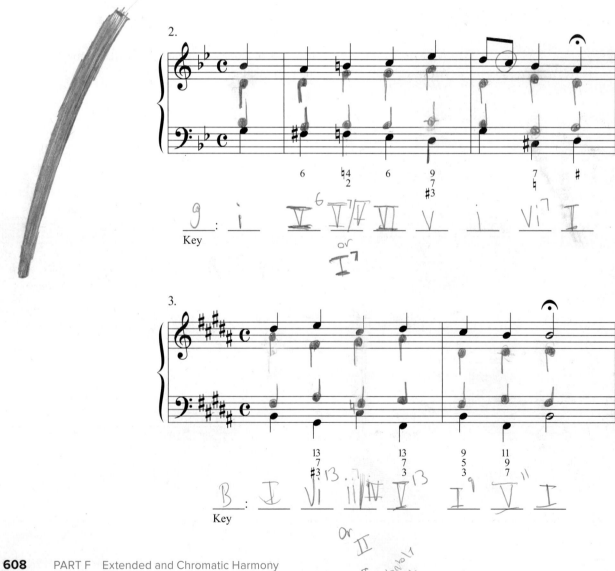

3.

4.

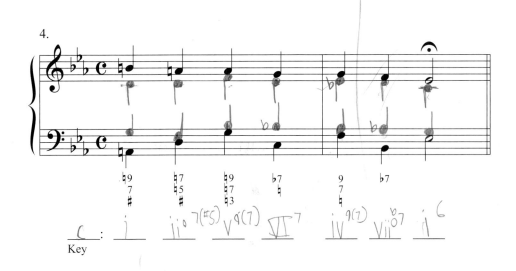

♭9   ♮7   ♮9   ♭7   9   ♭7
7   ♯5   ♮7   7
♯   ♮3

C : i   ii°7(♯5) V9(7) VI7 iv9(7) Vii°7 i6
Key

5.

♭9   ♮13   ♮9   ♮13   13   13   13
7   7   7   ♭7   9   ♭7   9

E♭ : I9(♯7) Vii°13(♭7) iii9(7) Vi13(7) ii13(9) V13(7) I
Key

6.

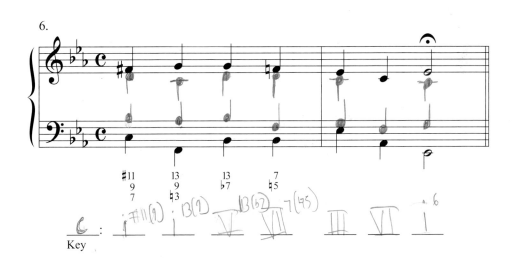

♯11   13   13   7
9   9   ♭7   ♮5
7   ♮3

C : i♯11(9) i13(7) V VII13(♭2) III7(♯5) III VI i6
Key

Assignment 27.4

The following excerpts are similar to music analyzed in this chapter.

1. Make a complete harmonic analysis of each excerpt using the illustrations as a guide.
2. In class or on a separate sheet of paper, discuss the 9ths, 11ths, and 13ths appearing in your analysis. Determine whether these intervals function as chord extensions or non-harmonic tones.

1. Mozart: Sonata in F Major, K. 332, II: Adagio, mm. 5–8.

2. Diabelli: Sonatina in C Major, op. 151, no. 4, II: Introduction, mm. 1–8.

3. Chopin: Nocturne in F Minor, op. 55, no. 1, mm. 5–8.

4. Grieg: *Vöglein* (Little Bird), op. 43, no. 4, mm. 33–36.

5. Grieg: *Det er den største dårlighed* (It Is the Greatest Foolishness), op. 66, no. 2, mm. 13–16.

Assignment 27.5

The excerpt on the following page is from *Pavane pour une Infante défunte,* written in 1899 by Maurice Ravel.

1. Make a complete analysis (macro or Roman numeral) according to the directions of your instructor.
2. When you find a 9th, 11th, or 13th chord, circle the analysis.
3. In class or on a separate sheet of paper, discuss the harmonic rhythm (how often chord changes occur); the kinds of 9th, 11th, and 13th chords that are present; the tonality; and the general use of dissonance.

Ravel: *Pavane pour une Infante défunte* (Pavane for a Dead Princess), mm. 1–12.

Altered Dominants

Important Concepts

Altered dominants are dominant triads and 7th chords that contain a raised or lowered 5th factor. One altered dominant type includes two lowered factors, the 3rd and the 5th, resulting in the half-diminished quality (vᵒ⁷). Figure 28.1 illustrates the five altered dominant types in common use.

Figure 28.1

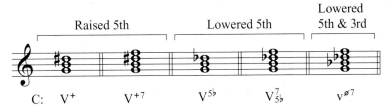

Raised 5th	Lowered 5th	Lowered 5th & 3rd

C: V⁺   V⁺⁷   V⁵♭   V⁷₅♭   vᵒ⁷

Characteristics

Altered dominants have the same function as their diatonic counterparts, but the alterations heighten the tension and increase the need for resolution to the tonic chord.

Position

Most often, altered dominants are found in root position, but they occasionally occur in inversion. When inverted, they can appear in any position.

Mode

Altered dominants are found in both major and minor keys; however, the altered dominant with a raised 5th does not occur in the minor mode because the raised 5th is enharmonic with the 3rd scale degree.

Progression

Altered dominants, like diatonic dominants, proceed in a circle progression to the tonic.
   The excerpt in Figure 28.2 provides an example of a dominant 7th chord with a raised 5th (V⁺⁷). The chord resolves as expected via circle progression to the tonic chord of a major key. The altered pitch (F×) resolves upward.

Figure 28.2

Brahms: "Wie Melodien zieht es mir" ("As if Melodies Were Moving"), op. 105, no. 1, mm. 6–9.

Figure 28.3 demonstrates a dominant 7th chord with a lowered 5th ($V^7_{5\flat}$). The chord resolves by circle progression to tonic, but the lowered pitch ($D\natural$) resolves downward. Notice that the analysis symbol indicates that the lowered pitch is altered with a natural ($V^7_{5\natural}$).

Figure 28.3

Chopin: Nocturne in C-sharp Minor, op. 27, no. 1, mm. 16–18.

The $V^7_{5\flat}$ in second inversion ($V^{4\ 3}_{1\flat}$) is identical in spelling to a French augmented 6th chord (Figure 28.4). The analysis should reflect the function of the chord to the surrounding harmony. If the chord functions as a dominant and resolves by circle progression, then the altered dominant analysis is appropriate.

Figure 28.4

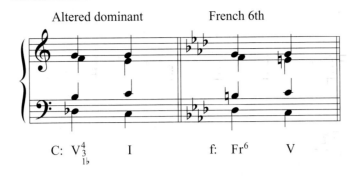

Figure 28.5 includes two examples of the dominant 7th chord with a lowered 5th. The second-inversion example is analyzed as an altered dominant because of its resolution to tonic.

Figure 28.5

Grieg: "Veslemøy" ("Little Maid") from *Haugtussa* (The Mountain Maid), op. 67, no. 2, mm. 38–42.

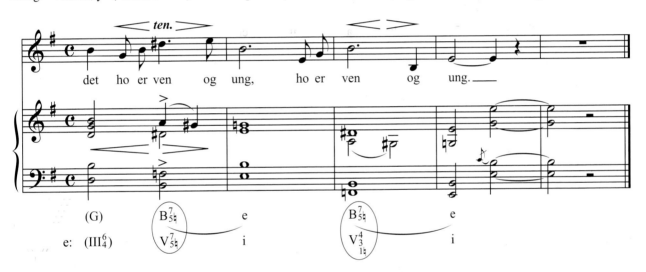

Secondary Dominants   Altered dominants are often used as secondary dominants (Figure 28.6). Secondary dominants that have been altered resolve in the same manner as their unaltered counterparts.

Figure 28.6

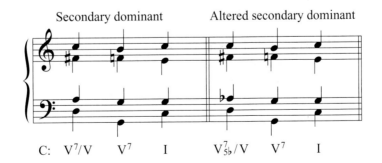

Altered dominants were virtually nonexistent during the baroque period. They began to appear in isolated instances during the classical period; their numbers did not increase considerably until the middle and late 1800s. Altered dominants represented a colorful and exotic addition to the harmonic vocabulary of the nineteenth century.

Figure 28.7 is from *Mörike Lieder,* a set of songs by Hugo Wolf. In the five measures shown, there are three altered dominants.

Figure 28.7

Wolf: "Das verlassene Mägdlein" ("The Forsaken Maiden") from *Gedichte von Eduard Mörike,* no. 7, mm. 26–30.

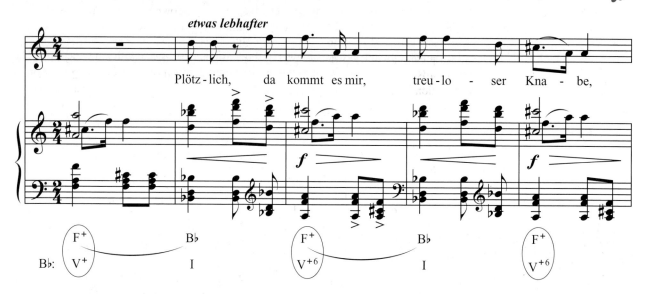

Altered dominants were employed in popular music and jazz beginning in the early twentieth century. Figure 28.8, an excerpt from a popular song published in 1923, illustrates an altered dominant extended to include the 9th. Despite the extended harmony, the altered dominant resolves as expected by way of circle progression root movement.

Figure 28.8

Freed, Arnheim, and Lyman: "I Cried For You," chorus mm. 5–8.

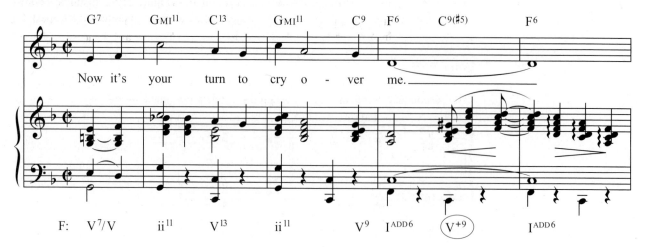

Altered dominants require careful treatment with regard to doubling and voice leading. Resolving the altered pitches sometimes results in doublings that differ from the unaltered dominants. The following guidelines apply when writing altered dominants.

Doubling

Altered tones are almost never doubled. Triads in this category typically double the pitch other than the altered pitch—the root of a root position chord, for example. Do not double the notes that have been altered.

Resolution

Resolve the altered 5th in the direction of the alteration—raised pitches up, lowered pitches down.

7th Resolution

In altered dominant 7th chords, resolve the 7th factor down one scale degree. This may result in either a doubled third or tripled root in the tonic triad that follows.

Figure 28.9 illustrates that the altered 5th resolves in the direction of the alteration: raised pitches resolve upward and lowered pitches resolve downward. In altered dominant 7th chords, remember to resolve the 7th factor down one scale degree (Figure 28.9b, d, e, f). Resolution of the altered tones and chord 7ths may result in either a doubled third or a tripled root in the tonic triad that follows (Figure 28.9b, c).

Figure 28.9

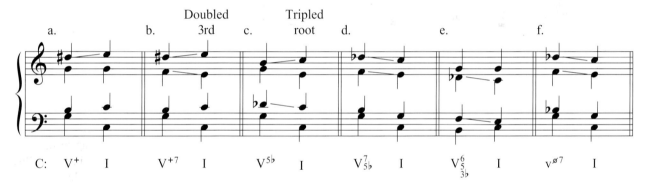

Summary

The five altered dominants, V^+, V^{+7}, $V^{5\flat}$, $V^7_{5\flat}$, and $v^{\varnothing 7}$, are modified versions of the dominant triad and dominant 7th chord. All five chords have a raised or lowered 5th. The half-diminished version ($v^{\varnothing 7}$) also includes a lowered 3rd.

Altered dominants function like their diatonic counterparts and typically resolve by circle progression. Although composers sometimes invert these chords, altered dominants usually appear in root position. They can be found in both major and minor keys, but V^+ and V^{+7} are avoided in minor keys because of the enharmonic equivalency with the 3rd scale degree.

Altered secondary dominants also occur in music and will resolve most often by circle progression. The $V^7_{5\flat}$ in second inversion shares note spelling with the French 6th chord, which means that harmonic surroundings need to be considered carefully when completing an analysis.

Voice-leading practices stipulate that altered tones need to receive specific resolutions. Raised notes should be resolved upward, and lowered notes downward. Irregular doublings may occur when accommodating the resolution of the altered note(s), the 7th of the chord, and the leading tone.

Practice

Side-by-side comparison of the diatonic dominant chords (V and V^7) with the altered versions is a simple way to become familiar with the chromatic alterations. To begin your practice, play the V triad in C major (G, B, D) on the piano or a keyboard. Alter the chord by raising and lowering the 5th. Follow this same process around the entire circle of fifths.

Figure 28.10

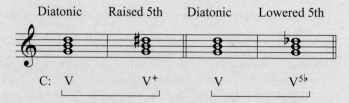

After you have completed this process of altering the triad, continue on to the 7th chords. Remember that three different alterations are possible with the 7th chords.

Figure 28.11

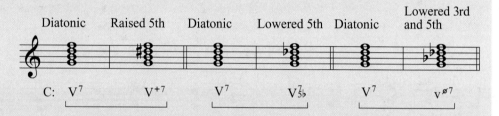

Altering the dominants results in heightened dissonance. After you play the chords, sing the pitches, bottom to top, to ensure that you fully understand the chords.

Assignment 28.1   Write the requested chord above the given tone. Indicate the major key in which this chord is found. The example illustrates the correct procedure.

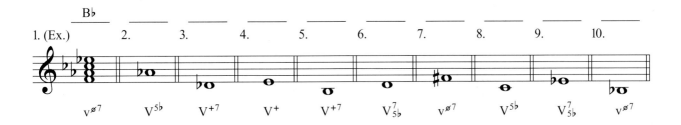

Assignment 28.2   Each of the following chords in four-part harmony is an altered dominant in a major key.

1. Determine the key and write it in the blank provided.
2. Write the most conventional resolution for each chord in four-part harmony.
3. Analyze the given chord and its resolution.

The example illustrates the correct procedure.

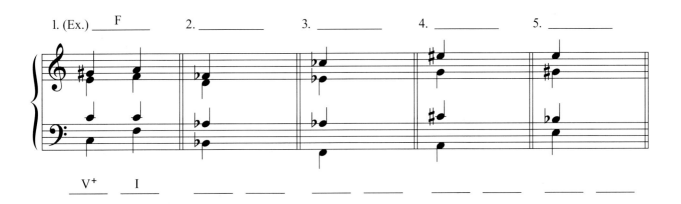

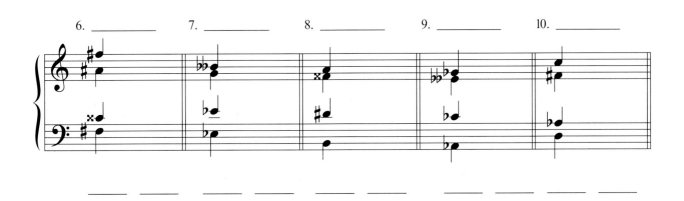

Assignment 28.3   Add alto and tenor voices to the following phrases.

1. Observe the voice-leading strategies listed in this chapter.
2. Make a complete harmonic analysis of each exercise.
3. Discuss different analyses that might be possible for some chords.

1.

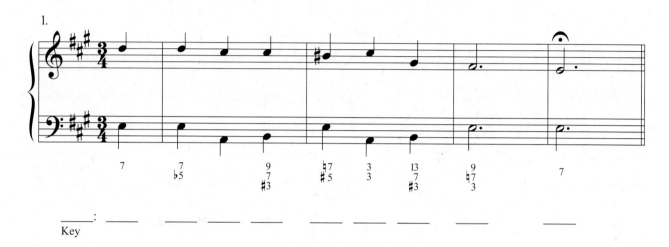

Key

2.

Key

3.

Key

Assignment 28.4   The following excerpts are similar to music analyzed in this chapter.

1. Make a complete harmonic analysis of each excerpt using the illustrations as a guide.
2. In class or on a separate sheet of paper, discuss the altered dominants appearing in the excerpts. Determine how chord function and voice leading are affected by the chromatic alterations.

1. Cécile Chaminade: "Rêve d'un soir" ("Dream of an Evening"), mm. 3–6.

2. Beethoven: Sonata in C Minor, op. 10, no. 1, II: Adagio molto, mm. 78–82.

3. Schubert: "Der Doppelgänger" ("The Double") from *Schwanengesang* (Swan Song), D. 957, no. 13, mm. 29–34.

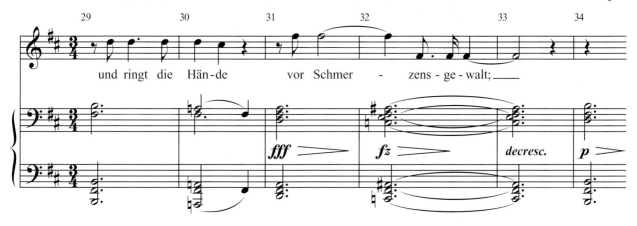

Assignment 28.5   The following excerpt is from a composition by George Gershwin. Make a complete analysis (macro or Roman numeral). The excerpt contains several chords discussed in this chapter, but also some that will test your ingenuity. Consider the possibility of more than one analysis. In class, discuss differences in analysis.

Gershwin: Prelude I from *Preludes for Piano,* mm. 50–62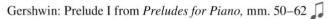

Chromatic Mediants

Important Concepts

Chromatic mediants are altered mediant and submediant chords. Because of their stability, major and minor triads constitute the largest number of chromatic mediants, but 7th chords may also be found in music literature (Figure 29.1).

Figure 29.1

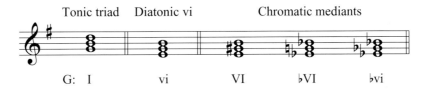

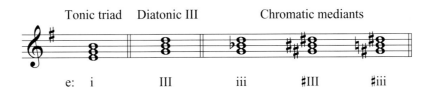

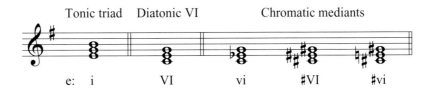

Some chromatic mediants are spelled the same as other altered chords.

Key	Chord	Other Function
Major	♭VI	Also a borrowed chord—from parallel minor (see Chapter 21)
Major	VI	Also a secondary dominant of ii (see volume 1, Chapter 14)
Major	III	Also a secondary dominant of vi (see volume 1, Chapter 14)

The analysis of these chords should reflect whatever function is evident from their relationship to the surrounding harmony. Figure 29.2 illustrates correct analysis. In Figure 29.2a, an E major triad (E, G♯, B) resolves to a ii triad, leaving no doubt that the chord is a secondary dominant, whereas in Figure 29.2b the same E major triad returns to the tonic triad, thus demonstrating the characteristics of a chromatic mediant. Always look carefully to determine the function of the chord.

Figure 29.2

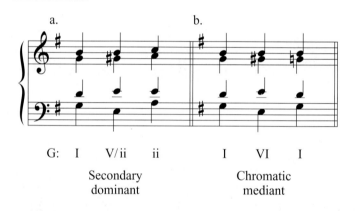

G: I   V/ii   ii   I   VI   I

Secondary dominant   Chromatic mediant

Characteristics

As the term chromatic mediant suggests, the mediants above and below the tonic are altered so that they are no longer diatonic. In addition, the mediant characteristic is frequently emphasized through approach by root movement of a third.

Position

Any position is possible, but root position is the most common.

Mode

As seen in the preceding examples, chromatic mediants and submediants may appear in either major or minor keys.

Function

Chromatic mediants are usually mediant or submediant chords that have been altered. They provide unusual color and interest while prolonging the tonic harmony.

Progression

Chromatic mediants usually have a 3rd relationship (of chord roots) with the tonic and most often proceed from and to the tonic triad. Less often, the dominant (V) is the pivot around which chromatic mediants move. Sometimes chromatic mediants are preceded or followed by their own secondary dominant and, in other instances, create a full-fledged modulation.

Figure 29.3 demonstrates the 3rd relationship of roots (F, D♭, F). Although the ♭VI spelling implies the possibility of a borrowed chord, the reiterated emphasis of I–♭VI–I is characteristic of chromatic mediant root movement.

Figure 29.3

Tchaikovsky: *Chant sans paroles* (Song Without Words), op. 2, no. 3, mm. 43–45.

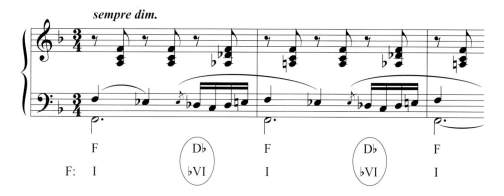

The chromatic mediant in Figure 29.4 begins as a triad and evolves into a 7th chord. Nevertheless, the resolution to the tonic chord by root movement of a 3rd emphasizes the mediant characteristic.

Figure 29.4

Shostakovich: No. 3 from *Three Fantastic Dances,* op. 5, mm. 41–42.

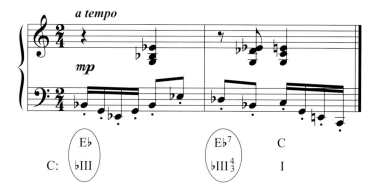

History

Chromatic mediants were rarely used during the baroque period. Although also a rarity in the classical period, the chromatic mediant relationship is occasionally found between sections of compositions. In Figure 29.5, the half cadence triad concluding the first section (F♯ major) has a chromatic mediant relationship with the beginning chord of the next section (D major).

Figure 29.5

Mozart: Fantasia in C Minor, K. 475, mm. 24–26. ♪

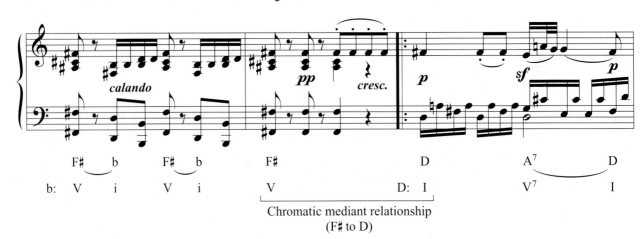

Chromatic mediant relationship
(F♯ to D)

Chromatic mediants became much more common in the romantic period. Figure 29.6 is from Brahms's Symphony no. 3. A chromatic mediant (♭VI) in C major occurs in the third measure. In this instance the A♭ major triad is both a chromatic mediant (because it returns to a C major triad immediately) and a borrowed chord (because it is borrowed from the parallel minor, C minor).

Figure 29.6

Brahms: Symphony no. 3 in F Major, op. 90, II: Andante, mm. 128–134. ♪

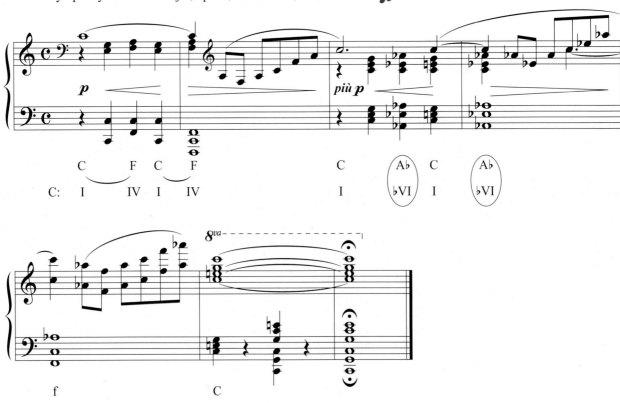

The chromatic mediant relationship was not limited solely to chord progressions in the romantic period. Key centers based on the chromatic third relationships were used to facilitate modulation. The excerpt in Figure 29.7 modulates from G major (I) to E♭ major (♭VI) to G minor (i). The brief modulation to E♭ major emphasizes the chromatic submediant relationship.

Figure 29.7

Schumann: *Vogel als Prophet* (The Prophet Bird) from *Waldszenen*, op. 82, mm. 23–25.

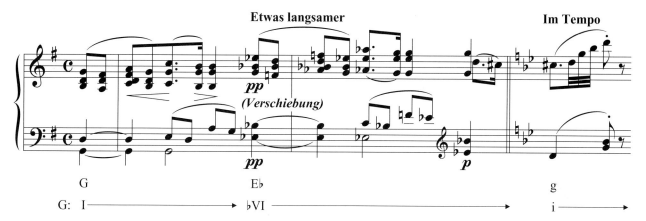

The 3rd relationship of chord roots in general and chromatic mediants in particular become even more prominent in the post-romantic and impressionistic period. Strict dominant–tonic relationships break down considerably and are replaced by chromatic mediants in many instances. Figure 29.8 is an illustration of a chromatic mediant that creates a 3rd-relationship cadence. Notice that the chromatic mediant (♮iii) is spelled enharmonically (A, B♯, E = A, C, E), a common practice in this style period.

Figure 29.8

Ravel: Sonatine, I: Modéré, mm. 81–84.

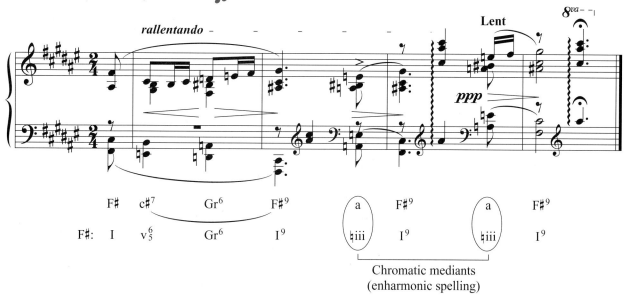

Because chromatic mediants are reached by 3rd-relationship progressions, chromatic movement, such as B to B♯, A to A♭, and F♯ to F in melodic lines, is common (Figure 29.9).

Chromatic mediants are either major or minor triads, so doubling patterns are often the same as for diatonic triads. Double the root whenever possible (Figure 29.9).

Figure 29.9 illustrates the preceding guidelines by way of the following examples:

a. Lowered minor-triad chromatic mediant
b. Lowered major-triad chromatic submediant
c. Raised major-triad chromatic mediant
d. Lowered minor-triad chromatic mediant with its secondary dominant

Figure 29.9

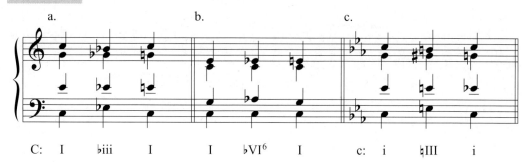

Summary

Mediant and submediant chords modified with nondiatonic alterations are known as chromatic mediants. These chords appear primarily as triads and in root position, but instances of inversion and the addition of a 7th do occur. Chromatic mediants progress most often to and from the tonic triad, but it is also possible for the chord to be tonicized with a secondary dominant. The chromatic-3rd relationship is not limited to chord progressions and can also be observed in key associations within a composition.

Practice

At this point in your theory studies, you are more than likely fluent at writing major and minor triads. This aspect of chromatic mediant spelling is not a significant challenge. What may pose difficulties for you is remembering which chromatic mediants are lowered and which are raised.

Before you complete any of the written assignments, spend time at the piano or keyboard playing both the diatonic and the chromatic mediants. Use Figure 29.1 as a guide to help you remember the 12 different chromatic variants in major and minor keys. Practice the major keys first, followed by a separate session with minor keys. Remember, when in major keys, lower four of the six mediants by a half step; when in minor keys, raise four of the six mediants by a half step.

Assignment 29.1 Write the six chromatic mediants related to the tonic triad for each of the keys indicated. The first exercise has been completed correctly as an example.

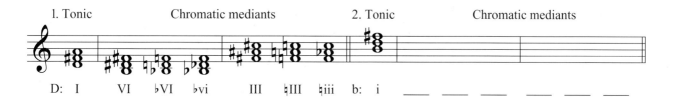

1. Tonic   Chromatic mediants   2. Tonic   Chromatic mediants

D: I   VI   ♭VI   ♭vi   III   ♮III   ♮iii   b: i   __ __ __ __ __ __

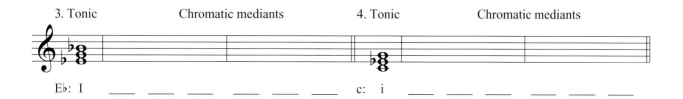

3. Tonic   Chromatic mediants   4. Tonic   Chromatic mediants

E♭: I   __ __ __ __ __ __   c: i   __ __ __ __ __ __

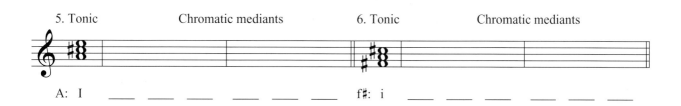

5. Tonic   Chromatic mediants   6. Tonic   Chromatic mediants

A: I   __ __ __ __ __ __   f♯: i   __ __ __ __ __ __

Assignment 29.2 Add alto and tenor voices to the following phrases. Analyze each chord.

1. Instead of figured bass, chord symbols are given above the soprano voice.
2. The bass melody is given and should not be altered. The placement of bass notes may indicate an inversion of the chord described by the chord symbol.
3. To refresh your memory regarding chord symbols, see Appendix C.
4. If your instructor requests, be prepared to categorize each altered chord—whether secondary dominant, altered dominant, borrowed chord, or chromatic mediant.

A: ____ ____ ____ ____ ____ ____ ____ ____

2.

A: _____ _____ _____ _____ _____ _____ _____ _____

3.

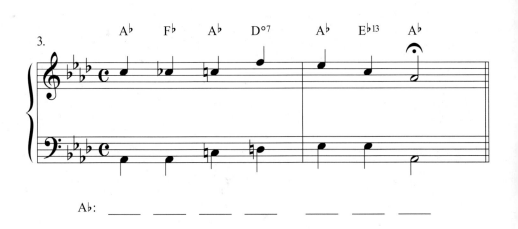

A♭: _____ _____ _____ _____ _____ _____ _____

4.

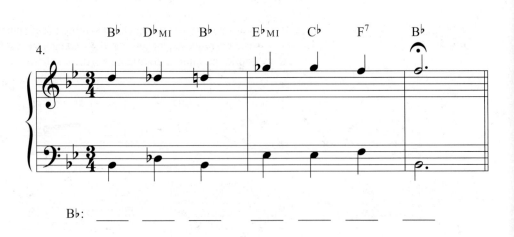

B♭: _____ _____ _____ _____ _____ _____ _____

Assignment 29.3

1. The following composition contains chromatic mediants. In this short work, Chopin includes chromatic mediants preceded by their secondary dominant. Be aware that some chromatic mediants may be enharmonically spelled. Neapolitan harmony also plays a role in the analysis.

2. Provide a complete analysis (macro or Roman numeral) of the composition with a single chord for each bracket.

3. Measures 4 (brackets 12–15) and 7 (brackets 22–25) are particularly difficult.

4. In one area that includes three adjacent brackets, the chords appear to be a byproduct of linear motion—circle progressions are absent. Besides indicating the chord analysis, label the area "linear."

5. Because there is more than one correct analysis for this composition, discuss alternative viewpoints and the merits of each in class.

Chopin: Prelude in E Major, op. 28, no. 9.

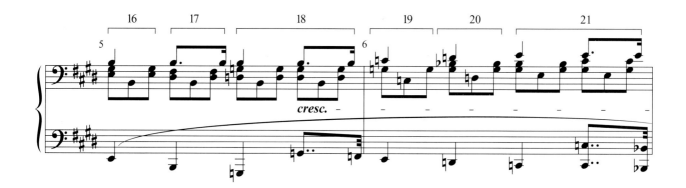

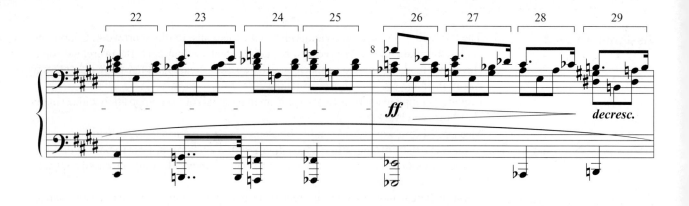

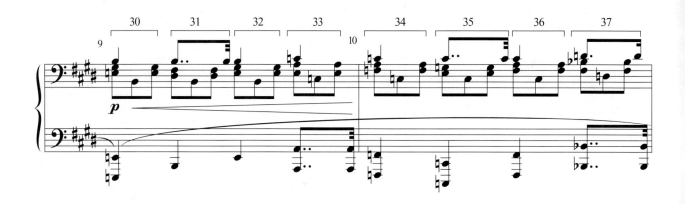

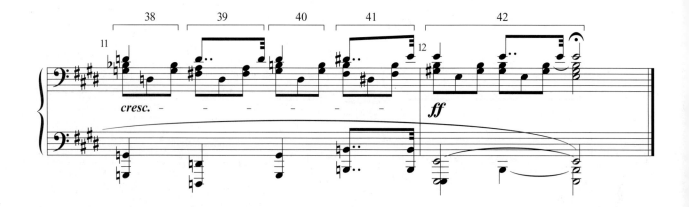

The Nineteenth and Twentieth Centuries

Romantic Period (1825–1900)

Music of the romantic period was dominated by a wider range of emotional expression, more individual styles, and greater subjectivity than the music of the classical period. Musical forms, such as the sonata and symphony, became longer and more involved, but shorter forms, especially piano compositions, were also numerous. Harmony and orchestration expanded to create a more colorful sound palette, which was used to create dramatic musical effects.

In contrast to the classic ideals of organization, symmetry, control, and perfection within acknowledged limits, romanticism sought independence, movement, and passion. It pursued the mysterious or exotic because they represented a distant and unattainable goal.

Post-Romantic and Impressionistic Period (1875–1920)

The post-romantic composers developed and extended the techniques of the romantic composers, resulting in a still more dramatic musical style. In contrast, a group of French composers, the impressionists, developed a musical style that renounced the clear phrases and goal-oriented harmonic idiom of romantic music. They replaced them with purposeful understatement and ambiguity that was evocative of, but very different in effect from, the romantic style. These impressionist composers abandoned traditional thematic development and became more concerned with the color or mood of a particular moment.

Contemporary Period (1920–Present)

The period from 1920 to the present has seen the development of great diversity in musical styles and techniques. Much of this development can be traced back to the upheavals following World War I (1914–1918) and World War II (1939–1945), which caused disruption of the established cultural institutions in Europe and at the same time brought people of diverse cultural backgrounds together for the first time. The development of recording technology, radio and television transmission, and rapid transportation created a sense of world community in which disparate cultures could freely intermingle. Modern technological advances have made possible the development of electronic and computer instruments for the composition, synthesis, and performance of music.

Popular song as we know it in the United States evolved during this period. Some notable composers of popular song were George Gershwin, Cole Porter, Richard Rodgers, Irving Berlin, Vernon Duke, and Burt Bacharach. Popular songs by these and other composers were the dominant popular music until rock music became firmly established in the 1960s.

African American music is among the most notable expressions of religious, folk, and art music in the United States. The blues, which arose from the gospel music of the South, has a unique style of its own. It has also infused and inspired nearly all types of African American music, some twentieth-century classical music, and the popular songs and rock music of the present day. Jazz, a general term for particular kinds of African American music, has undergone many changes in its brief history. It has now been accepted as a substantive art form and a unique American contribution to world culture.

In the 1960s, rock music, which developed out of the traditions of the blues, jazz, and popular music, became the dominant form of music with mass appeal. More recent popular music has been influenced extensively by electronics and the mass media, with developments such as new-age music, hip hop, and rap.

CHAPTER 30

The Romantic Period

Topics	Romanticism Modal Mixture Foreign Modulation	Nonfunctional Harmony Chromatic Nonharmonic Tones	Enharmonic Spelling Common-Tone Diminished 7th Chords

Important Concepts

Romanticism is the term applied to much of the music written between 1825 and 1900. The period could be seen as little more than an extension of the classical period, judging by the works of the more conservative composers, such as Franz Schubert (1797–1828) and Johannes Brahms (1833–1897), or as a major change in style, if the works of the more progressive composers such as Franz Liszt (1811–1886) and Richard Wagner (1813–1883) are considered. In spite of various national styles evident in the music of Polish composer Frédéric Chopin (1810–1849), Russian composer Alexander Borodin (1833–1887), and others, German-speaking composers dominated the music of the romantic period.

Expanded Chord Vocabulary

The harmonic materials discussed in the previous chapters—including borrowed chords; 9th, 11th, and 13th chords; the Neapolitan 6th; augmented 6th chords; chromatic mediants; and altered dominant chords—were used much more frequently during the romantic period.

Modal Mixture

The increasing use of borrowed chords resulted in a blending of the major and minor modes, sometimes to the point of modal ambiguity (Figure 30.1).

Figure 30.1

Schubert: Waltz no. 22 from *Original Tänze für Klavier* (Original Dances for Piano), op. 9, D. 365, mm. 1–4.

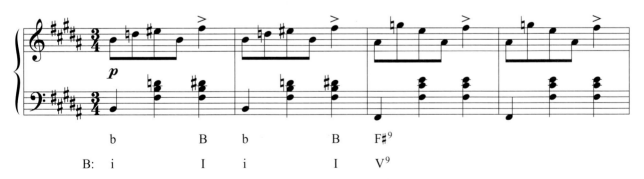

Modulation

Romantic composers often imply several keys in rapid succession. This has the effect of decreasing the influence of the central tonic. Notice the sudden modulation after only one measure and the equally sudden return in measure 3 in Figure 30.2 (see also Figure 30.7 on p. 638).

Figure 30.2

Chopin: Prelude in C Minor, op. 28, no. 20, mm. 1–3.

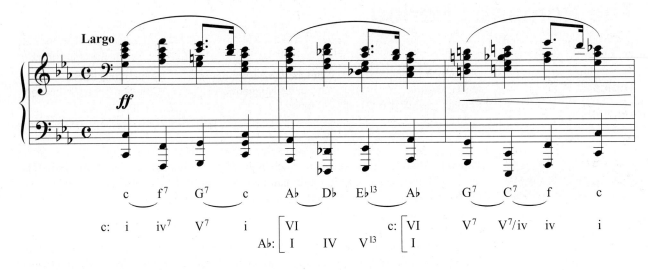

Foreign Modulation

Nineteenth-century composers exploited the full spectrum of keys, with modulations to keys quite distant from the tonic of the composition. These often necessitate enharmonic spellings of chords. In Figure 30.3, notice that measure 138 includes a V^7 chord in the key of G-sharp minor that is the enharmonic equivalent to the V^7 chord of the impending key of A-flat major.

Figure 30.3

Mendelssohn: Caprice in E Major, op. 33, no. 2, mm. 135–139.

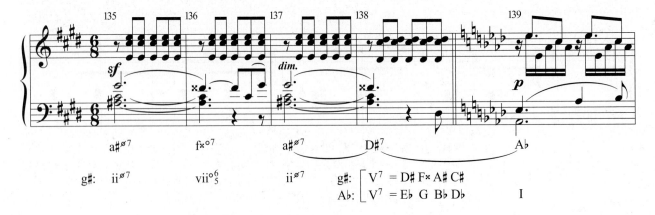

<table>
<tr><td>

**Unresolved
Dissonance**
</td><td>

Dissonant chords, which required resolution in earlier periods, were sometimes left unresolved by nineteenth-century composers. These unresolved dissonances were often exploited for their dramatic effect, as Figure 30.4 illustrates.
</td></tr>
</table>

Figure 30.4

Schubert: Symphony in B Minor ("Unfinished"), D. 759, I: Allegro moderato, mm. 60–64. ♪

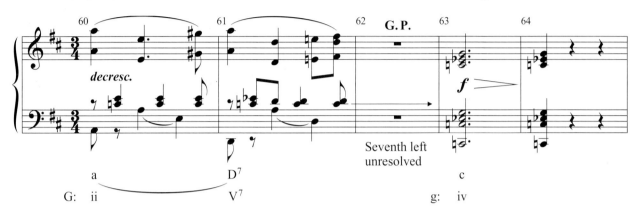

The tonic chord is clearly implied in measure 62 by the progression in the previous two measures (ii, V⁷). If this "missing chord" is filled in, a circle progression emerges (Figure 30.5).

Figure 30.5

Schubert: Symphony in B Minor ("Unfinished"), D. 759, I: Allegro moderato, mm. 60–64. ♪

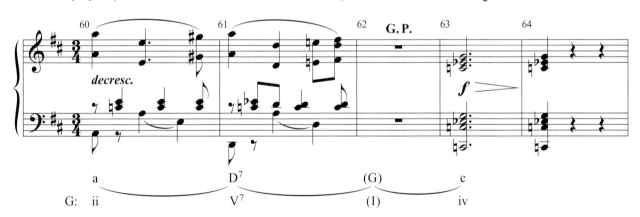

<table>
<tr><td>

**Nonfunctional
Harmony**
</td><td>

Romantic composers occasionally abandoned functional harmony for short periods. These passages were often organized around a segment of the chromatic scale, as Figure 30.6 illustrates. The chords have been given Roman numerals, but it is clear that they are not functionally related to each other. The passage is built around a descending chromatic pattern from the tonic in measure 5 to the dominant in measure 6.
</td></tr>
</table>

CHAPTER 30   The Romantic Period   **637**

Figure 30.6

Chopin: Prelude in C Minor, op. 28, no. 20, mm. 5–6.

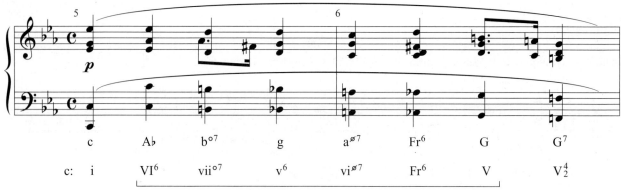

Linear chromatic steps

Chromaticism

The increased use of borrowed chords and augmented 6th chords along with modal mixture caused a general increase in chromaticism in the period. There also was an increase in the use of *chromatic nonharmonic tones,* particularly chromatic appoggiaturas and passing tones. Notice the chromatic appoggiaturas in measures 10 and 12 of Figure 30.7.

Figure 30.7

Schumann: "Im wunderschöen Monat Mai" ("In the Wonderful Month of May") from *Dichterliebe* (Poet's Love), op. 48, no. 1, mm. 9–12.

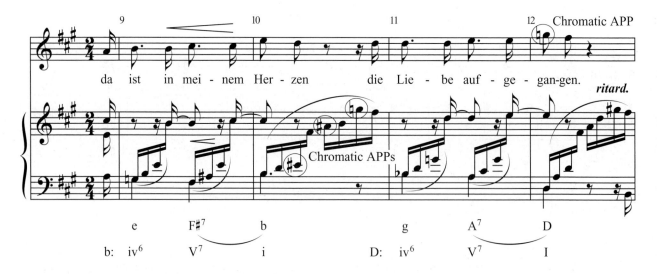

Chromatic passing tones are the central decorative devices in Chopin's Prelude in B-flat Major (Figure 30.8), occurring in nearly every measure of the work. The descending linear pattern coinciding with the chromatic passing tones serves as a unifying motivic element in the accompaniment.

Figure 30.8

Chopin: Prelude in B-flat Major, op. 28, no. 21, mm. 1–4.

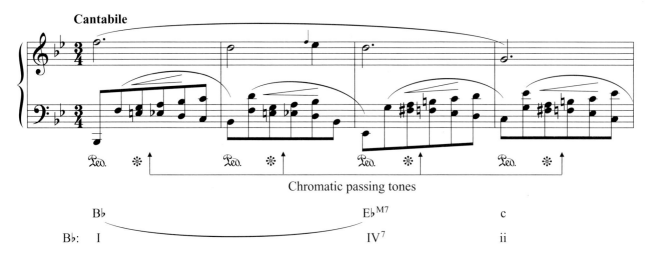

Chromatic passing tones

B♭	E♭^{M7}	c
B♭: I	IV^7	ii

**Increased
Dissonance**

More frequent use of 7th, 9th, 11th, and 13th chords and augmented 6th chords increased the general level of dissonance in nineteenth-century music. Composers came to favor the accented dissonances more and more, and these dissonances were often sustained much longer than their resolutions. In Figure 30.9, notice the accented neighboring tone to the 9th of a dominant 9th chord in measure 16 and the accented appoggiatura on the downbeat of measure 17. These nonharmonic tones greatly increase the dissonance level of the passage.

Figure 30.9

Wagner: *Tristan und Isolde,* Prelude to act I, mm. 15–17.

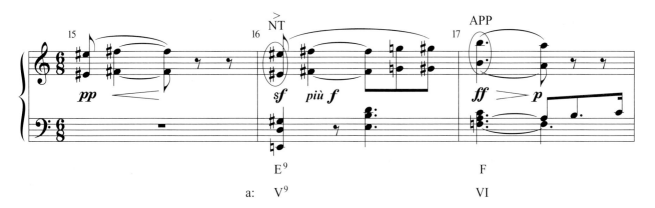

a: V^9   VI

E^9   F

**Enharmonic
Spelling**

The increased chromaticism of the nineteenth century complicated the notation of music, with the result that enharmonic spellings of chords and melodic lines became more frequent. (See measures 8 and 9 of Schumann's "Am leuchtenden Sommermorgen," Figure 30.18, on page 644, where the vocal part remains in flats while the accompaniment is written in sharps.) It is important that you develop skill in thinking enharmonically when analyzing the music of the nineteenth and twentieth centuries. The examples of enharmonic spelling of chords in Figure 30.10 by no means exhaust the possibilities, but they furnish models of what you will need to be aware of in future analyses.

Diminished 7th Chords Because all diminished 7th chords result from enharmonic spellings of three basic chords, composers often write them enharmonically.

Figure 30.10

The three basic diminished 7th chord sounds:

Enharmonic spellings:

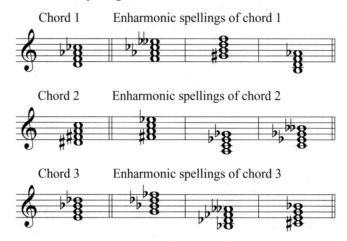

Any tone of a diminished 7th chord is a potential leading tone, and the chord may resolve to any of four roots. The chord may or may not be spelled to agree with its resolution, and enharmonic spelling must be considered in arriving at a correct analysis (Figure 30.11).

Figure 30.11

Four resolutions of Chord 1

Figure 30.12 illustrates the enharmonic spelling of a diminished 7th chord to facilitate a modulation from A minor to E-flat minor.

Figure 30.12

Schubert: String Quartet in A Minor, op. 29, D. 804, I, mm. 144–149. ♪

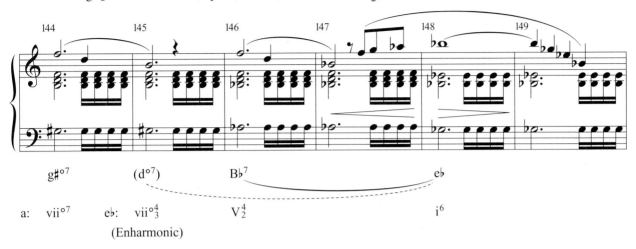

a: vii°7   e♭: vii°4/3   V4/2   i6
(Enharmonic)

Common-Tone Diminished 7th Chords

An alternative resolution of a diminished 7th chord is to a major triad or major-minor 7th chord whose root is one of the tones of the diminished 7th sonority. In Figure 30.13a, a diminished 7th chord embellishes the tonic chord with neighboring motion. In Figure 30.13b, chromatic passing motion in the bass is the result of a diminished 7th chord resolving to a dominant 7th chord. Both progressions retain a common tone before and after the diminished 7th chord.

Figure 30.13

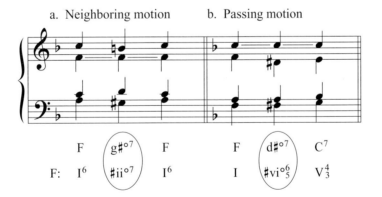

a. Neighboring motion   b. Passing motion

F: I6   g♯°7   F   F   d♯°7   C7
         ♯ii°7 I6   I   ♯vi°6/5 V4/3

Although these chords can function in a number of ways, the most common are (1) the raised supertonic 7th, which resolves to the tonic chord in major keys (Figure 30.14a), and (2) the raised submediant, which resolves to the dominant triad or 7th chord in major keys (Figure 30.14b).

Figure 30.14

$$\text{g\#}^{\circ 7} \qquad \text{F} \qquad\qquad \text{g\#}^{\circ 7} \qquad \text{F}^7$$
$$\text{F: } \text{\#ii}^{\circ 4}_{2} \qquad \text{I} \qquad \text{B\flat: } \text{\#vi}^{\circ 4}_{2} \qquad \text{V}^7$$

Notice in Figure 30.14 that the tones that are raised resolve a half step upward. This follows the general principles outlined in previous chapters for resolving altered tones. Although these chords were known to composers in the baroque and classical periods, they became much more common during the nineteenth century (see Figures 30.15a and b).

Figure 30.15

a. Josephine Lang: "Fee'n-Reigen" ("The Dance of the Fairies"), mm. 18–22. 🎵

Die   sil - ber - nen   Glöck-chen der   Blu - me — des — Mai's

$$\text{D} \qquad \text{e\#}^{\circ 7} \qquad\qquad \text{D} \qquad \text{A}^7$$
$$\text{D: } \text{I} \qquad \text{\#ii}^{\circ 4}_{2} \qquad\qquad \text{I} \qquad \text{V}^7$$

b. Tchaikovsky: *Nutcracker Suite*, op. 71a, III: *Valse des Fleurs*, mm. 1–4. 🎵

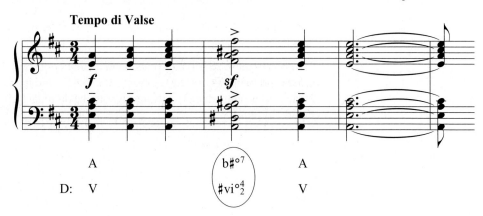

$$\text{A} \qquad \text{b\#}^{\circ 7} \qquad \text{A}$$
$$\text{D: } \text{V} \qquad \text{\#vi}^{\circ 4}_{2} \qquad \text{V}$$

The raised supertonic and raised submediant diminished 7th chords are very common in twentieth-century "barbershop" quartet music, as shown in Figure 30.16.

Figure 30.16

"In the Good Old Summertime" from *Strictly Barbershop,* S. P. E. B. S. Q. S. A., Folio 6049. ♪

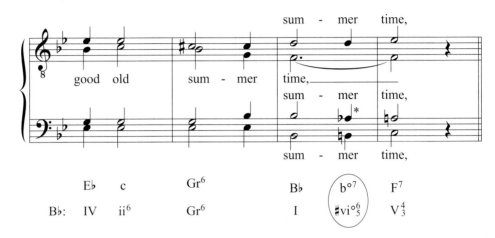

*A♭ should be read enharmonically as G♯ for purposes of analysis.

German 6th Chords

The enharmonic relationship between the dominant 7th and the German 6th chords led composers to spell these chords enharmonically (Figure 30.17).

Figure 30.17

Dominant 7th and German 6th chords

Dominant 7th (major-minor)	German 6th	German 6th spelled with AA4

In Figure 30.18, the German 6th chord in measure 6 is respelled as a dominant 7th in measure 8.

| Measure 6: | G♭ | B♭ | C♯ | E |
| Measure 8: | F♯ | A♯ | C♯ | E |

Notice that the enharmonic relationship is apparent in the notation. The vocal part is written using flats even though the accompaniment changes to sharps.

Figure 30.18

Schumann: "Am leuchtenden Sommermorgen" ("On a Shining Summer Morning") from *Dichterliebe* (Poet's Love), op. 48, no. 12, mm. 6–11.

Be alert for dominant 7th chords where the root resolves downward by a half step. Most of these chords are functioning as German 6th chords. When the enharmonic relationship between dominant 7ths and the augmented 6th chords is used as a modulatory device, the chord may be spelled correctly in one key but not in the other, as demonstrated in Figure 30.19.

Figure 30.19

Schubert: Waltz no. 14 from *Original Tänze für Klavier* (Original Dances for Piano), op. 9, D. 365, mm. 17–24.

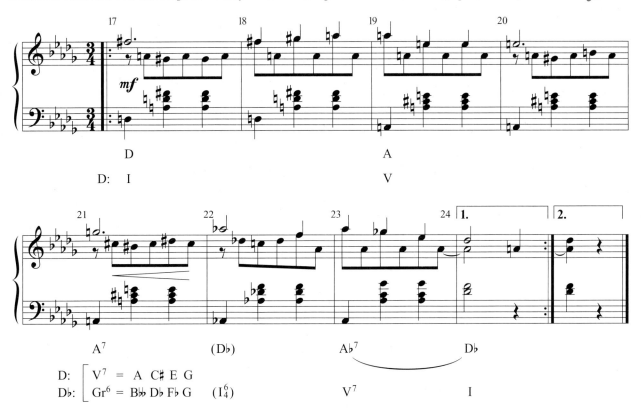

Summary

Music of the romantic period has an expanded chromatic chord vocabulary that includes common-tone diminished 7th chords (♯ii°7 and ♯vi°7) and enharmonic chord spellings. Modal mixture is the byproduct of frequent borrowing from parallel keys, and increased chromaticism—often accompanied by stepwise linear motion—results in nonfunctional harmony. Rapidly changing tonal centers, modulations to foreign keys, and unresolved dissonances all characterize this style period with its heightened chromatic tension.

Practice

The concept of enharmonic equivalency is not a difficult idea to grasp, but because your studies have been devoted to spelling intervals, triads, and 7th chords using correct note names (while avoiding enharmonic spellings), you may now find it difficult to embrace the enharmonic chords presented in this chapter.

Before you attempt your first written assignment, use the piano or a keyboard to review the enharmonic spellings of the three basic diminished 7th chord sounds (see Figure 30.10 on p. 640). Begin with a fully diminished 7th chord, and reconfigure the chord to arrive at enharmonic spellings. This can be done by moving the root of the chord up an octave to reassign the note as the 7th of the enharmonic chord (see Figure 30.20).

Figure 30.20

a.   b.   c.

D = E♭♭   F = G♭♭

d.   e.   f.

C× = D   E♯ = F

After you have practiced the enharmonic spellings of the diminished 7th chord, do the same with the dominant seventh and German 6th enharmonic spellings in all keys (Figure 30.21).

Figure 30.21

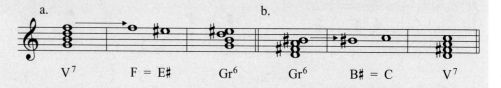

a.   b.

V⁷   F = E♯   Gr⁶   Gr⁶   B♯ = C   V⁷

Assignment 30.1

Because enharmonic spelling of diminished 7th chords is quite common, it is important that you become accustomed to thinking of the enharmonic equivalents of these chords. The following chord represents one spelling of a diminished 7th chord. Analyze this chord (or its enharmonic equivalent) in as many ways as possible in each of the given keys. The first problem is completed as an example.

1. F: $\underline{\text{vii}^{\circ 7}/\text{V}}$ $\underline{\sharp\text{ii}^{\circ 7}}$ $\underline{\text{vii}^{\circ 7}/\text{N}}$ $\underline{\text{vii}^{\circ 7}/\text{iii}}$

2. C: _____ _____

3. D: _____ _____ _____ _____

4. G: _____ _____ _____

5. A♭: _____ _____ _____ _____

6. B♭: _____ _____ _____

7. E♭: _____ _____

Assignment 30.2

Resolve each of the following "common-tone" diminished 7th chords to its normal chord of resolution using Figure 30.14 as a model. Provide a Roman numeral analysis of the second chord.

B: $\times\text{ii}^{\circ 4}_{2}$ I   F: $\sharp\text{vi}^{\circ 7}$ _____   G: $\sharp\text{ii}^{\circ 4}_{2}$ _____   D♭: $\natural\text{vi}^{\circ 6}_{5}$ _____

E: $\times\text{vi}^{\circ 4}_{3}$ _____   A♭: $\natural\text{ii}^{\circ 7}$ _____   D: $\sharp\text{vi}^{\circ 4}_{2}$ _____   B♭: $\sharp\text{ii}^{\circ 7}$ _____

Assignment 30.3   Because the German augmented 6th and the dominant 7th chords sound the same (B♭–D–F–G♯ = B♭–D–F–A♭), composers of this period occasionally spelled these chords enharmonically. Analyze each of the following chords as either dominant 7th or German 6th chords in the keys indicated and resolve each chord to the logical diatonic chord in the key. Some augmented 6ths may be spelled as dominant 7ths, and vice versa, so it is important that you consider various spellings in completing the exercise.

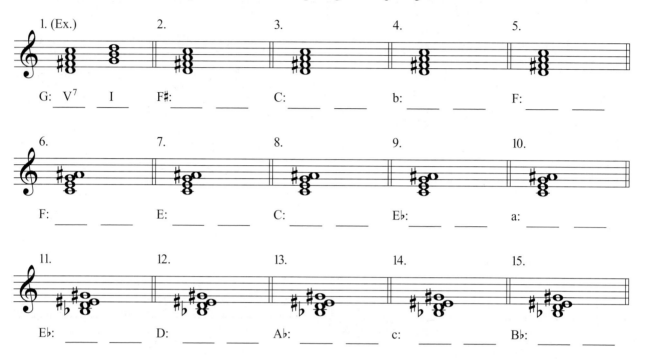

1. (Ex.)   2.   3.   4.   5.

G: V⁷ I   F♯: ___ C: ___ b: ___ F: ___

6.   7.   8.   9.   10.

F: ___ ___   E: ___ ___   C: ___ ___   E♭: ___ ___   a: ___ ___

11.   12.   13.   14.   15.

E♭: ___ ___   D: ___ ___   A♭: ___ ___   c: ___ ___   B♭: ___ ___

Assignment 30.4   Complete each of the following figured basses and do a Roman numeral analysis. Each progression involves a foreign modulation and may involve enharmonic spelling of chords. Indicate the new key and analyze each modulation with a pivot chord. These progressions may be transposed to a variety of keys as a keyboard assignment.

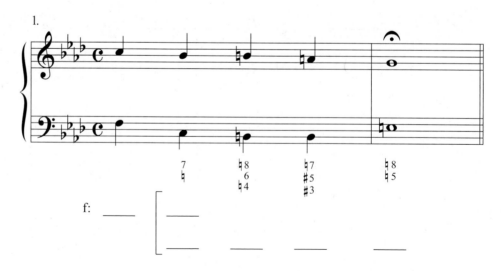

1.

f: ___

2.

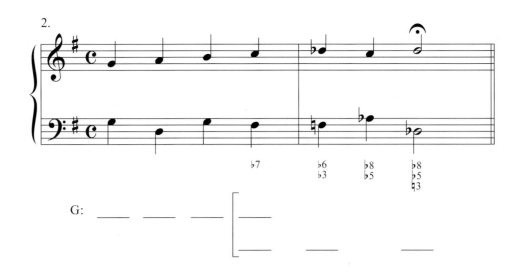

G: ____ ____ ____ [____
    ____ ____ ____

3.

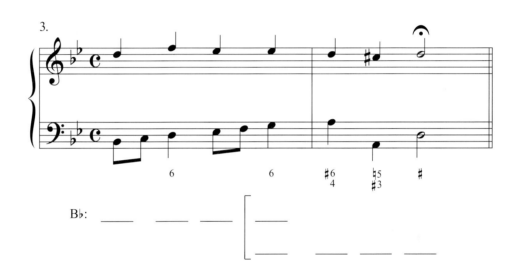

B♭: ____ ____ ____ [____
     ____ ____ ____

4.

d: ____ ____ ____ [____
    ____ ____ ____

Assignment 30.5   Make an analysis (Roman numeral or macro) of the excerpt from Franck's Choral no. 1, which follows. This chromatic work includes passages of nonfunctional harmony, making multiple analyses possible. Discuss the merits of your preferred analysis in class.

Franck: Choral no. 1 from *Trois Chorals pour Grand Orgue*, mm. 1–23.

Assignment 30.6   Make an analysis (Roman numeral or macro) of Chopin's Prelude in E Minor, op. 28, no. 4, which follows. This work contains nonfunctional harmony and enharmonic spelling of chords. Compare your analysis with that of other class members and discuss the relative merits of the various analyses. There is no single "correct" analysis of this work.

Chopin: Prelude in E Minor, op. 28, no. 4.

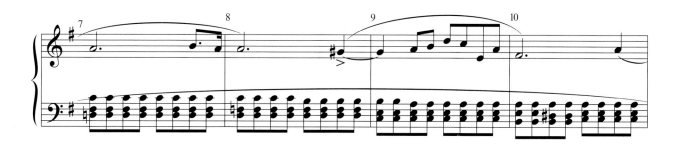

Assignment 30.7   The following excerpt is from the opera *Tristan und Isolde*, completed by Wagner in 1859.

1. Provide a complete analysis (Roman numeral or macro) for the passage.
2. The first six measures are analyzed for you. These measures form the basis of a pattern that continues throughout the excerpt. Trace this pattern.
3. Discuss the general style of the music. Indicate salient features that make the style distinctive.
4. Perform the excerpt in class, with piano accompaniment. Have the men sing the part of *Tristan* and the women the part of *Isolde*.
5. Listen to this excerpt on recordings.

Wagner: *Tristan und Isolde,* act II, scene 2, mm. 615–631.

CHAPTER 31

The Post-Romantic Style

Topics	Post-Romanticism	Nonfunctional Harmony	Blurred Cadence
	Tonal Instability	Omnibus Progression	Augmented Triads

Important Concepts

The term *post-romantic* is applied to the music of composers such as Hugo Wolf (1860–1903), Gustave Mahler (1860–1911), and Richard Strauss (1864–1949), who carried the musical style developed by the romantic composers (Richard Wagner in particular) to the outer limits of a tonal system based on the major and minor scales and functional harmony. Although tertian harmony remains an integral part of the harmonic system, *post-romanticism* reflects a compositional style characterized by tonal instability and nonfunctional harmony.

Tonal Instability

The post-romantic composers were greatly influenced by the music of Richard Wagner, who was able to sustain high levels of tension for long periods of time by avoiding resolution of the dominant function. Notice that each dominant 7th in Figure 31.1 is followed by silence and not resolved in the expected way.

Figure 31.1

Wagner: *Tristan und Isolde,* Prelude to act I, mm. 1–11. ♩

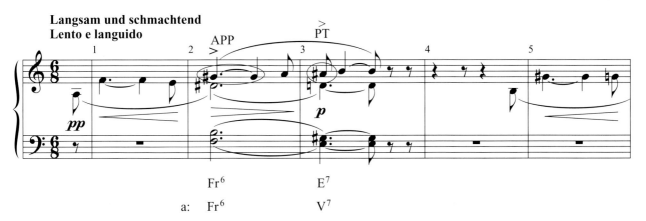

The use of chromatic harmony and nonharmonic tones, plus the absence of the tonic chord, creates tonal instability in this passage. This passage is one of the most discussed and analyzed passages in all Western music, and the analysis just presented is only one possible interpretation.

The following excerpt from a Wolf song (Figure 31.2) creates tonal instability at the outset of the song through thin textures, chromaticism, incomplete chords, and lack of strong moves toward the tonic. The music arrives at a clear tonal center only in measure 9 through a circle progression in the previous measure (V/V–V^7–i), and even here the tonic is somewhat obscured by nonharmonic tones.

Figure 31.2

Wolf: "Der Knabe und das Immlein" ("The Boy and the Bee") from *Gedichte von Eduard Mörike,* mm. 1–9. ♪

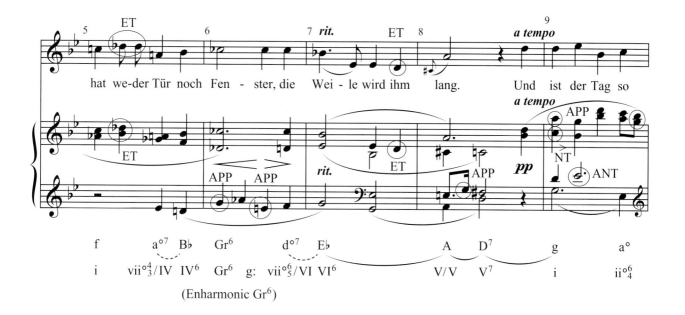

Nonfunctional Harmony

The post-romantic composers often used foreign modulation to create tonal instability. Figure 31.3 is the beginning of a passage that does not return to the tonic for 16 measures. Notice the movement toward G major and D-flat major and the chromatic passage in measures 13 to 15.

Figure 31.3

Strauss: "Allerseelen" ("All Souls Day"), op. 10, no. 8, mm. 11–17.

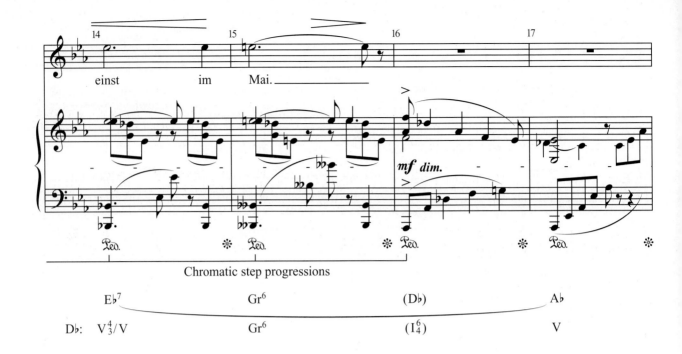

Chromatic step progressions

| | Eb⁷ | | Gr⁶ | | (Db) | | Ab |
| Db: | V$^4_3$/V | | Gr⁶ | | (I$^6_4$) | | V |

Omnibus Progression

The so-called *omnibus progression* is a specific nonfunctional harmonic progression based on the chromatic scale. In Figure 31.4, notice how the descending chromatic bass line accompanies a sequential harmonic pattern whose repetition divides the octave into four similar parts.

Figure 31.4 ♫

Augmented 6th and 7th chord resolutions

This progression, which occurred occasionally in romantic period music and more frequently in post-romantic music, takes advantage of the dual resolution tendencies of the major-minor 7th chord and the German 6th chord. In chord 1, the minor 7th (G–F) is resolved as an augmented 6th (G–E♯). In chord 3, the F is resolved as the 7th of a chord. At the point of resolution in chord 4, another German 6th/dominant 7th sonority is created, and the process continues until the first chord returns, creating an endless cycle. Figure 31.5 shows a passage from Mussorgsky's *Boris Godunov* that uses seven chords of the omnibus cycle.

Figure 31.5

Mussorgsky: *Boris Godunov,* act III, scene I, mm. 210–217.

Blurred Cadence

The tonic is sometimes in doubt during most of a composition in this period, but it normally returns at the end to create closure. At the end of a composition, strong cadences are often blurred when other chords (particularly the V/iv) are inserted between the dominant and the tonic chord, as shown in Figure 31.6. The authentic cadence was too simple, following the highly chromatic music earlier in this song.

Figure 31.6

Strauss: "Zeitlose" ("Meadow Saffron"), op. 10, no. 7, mm. 22–27.

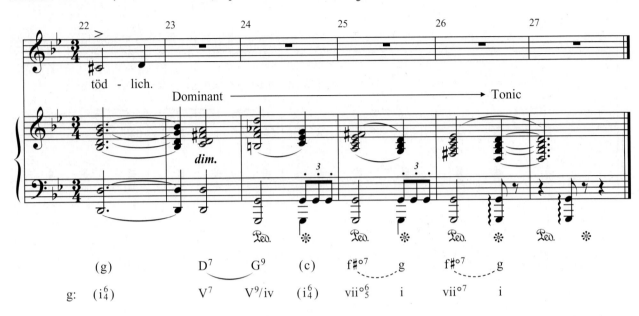

Augmented Triads

The post-romantic composers added the augmented triad to their vocabulary of ambiguous chords. It appeared both as an altered dominant and as a nonfunctional chord. In Figure 31.7, nonfunctional augmented chords are treated with the same sliding chromaticism as the diminished 7th chord in earlier times.

Figure 31.7

Wolf: "Das verlassene Mägdlein" ("The Forsaken Maiden") from *Gedichte von Eduard Mörike*, no. 7, mm. 19–26.

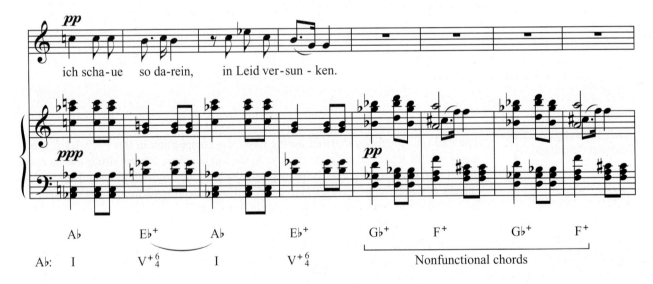

Summary

Composers of post-romantic music embraced tertian harmony and utilized the tonal system of major and minor scales, but the style is characterized by tonal instability resulting from chromaticism and delayed resolution. Although analytical systems such as Roman numeral analysis and macro analysis can be applied to compositions from this style period, the frequent key changes, irregular resolutions, chromatic inflections, and enharmonic relationships require a broad-visioned perspective when assessing compositions of this style period.

Assignment 31.1

The following song by Hugo Wolf includes nonfunctional harmony and foreign modulations.

1. Prepare a complete analysis (Roman numeral or macro) according to the directions of your instructor.
2. In class or on a separate sheet of paper, discuss the types of harmonic progressions appearing throughout the song. Determine how nonharmonic tones relate to harmonic patterns. Assess the tonal centers and key relationships. Consider how the melody interacts with the framework of the harmony and discuss the impact of the relationship.
3. Before preparing the analysis, have two students perform the song in class or listen to a recording until the work is familiar. (It is fruitless to attempt the analysis of a composition unless you know it thoroughly.)

Wolf: "Der Mond hat eine schwere Klag' erhoben" ("The Moon Hath Been Most Grievously Complaining") from *Italienisches Liederbuch.*

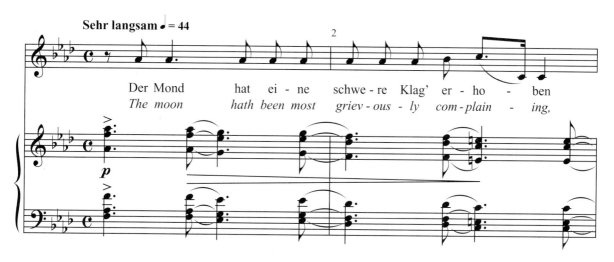

Er wol - le nicht mehr stehn_____ am Him - mel dro - ben,
she feels that in the Heav'ns_____ her glo - ry's wan - ing,

du ha - best ihn um sei - nen Glanz_____ ge - bracht.
since of her lu - stre she's by thee_____ be - reft.

Als er zu - lezt das Ster - nen - heer ge - zählt,_____
When last she came to count_____ her star - ry le - gions,

da hab' es an der vol - len Zahl ge - fehlt; —
some stars were miss - ing from _____ the heav'n - ly re - gions;

zwei von den schön - sten ha - best du ent - wen - det:
two bright - est stars had left _____ her at thy woo - ing;

die bei-den Au - gen dort, die mich ver - blen - det.
those eyes of thine, that proved my heart's un - do - ing. (Lily Henkel)

Assignment 31.2   Compose a short song in the post-romantic style.

1. Select a short poem you particularly like as the basis for your song.
2. Pattern the harmonic vocabulary after Wolf's "Der Mond hat eine schwere Klag' erhoben" ("The Moon Hath Been Most Grievously Complaining") from *Italienisches Liederbuch*. Use a recurring motivic pattern in the accompaniment.
3. Be sure to include frequent key changes and include modulations to foreign keys.
4. Perform the composition in class with a voice major singing the vocal line.

CHAPTER 32

Impressionism and Related Styles

Topics		
	Impressionism	Quartal and Quintal Chords
	Church Modes	Traditional Cadences
	Pentatonic Scale	Linear Cadence
	Whole-Tone Scale	3rd-Relationship Cadence
	7th, 9th, 11th, and 13th Chords	Cadences with Added or Omitted Tones
	Chords of Addition and Omission	Melodic Doubling in Parallel
	Split 3rds	Parallel Chords (Planing)

Important Concepts

The term *impressionism* was first applied to a group of French painters, including Édouard Manet, Claude Monet, and Auguste Renoir. Their interest in light and color led to a style characterized by blurred images that convey the "impression" of a scene instead of an actual representation. The term was first used in music to describe the work of Claude-Achille Debussy (1862–1918) and his followers, principally Maurice Ravel (1875–1937).

Like the post-romantic composers, Debussy also felt the influence of Wagner, but his response was a conscious attempt to remove "Wagnerisms" from his music. In a letter to a friend during the composition of his opera *Pelléas et Mélisande,* he complained, "I was too hasty to crow over *Pelléas et Mélisande.* . . . The ghost of old Klingsor, alias *R. Wagner,* appeared at the turn of a measure, so I tore it all up." Debussy created a unique musical style that has come to be called impressionism. It is a blend of elements borrowed from Eastern and Western music as well as those of his own invention. Many composers in the early twentieth century were influenced by impressionism.

Scale Resources

Church Modes

Composers of this time often utilize modal resources originating from the *church modes* to create new and unusual melodic effects. Figure 32.1 (pp. 665–666) illustrates the use of the Dorian mode as it appears in Ernest Bloch's *Chanty.*

Figure 32.1

Dorian mode beginning on A

Bloch: *Chanty* from *Poems of the Sea*, mm. 1–8.

Figure 32.2 illustrates the use of the Phrygian mode beginning on A.

Figure 32.2

Respighi: *Trittico Botticelliano* (Botticelli Triptych).

Pentatonic Scale

The *pentatonic scale* (five-tone scale) was frequently used in compositions of this period. Because it is a gapped scale (containing intervals larger than a whole step between adjacent tones), there are several possible forms. Two of the more frequently used pentatonic scales are shown in Figure 32.3.

Figure 32.3

Figure 32.4, an excerpt from one of Debussy's Preludes, demonstrates the use of the pentatonic scale.

Figure 32.4

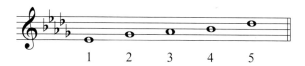

Debussy: *Voiles* (Sails*) from Preludes, Book I, no. 2, mm. 43–45 (modified). ♪

*Voiles can also be translated as "Veils."

Whole-Tone Scale

The *whole-tone scale* is a scale in which each degree is a whole step from the next. The whole-tone scale has only six tones—it is a hexatonic scale. Only two different whole-tone scales are possible. The two scales illustrated form an aggregate of the chromatic scale.

Figure 32.5 is a whole-tone scale utilizing the tones C, D, E, F♯/G♭, G♯/A♭, and A♯/B♭ (any pitch may be spelled enharmonically).

Figure 32.5

Figure 32.6 shows the remaining tones of the chromatic scale (any pitch may be spelled enharmonically).

Figure 32.6

There are no P5ths or P4ths between any two degrees of the whole-tone scale. The whole-tone scale is not diatonic—it contains no key or tonal center and may begin on any of the six tones. Figure 32.7 illustrates Debussy's use of the whole-tone scale.

Figure 32.7

Debussy: *Voiles* (Sails) from Preludes, Book I, no. 2, mm. 1–4.

Chords

*7th, 9th, 11th, and
13th Chords*

The *7th, 9th, 11th, and 13th chords* are employed with considerably greater frequency during the impressionistic period and with much less tendency to resolve the dissonant factors. Figure 32.8, from Ravel's Sonatine (1903), illustrates the use of 7th and 9th chords in succession. Note the circle progression, a vestige of the baroque, classical, and romantic periods.

Figure 32.8

Ravel: Sonatine, II: Mouvement de Menuet, mm. 6–12.

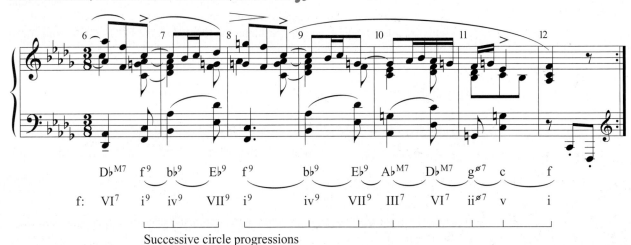

Successive circle progressions

**Chords of Addition
and Omission**

Chords of addition and omission are chords with added or deleted tones. To enrich the sound of some sonorities, composers of the period often added a 6th, a 4th, or a 2nd to the traditional triad. Similarly, tones were, on occasion, deleted from chords, thus thinning the sound. Some common examples are found in Figure 32.9.

Figure 32.9

Added 6th   Added 4th   Added 2nd   Omitted 3rd   Omitted 3rd

Chords with added tones often appear very similar to 9th, 11th, and 13th chords, but when the highest factor (9th, 11th, or 13th) is in a lower voice, the tendency is to hear it as an added tone (Figure 32.10).

Figure 32.10

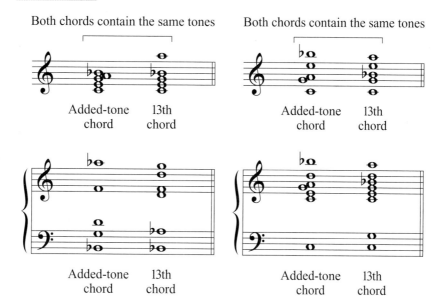

In this book we use the word ᴼᴹᴵᵀ plus the chord factor missing to indicate tones omitted from chords and the word ᴬᴰᴰ plus the interval added for tones added to chords. For example, a chord with a missing third will be labeled ᴼᴹᴵᵀ ³, and a chord with an added sixth will be labeled ᴬᴰᴰ ⁶.

The added 6th chord is especially prominent in Figure 32.11.

Figure 32.11

Ravel: Sonatine, I: Modéré, mm. 22–26.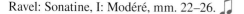

The excerpts in Figure 32.12 contain both chords of omission and added tones.

a. Debussy: *La Soirée dans Grenade* (Evening in Granada) from *Estampes* (Prints), mm. 1–4. ♪

b. Debussy: *La Soirée dans Grenade* (Evening in Granada) from *Estampes* (Prints), mm. 38–39. ♫

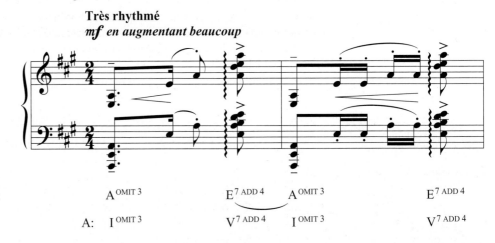

Split 3rds

The preceding examples of added tones were diatonic, but chromatic added tones are also found. Such chromatic tones often produce double inflections of chord tones. Double inflection of the 3rd of the chord produces a combination of major and minor, which is called a *split 3rd*. Figure 32.13 contains five chromatic added tones.

Figure 32.13

Ravel: *Valses nobles et sentimentales* (Noble and Sentimental Waltzes), I, mm. 57–58.

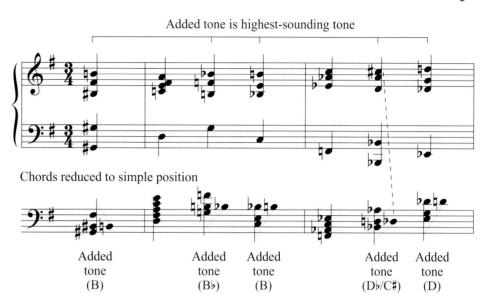

Added tone is highest-sounding tone

Chords reduced to simple position

| Added tone (B) | Added tone (B♭) | Added tone (B) | Added tone (D♭/C♯) | Added tone (D) |

Quartal and Quintal Chords

Quartal chords are chords built in 4ths, whereas *quintal chords* are based on 5ths. Although by no means a common occurrence, quartal and quintal chords can be found in this style period. Two distinct types can be identified: "consonant" and "dissonant" quartal/quintal sonorities. Consonant quartal/quintal chords usually contain three to five factors built in P4ths (or P5ths), whereas dissonant quartal/quintal chords contain one or more A4ths (or d5ths) or five or more P4ths (or P5ths). Examples are shown in Figure 32.14.

Figure 32.14

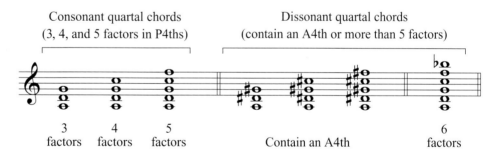

Consonant quartal chords (3, 4, and 5 factors in P4ths)

Dissonant quartal chords (contain an A4th or more than 5 factors)

| 3 factors | 4 factors | 5 factors | Contain an A4th | 6 factors |

Quartal and quintal chords are not particularly common in impressionistic music, although they sometimes appear as parallel chords in nonfunctional harmony. Figure 32.15 illustrates such use.

Figure 32.15

Debussy: *La Cathédrale engloutie* (The Engulfed Cathedral) from Preludes, Book I, no. 10, mm. 85–86.

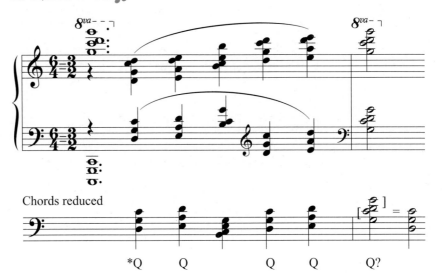

*Quartal chords

Cadences

Traditional Cadences

A variety of cadences are found in this style period, ranging from the traditional authentic cadence to the 3rd-relationship cadence. The traditional authentic cadence is frequently adorned with 7th, 9th, 11th, or 13th chords (Figure 32.16).

Figure 32.16

Debussy: *Pelléas et Mélisande,* act I, scene 1, mm. 131–132.

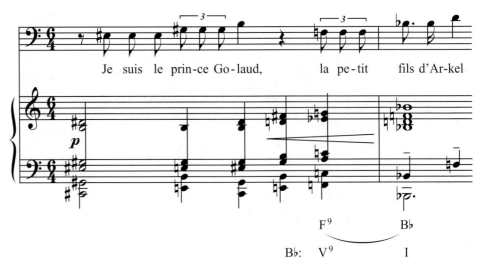

Linear Cadences

A *linear cadence* consists of melodic lines that converge or diverge to form cadence points. These cadences are reminiscent of cadences in early music, before the development of the major/minor tonal system. (See clausula vera, Chapter 1.) Figure 32.17 contains examples of linear cadences.

Figure 32.17

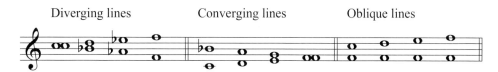

In Figure 32.18, the final cadence results from oblique motion.

Figure 32.18

Debussy: *Le vent dans la plaine* (Wind on the Plain) from Preludes, Book I, no. 3, mm. 57–59. ♩

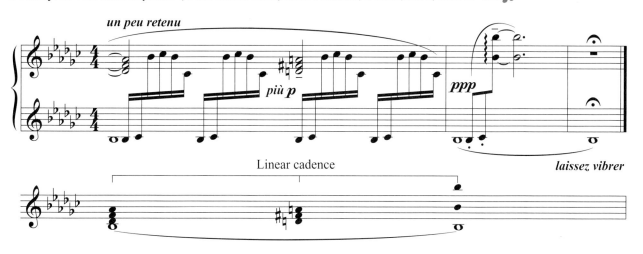

3rd-Relationship Cadences

A cadence that results from a harmonic progression in which the roots lie a 3rd apart is very common. Figures 32.19 to 32.21 illustrate *3rd-relationship cadences*.

Figure 32.19

Ravel: Sonatine, II: Mouvement de Menuet, mm. 77–82 ♩.

Figure 32.20

Debussy: *Clair de lune* (Moonlight) from *Suite Bergamasque,* mm. 70–72.

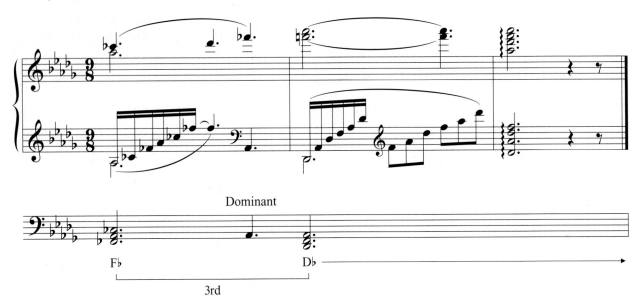

Figure 32.21

Ravel: Sonatine, I: Modéré, mm. 79–84.

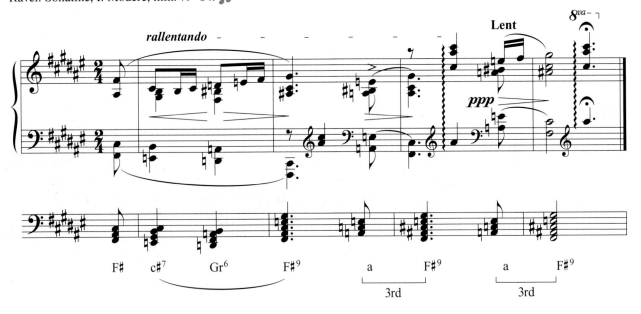

Cadences with Added or Omitted Tones

Although the authentic cadence of the late eighteenth and nineteenth centuries is sometimes found in its unaltered state in this style period, chords to which additional factors have been added or from which they have been deleted often camouflage the dominant–tonic function. The final cadence in Figure 32.22 contains a dominant 7th chord with an added 4th. This chord thus contains elements of both dominant and tonic harmony.

Figure 32.22

Debussy: Menuet from *Petite suite,* mm. 86–88.

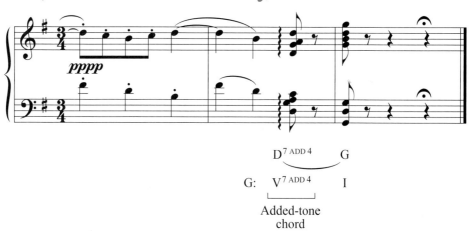

G: V$^{7\ \text{ADD}\ 4}$ I

Added-tone
chord

Other Cadences

A variety of other cadences are also a part of the late nineteenth- and early twentieth-century style. Most are simply variations of traditional cadences. Figure 32.23 ends with a dominant–tonic cadence in the Mixolydian mode.

Figure 32.23

Satie: *Gymnopedie* no. 2, mm. 61–65.

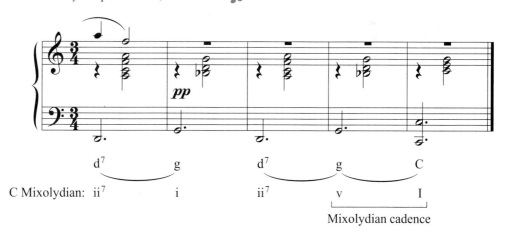

C Mixolydian: ii^7 i   ii^7 v   I

Mixolydian cadence

**Textural
Considerations**

Melodic doubling in parallel refers to the doubling of melodic lines to create parallel movement. The doubling may be simply the addition of a single tone at a fixed harmonic interval (Figure 32.24).

Figure 32.24

Melody

Same melody with melodic doubling

Although treated in a unique way in this period, melodic doubling is by no means the invention of twentieth-century composers. Such doubling has been in existence for many centuries and can be found in fauxbourdon and English descant of the fifteenth century (Figure 32.25).

Figure 32.25

Dufay: *Missa Sancti Jacobi,* Communio, mm. 21–23. ♪

Figure 32.26 illustrates the use of melodic doubling at the interval of the 2nd.

Figure 32.26

Debussy: *Ce qu'a vu le vent de l'Ouest* (What the West Wind Saw) from Preludes, Book I, no. 7, mm. 10–13. ♪

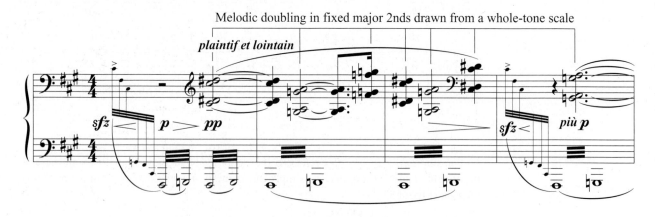

Parallel Chords (Planing)

Similar to melodic doubling, *parallel chords* are chords in which all factors or voices move in parallel motion. This motion is called *planing*. Generally, planing reduces or negates the effect of harmonic progression, but occasionally chords such as the tonic and dominant may create the sense of harmonic progression (Figure 32.27).

Figure 32.27

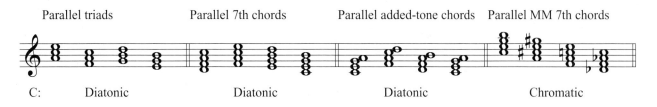

The example of planing in Figure 32.28 contains only major-minor 7th chords.

Figure 32.28

Debussy: Sarabande from *Pour le Piano* (For the Piano), mm. 9–12.

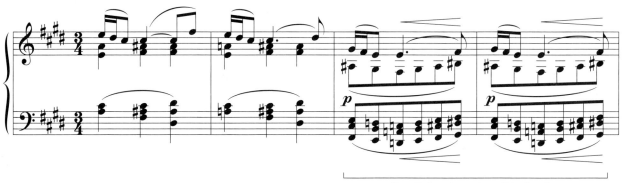

Parallel major-minor 7th chords

Figure 32.29 contains mixed major and minor triads in first inversion.

Figure 32.29

Debussy: *La Soirée dans Grenade* (Evening in Granada) from *Estampes* (Prints), mm. 80–81.

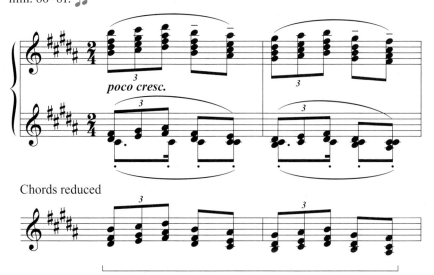

Chords reduced

Planed first inversion major and minor triads

The romantic period's emphasis on individual expression rested heavily on composers at the turn of the twentieth century. Wagner had explored the outermost boundaries of the major/minor tonal system, and the music of all cultures was becoming known. (It is well known, for example, that Debussy was influenced by the pentatonic music of the Javanese gamelan, which he heard at the Paris *Exposition Universelle* in 1889.) The study of history had brought much of the music of earlier times to the attention of musicians. The composer was faced with the daunting task of creating a "new" music. The statements of Ferruccio Busoni are typical of the period: "The function of the creative artist consists in making laws, not in following laws ready made. He who follows such laws, ceases to be a creator. Creative power may be the more readily recognized, the more it shakes itself loose from tradition. But an intentional avoidance of the rules cannot masquerade as creative power, and still less engender it" (from *Sketch of a New Esthetic of Music*). The paradox of "not following laws ready made," although not "intentionally" avoiding tradition, was a nearly insurmountable obstacle and may be responsible, in part, for the note of regret and nostalgia that comes through in much late nineteenth-century music. The music of this period presents unique challenges to analysis. It is much more diverse and not as systematized as the music of the baroque, classical, and early romantic periods. It should not be surprising that new analytical strategies must be created to deal with music from the late nineteenth century to the present.

Applications

Scale Vocabulary

In previous analyses the major or minor scales could be assumed to be the tonal basis, but no such assumption can be made with music of the late nineteenth and early twentieth centuries. Instead, the identification of the scale basis (major, minor, modal, chromatic, pentatonic, or whole tone) will be an important step in analysis. If the music is not based in some way on the major/minor tonal system, then traditional Roman numeral analysis is not likely to prove fruitful. (In some cases, modal materials can be successfully analyzed with Roman numerals.)

Chord Vocabulary

The introduction of quartal chords raises questions concerning the interval basis of harmony. Roman numeral analysis assumes a tertian system (a harmonic system based on thirds) and is not appropriate for quartal harmonic materials. Chords of addition and omission present new problems in chord labeling.

The following suggestions are intended to help you recognize and label the tonal materials you will encounter in studying the music of this period.

Suggested Approach to Analysis

1. Establish the scale basis by examination of the music. If the music is chromatic, try to determine whether the chromaticism is the result of functional chromatic harmony or is nonfunctional. If the music seems diatonic, check first to see if it may be pentatonic. Because the pentatonic scale is a subset of the diatonic scale, it is easily overlooked. If the music proves to be diatonic, check for a modal versus a major/minor basis.
2. Examine the harmonic vocabulary by looking at prominent chords. Check particularly for quartal/quintal sonorities.
3. If the music is major/minor or functional chromatic, then Roman numeral analysis is appropriate. Complete an analysis (Roman numeral or macro) below the staff.
4. If the music contains passages of nonfunctional harmony, do a harmonic reduction and identify each chord by quality, with either Roman numerals or direct labeling (A^7, d^7, etc.). Check carefully for functional relationships that may be masked by enharmonic spellings.

5. If the music falls outside steps 3 and 4, do a harmonic reduction and resort to direct labeling of scales and chords.
6. Melodic and rhythmic analysis is little affected by the introduction of new tonal materials and can be done in the usual way.

Specimen Analysis

The following analysis of a well-known composition by Debussy, *La Cathédrale engloutie*, provides an example of the analytical technique that can be applied to late nineteenth- and early twentieth-century music (Figure 32.30).

Figure 32.30

Debussy: *La Cathédrale engloutie* (The Engulfed Cathedral) from Preludes, Book I, no. 10.

(E Lydian)

(Melody against E pedal)

(E Lydian)

pp

pp   *sans nuances*

$E^{OMIT\ 3}$

C^{M7} Q   Q   Q   Q   Q   Q   Q   Q

C major

(C–G pedal established)

② 16

sempre ***pp***

p marqué

pp

B pentatonic (B–C♯–D♯–F♯–G♯)

B   (Added tones)

$B^{ADD\ 6}$

(B pentatonic)

E♭ major

B^ADD 6

E♭   (Added tones)

(E♭ major)

E♭

E♭

C major

Q

d^{7 ADD 4}

(C: ii^{7 ADD 4})

(d^{7 ADD 4})

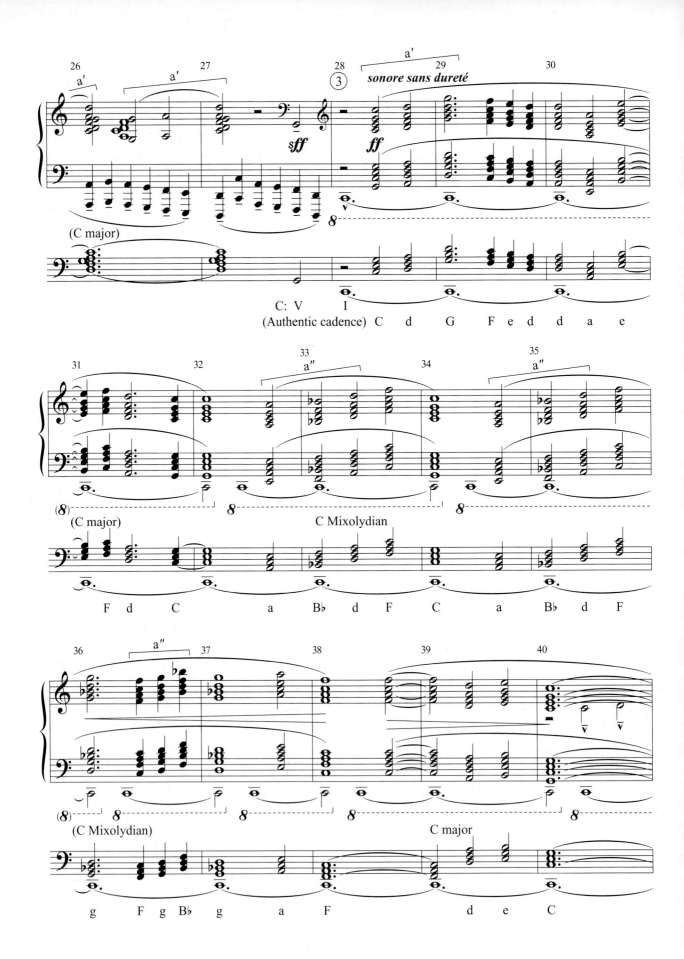

Tonality

Although not based, for the most part, on functional harmony, an overall tonal center of C emerges. This is primarily due to a bass line in the opening section that descends in step-wise motion from G to C (Figure 32.31a), a strong authentic cadence in measures 27 to 28 (Figure 32.31b), and sustained C pedals in measures 28 to 41 and 72 to 89.

Figure 32.31

The C tonal center is relieved by passages centered around B (mm. 16–18), E♭ (mm. 19–21), and G♯ (mm. 47–67). Notice the extensive 3rd relationships among these centers (C–E♭, B–E♭, G♯–C), even though they may be spelled enharmonically.

Chord Progressions

The effect of regularly recurring harmonic progressions is minimized in this composition. The reasons are as follows:

1. The actual progressions occur at widely spaced intervals of at least 2 measures, and in one instance at a distance of 13 measures. The harmonic rhythm is extremely slow.
2. Some of the harmonic progressions (such as from measures 18 to 19 and 21 to 22) contain chords whose roots lie in 3rd relationship to each other. When the 3rds are ascending, the harmonic strength is weakened considerably.

Cadences

Traditional harmonic cadences are suggested but are seldom stated clearly as in earlier styles. (The authentic cadence at measures 27 to 28 is veiled with added-tone chords and a running figure in the lower voice.) The cadence points are as follows:

Measures	Cadence Type	Tonality	Chords
27–28	Authentic	C	V (implied) to I
39–40	Linear (parallel motion)	C	I (pedal)
64–66	Half	C♯	V^7/V to V^7
86–89	Authentic (modified dominant)	C	V (or quartal) to I

Melodic Material

The melodic material is quite similar throughout the work. There is a prominent three-note motive that appears in various guises in most sections of the piece (Figure 32.32). The similarity of melodic material creates an organic unity that ties the work together.

Figure 32.32

Meter and Rhythm

The meter $\frac{6}{4} = \frac{3}{2}$, indicated at the beginning of this composition, is normally interpreted to mean that the quarter-note values remain fixed and that in some measures they will be grouped in duples and in others as triplets. However, in his own performance of this work, Debussy played in a fashion that would indicate the following:

♩ in $\frac{6}{4}$ meter = ♩ in $\frac{3}{2}$ meter

Because the meter vacillates somewhat between groupings of two and groupings of three, the rhythm, although interesting and diverse, is not stressed. In its subtler aspects, however, rhythm plays a role as part of the total "color" in this work.

Texture

The texture of this composition is the antithesis of polyphony. With the numerous pedal tones and the parallel movement of chords (planing), conflict of opposing melodies is almost totally absent. The motion is predominantly parallel or oblique, as shown in Figure 32.33, in a typical measure (14).

Figure 32.33

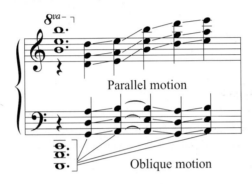

Form

In 1907 Debussy wrote to his publisher, "I am more and more convinced that music is not, in essence, a thing that can be cast into a traditional and fixed form. It is made up of colors and rhythms." Any attempt to cast this music into a traditional form would seem doomed to failure. Nevertheless, several points within the work seem to be the beginnings of important statements or seem to contrast in one way or another with previous sections. These points are identified in the score as points of formal articulation. The following table lists these points and musical elements that support the perception of the beginning of a statement.

Articulation Point	Measure	Elements Creating the Formal Articulation
1	1	Beginning of the work
2	16	New accompaniment texture; tonal center B
3	28	Strong cadence; new planed triad texture
4	47	Tonal center G♯; previous passage is "transitional"
5	72	Return to C tonal center; previous passage is "transitional"
6	84	Eighth-note accompaniment texture replaced by quarter-note motion; planed quartal texture

It is clear that articulation point 6 is like number 1 (the beginning of the work), creating a sense of return. Articulation point 3 is also similar to number 5 (compare right-hand parts). This has led at least one theorist to see an arch form in which the second part of the work represents a mirror image of the first part of the work.

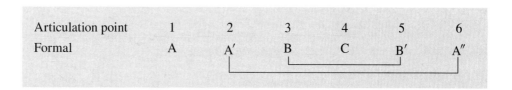

Articulation point	1	2	3	4	5	6
Formal	A	A'	B	C	B'	A''

Although it may not be possible to state with certainty which formal outline best fits this prelude, it is clear that the work is carefully constructed and presents a unified impression. Judging by Debussy's statements on the subject of form, this should be sufficient.

Summary

The compositional devices illustrated in this chapter are an integral part of the musical style known as impressionism first made famous by Debussy. Some of the basic elements of impressionism are present in earlier musical styles, but the unique application within a new context requires a flexible approach when attempting an analysis.

The following list represents the more common scales, chords, and procedures associated with impressionism.

Scales:
    Church modes
    Pentatonic scale
    Whole-tone scale
    Major and minor scales

Chords:
    Triads
    7th, 9th, 11th, and 13th chords
    Chords of addition (added 6th, 4th, and 2nd)
    Chords of omission (omitted 3rd)
    Split-3rd chords
    Quartal and quintal chords

Cadences:
    Traditional cadences
    Linear cadences
    3rd-relationship cadences
    Cadences with added or omitted tones
    Varied traditional cadences

Compositional techniques:
    Melodic doubling in parallel
    Parallel chords (planing)

Practice

It may have been a while since you have had to write or analyze a church mode, pentatonic scale, or whole-tone scale. If you have forgotten how to construct these scales, review the previous chapters as a refresher. Information on the modal scales can be found in volume 1, Chapters 2 and 8, and volume 2, Chapter 18. The pentatonic and whole-tone scales are described in volume 1, Chapter 2.

Throughout much of this text, the music presented is based on the tonal system of major and minor scales. With this chapter, new methods for assessing tonal concepts are introduced. Be sure to review items such as the 7th, 9th, 11th, and 13th chords that continue to be part of the style vocabulary.

Take time to scrutinize the structure of the chords newly presented in this chapter. At the piano or a keyboard, practice stacking chords in 4ths and 5ths to construct quartal and quintal chords. Be aware of the differences between the chords of addition with the added 2, 4, and 6, and their extended counterparts, the 9th, 11th, and 13th chords. Practice split-3rd chords by playing triads that include both a major and minor 3rd.

Aural assessment of the scales, chords, cadences, and techniques associated with impressionism will help prepare you for written analysis. Become familiar with impressionism by listening to live performances or recordings of Debussy's music. Any composition by Debussy will do, but if you are at a loss to pick a work, the *Trois Nocturnes* (Three Nocturnes) and Preludes Books I and II provide excellent examples of the impressionism procedures outlined in this chapter.

Assignment 32.1

Using the suggestions in the applications section of this chapter (p. 678), do an analysis of the following excerpt from *Pour le Piano* by Debussy. Before preparing the analysis, have a student perform the composition several times in class or listen to a recording until the work is thoroughly familiar to you.

Debussy: Sarabande from *Pour le Piano* (For the Piano).

Assignment 32.2

Using the suggestions in the applications section of this chapter, do an analysis of "Je garde une médaille d'elle" by Lili Boulanger (1893–1918). Before preparing the analysis, have a student perform the composition several times in class or listen to a recording until the work is thoroughly familiar.

Translation of the lyrics:
I keep a medal of hers on which are engraved a date, and the words: "pray, believe, hope." But, as for me, I see above all that the medal is dark; its silver has tarnished on her dovelike neck.

Boulanger: "Je garde une médaille d'elle" ("I Keep a Medal of Hers").

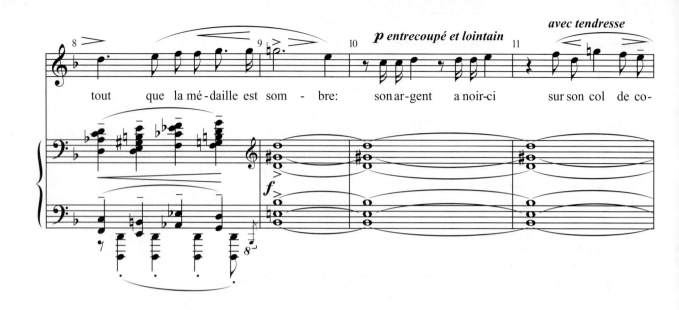

tout   que la mé - daille est som - bre: son ar-gent   a noir-ci   sur son col   de co-

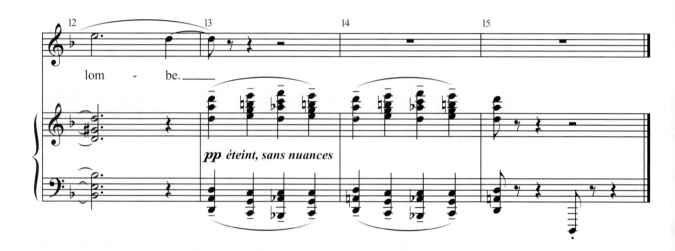

lom - be._____

Assignment 32.3   Using some of the following devices, write a short composition of 16 to 30 measures in the style of Debussy.

3rd-relationship cadence	Melodic doubling
Parallelism (planing)	Altered dominants or tonics
Modal melody	Changing meters
Pedal tones	7th, 9th, 11th, and 13th chords
Chords of addition and omission	Pentatonic scale

1. Write for any combination of instruments played by class members.
2. Perform the compositions in class.
3. After each student composition is performed, members of the class should enumerate (from listening only) the various devices employed in the work.

CHAPTER 33

The Early Twentieth Century

Topics

Primitivism
Neoclassicism
Pandiatonicism
Polytonality
Dual Modality

Shifted Tonality
Free Tonality
Polychords
Quartal Chords
Clusters

Changing Meter
Additive Rhythm
Asymmetric Meters
Nonaccentual Rhythms

Important Concepts

Concurrent with the surge of post-romantic and impressionistic music, several other, quite different styles began to surface. At the same time that the works of Debussy, Delius, Wolf, Fauré, and Richard Strauss were receiving their premieres, other composers such as Arnold Schoenberg (1874–1951), Charles Ives (1874–1954), Béla Bartók (1881–1945), and Igor Stravinsky (1882–1971) were writing music in distinctly different idioms. Some composers maintained tertian chord structures but abandoned functional harmony, whereas others experimented with chords constructed in 4ths, 5ths, or combinations of several intervals. Some preserved tonality, others discarded it in favor of atonality. Experimentation ranged even to the tuning system itself, leading to the development of microtonal systems based on more than 12 different pitches per octave. Chapters 33 and 34 deal with the music of Stravinsky, Bartók, and composers with similar styles; Chapter 35 discusses the work of Schoenberg and the other composers who evolved a music based on *twelve-tone technique,* a compositional technique in which all pitches are related to a fixed ordering of the 12 tones of the chromatic scale.

Major Styles

Primitivism

Primitivism provided a contrast to the extremely refined and fragile music of such composers as Debussy and Ravel. Rhythm was the primary structural element of this music, and driving rhythms were combined with simple and clearly defined melodies, often of a folk nature, that operated within a narrow pitch range. Sharp percussive effects with thick chords and much parallel movement typified the style. Bartók's *Allegro Barbaro* (1911) and Stravinsky's *The Rite of Spring* (1913) represent examples of this movement, which flourished in the early years of the twentieth century.

Neoclassicism

The term *neoclassicism* refers to the music of composers such as Stravinsky and Hindemith, who sought to return to the classical values of symmetry and balance while maintaining more contemporary tonal materials. This movement, which began just after World War I, was quite important through the first third of the twentieth century.

Tonal Basis

Pandiatonicism

Pandiatonicism is the use of the tones of a diatonic scale in such a way that each tone is stripped of its traditional function. The style is characterized by the absence of functional harmony, little or no chromaticism, and thick harmonies. Figure 33.1 is a typical example of pandiatonicism.

Figure 33.1

Stravinsky: Sonata for Two Pianos, II: Variation 1, mm. 4–7.

Polytonality

Polytonality is the use of two or more tonalities at the same time. The simultaneous use of two tonalities is often called *bitonality* (Figure 33.2).

Figure 33.2

C major

G♭ major

Dual Modality

The simultaneous use of a pair of major and minor modes or combinations of Gregorian modes is called *dual modality*. Usually the two modes have the same tonic (Figure 33.3).

Figure 33.3

Bartók: *Major and Minor* from *Mikrokosmos,* vol. II, no. 59, mm. 1–3. ♪

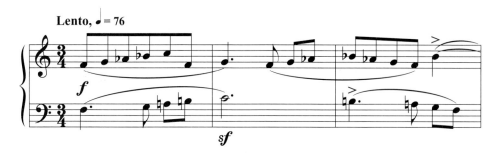

Treble clef notes: Dorian

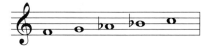

Bass clef notes: Lydian

Shifted Tonality

Shifted tonality refers to a sudden change of tonality without preparation, as occurs in the excerpt in Figure 33.4.

Figure 33.4

Prokofiev: Piano Sonata no. 8 in B-flat Major, op. 84, II: Andante sognando, mm. 7–10. ♪

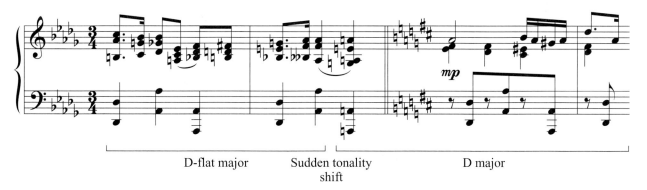

Free Tonality

Free tonality has the following characteristics:

1. No conventional mode or key is used.
2. A clear tonal center is present.
3. Any combination of the 12 tones of the octave may be used.
4. The traditional functioning of the diatonic tones of a key based on that same tonal center is minimized or avoided entirely.
5. The dominant-tonic relationship of key-centered tonality is absent.

In Figure 33.5, 11 of the 12 tones are present, the tonality of F is achieved without a single dominant–tonic progression, and the Phrygian mode is suggested but not confirmed.

Figure 33.5

Hindemith: Piano Sonata no. 2, I, mm. 41–48.

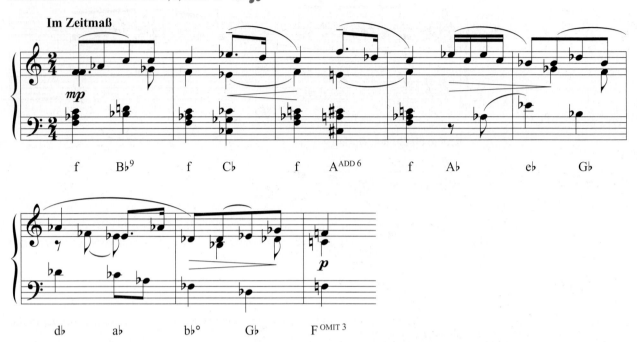

Harmony
Polychords

A *polychord* consists of two or more triads, 7th chords, or other chords sounded simultaneously and spaced far enough apart to make each recognizable as a separate structure. Two triads containing common tones and spaced a distance apart may not be perceived as separate structures if the combination of the two forms a chord very familiar to us. But if the triads contain no common tones and are of sufficiently contrasting nature, fusion will not result, and each triad will maintain its identity, as shown in Figure 33.6.

Figure 33.6

Polychord

No common tones.
Each chord retains separate sound.
Polychordal effect is emphasized.

Single chord implied

Chords contain two common tones.
Tones fuse into Mm 7th chord.
Little polychordal effect.

Figure 33.7 illustrates the wide spacing and contrasting nature of the simultaneous chords making up polychords.

Figure 33.7

Schuman: No. 2 from *Three Score Set*, mm. 1–4.

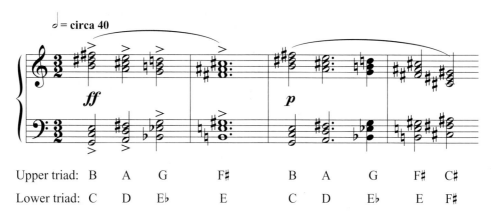

| Upper triad: | B | A | G | F♯ | | B | A | G | F♯ | C♯ |
| Lower triad: | C | D | E♭ | E | | C | D | E♭ | E | F♯ |

Quartal Chords

Quartal chords are common in music of the early twentieth century. Figure 33.8 contains pure quartal chords almost exclusively throughout the composition, which makes it a rare example of quartal chord treatment.

Figure 33.8

Ives: "The Cage," no. 64 from *114 Songs*, m. 2.

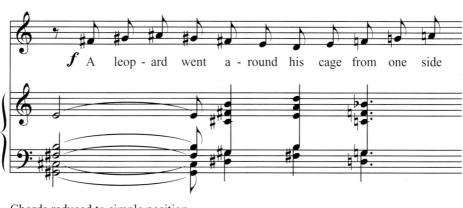

Chords reduced to simple position

All are 5-factor consonant quartal chords.

Frequently, quartal chords are not pure—that is, other intervals are included in the chord, thus creating a mixture of quartal and tertian harmony. The following excerpt (Figure 33.9) from Alban Berg's opera *Wozzeck* (1921), illustrates the intermixing of 3rds and 4ths. The parallel 4ths in contrary motion (treble against bass) create a counterpoint that adds to the interest of the composition.

Figure 33.9

Berg: *Wozzeck,* op. 7, act I, scene 3: "Marie's Lullaby," mm. 372–374.

*Predominantly quartal.

Both quartal and tertian harmony often contain the same tones, each distinguished only by the arrangement of the chord factors (Figure 33.10).

Figure 33.10

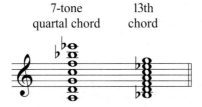

Both contain the same pitches

Clusters

Chords containing three or more factors of which each is no more than a whole step from its adjacent factor are called *clusters* (Figure 33.11).

Figure 33.11

Rhythm

Changing Meter

Meter changes from measure to measure within a composition show shifting rhythmic patterns more clearly than would a single governing meter. The signature is changed as often as necessary to clarify rhythms. *Changing meter* often occurs in music with *additive rhythm,* where the pulse is irregular in length, varying between groups of two and three regular divisions (Figure 33.12).

Figure 33.12

Stravinsky: *Triumphal March of the Devil* from *L'Histoire du Soldat* (The Soldier's Tale), violin part, mm. 1–7.

Asymmetric Meters

Asymmetric meters, also known as irregular meters or combination meters, are meters in which the beats are not grouped into units divisible by two or three. These meters are a common way of notating additive rhythm, particularly when there is a recurring pattern of beats (Figure 33.13).

Figure 33.13

Nonaccentual Rhythms

Nonaccentual rhythms are characterized by the absence of dynamic accents, which focuses the listener's attention on agogic accents (accents by virtue of duration) (Figure 33.14).

Figure 33.14

History

Increasing stylistic divergence marked the music of the early twentieth century. Rapid transportation, radio communication, the development of audio recording technology, and the sound film brought the rich diversity of the world's cultures to the attention of the general public. At the same time, World War I in Europe devastated established cultural institutions, leaving a culture that was undergoing rapid change while losing some of its own traditional base. The composers of this period were affected in many ways by these upheavals, as the brief biographies in this and the following chapters illustrate.

**Igor Stravinsky
(1882–1971)**

Igor Stravinsky's professional activity lasted nearly 60 years and evolved through many styles. Born in St. Petersburg, Russia, in 1882, he began studying with Rimsky-Korsakov in 1907. By 1911 Stravinsky had achieved success in Paris with two ballets, *The Firebird* and *Petrushka.* A third ballet, the initially controversial *The Rite of Spring,* received its first performance in 1913 and has since become one of the landmarks of twentieth-century music. Just before World War I, Stravinsky left Russia and took up residence in Switzerland, where he remained until 1920. After a long residence in France (1920–1939), he moved to the United States and became an American citizen in 1945. Perhaps the capstone of his career are the 21 works for the theater and 19 orchestral compositions, but he published chamber music, concertos, sacred choral–orchestral works, solo songs, and piano music. Stravinsky is considered by many to be the most important figure in twentieth-century music.

The following table provides an overview of the various phases of Stravinsky's professional life.

Approximate Years	Period	Representative Compositions	Brief Description of Techniques
1904–1913	Post-romantic Nationalistic	*The Firebird* *Petrushka* *The Rite of Spring*	Extreme modulations; rich harmonic schemes; full orchestral sounds; changing and asymmetrical meters.
1913–1923	Transition to Neoclassic	*L'Histoire du Soldat* *Les Noces*	Chromaticism, polytonality; more dissonant harmony; use of polyrhythms; thinner textures.
1923–1951	Neoclassic	*Symphony of Psalms, Symphony in Three Movements*	Somewhat less chromaticism; use of pandiatonicism; thin textures; use of song and sonata-like forms.
1952–1971	Serial technique	*In Memoriam Dylan Thomas Orchestral Variations*	Tone rows of five to seven tones; also fully developed serial technique; suggested by a study of Webern's music.

Application

The diversity of style in the music of the twentieth century requires more than one system of analysis. Several systems have been proposed, but none appears to be useful for all styles of music. In the face of such diversity, it becomes important to choose analytical methods that reveal the underlying structure of a given work. Thus the choice of analytical method becomes the first and most important decision you must make when approaching a composition from this time period. The following specimen analysis of the *Marche du Soldat* from Stravinsky's *l'Histoire du Soldat* (1919) illustrates one possible approach to the analysis of twentieth-century music.

Marche du Soldat by Stravinsky

L'Histoire du Soldat (The Soldier's Tale), a work intended "to be read, played, and danced," was written in 1918 for a small touring theater company composed of a few actors, dancers, and a chamber ensemble consisting of clarinet in A, bassoon, cornet in A, trombone, percussion, violin, and double bass. The percussion instruments include two snare drums, two tenor drums, bass drum, cymbals, tambourine, and triangle, all to be played by one player. This limited ensemble was clearly chosen to emphasize diversity of color, but the woodwinds, brass, and string sections are each represented by one high- and low-pitched instrument, and the ensemble covers the entire orchestral range. Swiss author C. F. Ramuz prepared the libretto and, because he was not a dramatist, a mimed narration (narrator and mime) supported by dancers and orchestra was prepared. Currently the work is sometimes performed without the staging.

Because the work is heterogeneous (consisting of many diverse elements), a descriptive analysis is the best choice (Figure 33.15).

Figure 33.15

Stravinsky: *Marche du Soldat* (Soldier's March) from *L'Histoire du Soldat* (The Soldier's Tale) ♩.

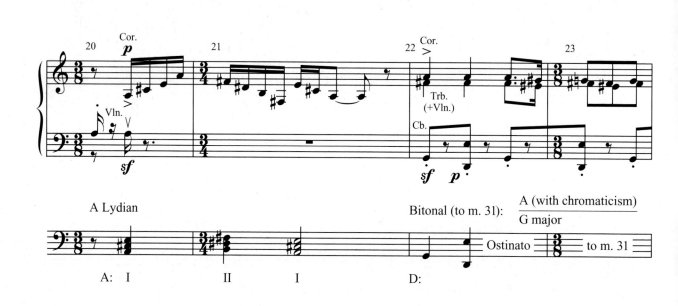

A Lydian

Bitonal (to m. 31): $\dfrac{\text{A (with chromaticism)}}{\text{G major}}$

A: I   II   I   D:

Ostinato   to m. 31

Quinze   jours
Ten   *days*

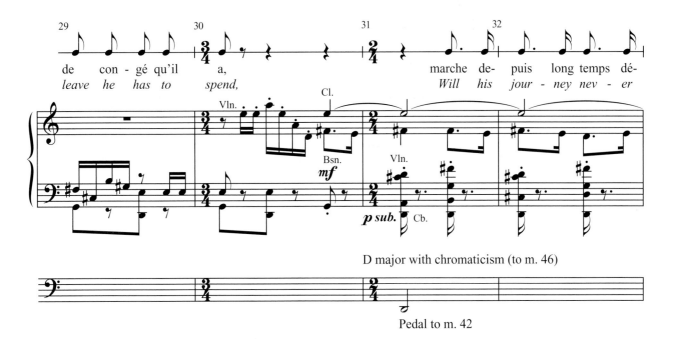

de con - gé qu'il a, marche de- puis long temps dé-
leave he has to spend, Will his jour - ney nev - er

D major with chromaticism (to m. 46)

Pedal to m. 42

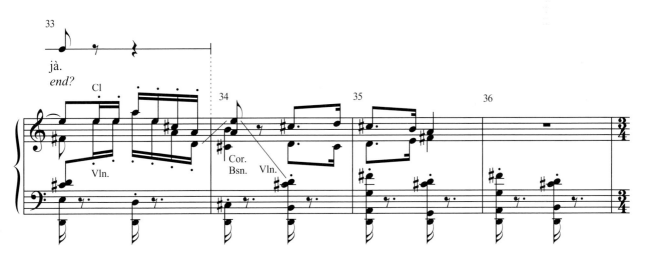

jà.
end?

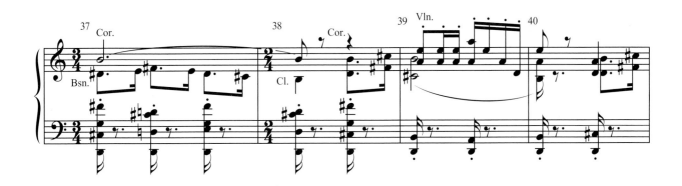

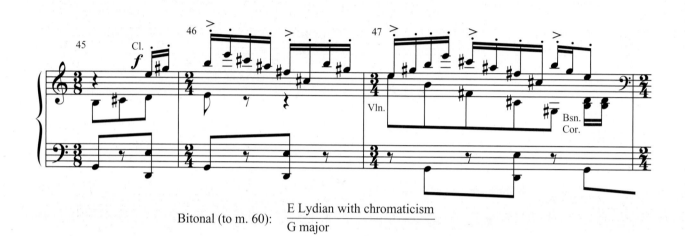

Bitonal (to m. 60): $\frac{\text{E Lydian with chromaticism}}{\text{G major}}$

A mar- ché, a beau-coup mar- ché,

March-ing home, *March-ing on his way.*

G major (to m. 64)

Bitonal (to m. 84)

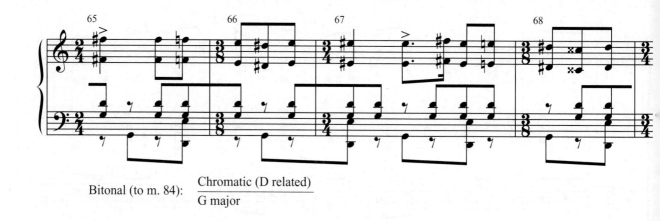

Bitonal (to m. 84): $\dfrac{\text{Chromatic (D related)}}{\text{G major}}$

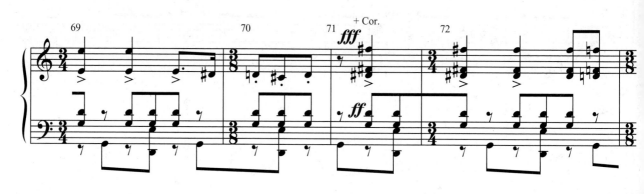

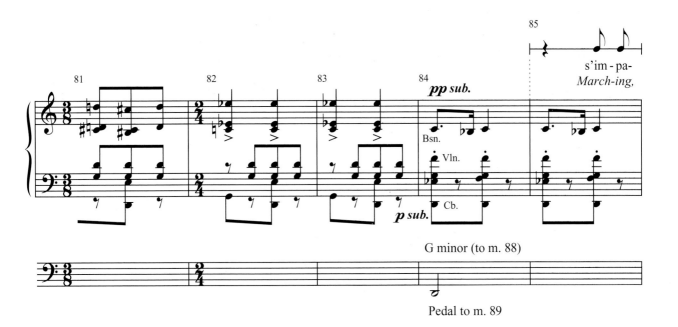

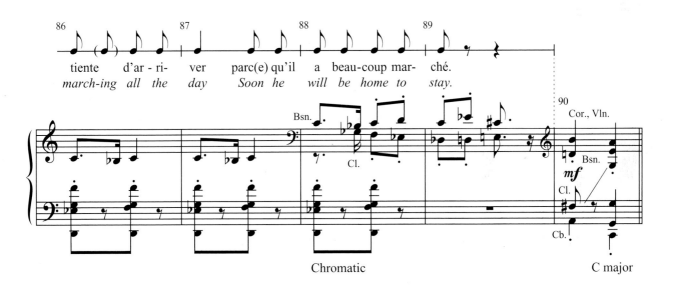

Melody

The characteristics of the melody are as follows:

1. The melody is in the top part, often with contrapuntal accompaniment.
2. A mixture of homophonic and contrapuntal texture applies throughout most of the composition.
3. The melody is based essentially on diatonic scales.

The Motives

The melody utilizes three motives. Motive A is simply a diatonic, conjunct passage that first descends and then ascends. Figure 33.16 shows examples of variations of this motive.

Figure 33.16

Motive A

Motive B, by contrast, consists of outlined chords (Figure 33.17).

Figure 33.17

Motive B

Motive C is very similar to motive A but differs in that it is made up entirely of repeated notes and half steps (Figure 33.18).

Figure 33.18

Motive C

A close look at measures 64 to 79 reveals the technique of phrase extension using motive C. Figure 33.19 compares measures 64 to 70 with measures 71 to 79. Whole notes are used to represent all tones so that rhythmic factors will not obscure the pitch relationships.

Figure 33.19

Phrase extension (melodic extension):

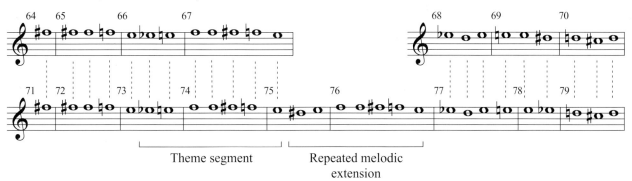

Theme segment | Repeated melodic extension

Form

The composition does not divide itself easily into clearly defined sections because it is strongly influenced by the spoken narrative (The Soldier's Tale). It is designed to accompany and strengthen the plot. An ostinato figure and a pedal tone on D are two of the most easily identified musical components of the work. If these two factors were considered alone, the form might suggest the following:

Measures	Lower Voice	Section
1–30	Ostinato figure	A
31–41	Pedal tone	B
42–83	Ostinato figure	A
84–90	Pedal tone	B

Another approach would use motive order as a way of organizing the composition:

Measures	Motive	Measures	Motive
1–18	A	39–43	B
20–21	B	44–46	A
22–26	C	45–47 (overlap)	B
26–30	B	47–57	A
31–32	A′	57–59	B
33–34	B	64–83	C
34–38	A′ (inv.)	84–90	Related to A

Harmony	The harmonic material is mostly the result of the bitonal mix, except for clear chords in measures 4, 20 to 21, and 90 (Figure 33.20).

Figure 33.20

Measure 4

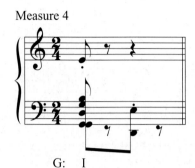

G: I

Measures 20–21

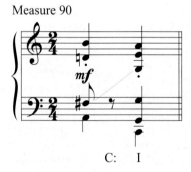

A: I   II   I

Measure 90

C: I

Phrase Structure	Melodic cadences, such as in Figure 33.21, often mark the end of phrases in the upper voices but are not often supported by the lower voices because of the continuing ostinato figure.

Figure 33.21

Melodic cadence

Overlapping phrases are fairly common. A melodic cadence is completed in one voice while a new phrase begins in another voice (Figure 33.22).

Figure 33.22

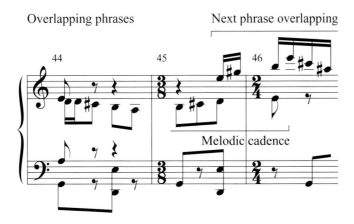

Meter

There are frequent meter changes, but in most instances the steady ostinato figure disregards these and plods on as if the $\frac{2}{4}$ meter had not been altered. Figure 33.23 is an example showing Stravinsky's actual notation along with another version illustrating how it might have been written keeping the steady $\frac{2}{4}$ meter intact.

Figure 33.23

The passage as written

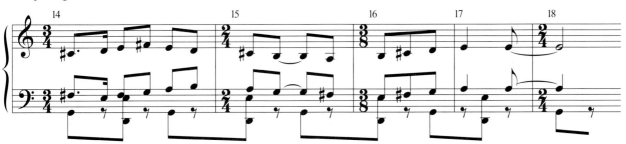

The same passage in strict $\frac{2}{4}$ meter

Texture

A thin, homophonic texture persists throughout. The upper voices occasionally engage in counterpoint (as in mm. 11–18).

Summary

The analytical approach presented in this chapter emphasizes the identification of compositional devices. Due to the breadth of differing styles, music of the early twentieth century requires a flexible approach. Tonality continues to be a part of music, but the tonal system expands to include pandiatonicism, polytonality, dual modality, shifted tonality, and free tonality. The harmonic vocabulary includes polychords and chord clusters, and quartal chords are juxtaposed with tertian structures. Rhythm becomes increasingly complex with changing meters, asymmetric meters, and nonaccentual rhythms. All of these varied elements require the analyst to consider carefully the best approach when engaging in analysis.

Practice

Obtain from your music library or the internet a score and recording for one or more of the following works by Stravinsky. Select a small section to analyze. Listen to your chosen excerpt(s) several times and make an aural analysis using the approach presented in this chapter. Attempt to identify the compositional techniques you hear.

Le Sacre du Printemps (The Rite of Spring) (either full score or a piano arrangement).
Petruchka (either full score or excerpts arranged for two pianos by Victor Babin).
Circus Polka (either full score or arranged for piano solo, violin and piano, or two pianos).
L'Oiseau de Feu (The Firebird) suite.

Assignment 33.1   The following excerpts include compositional devices presented in this chapter.
1. Make a complete analysis of each excerpt using the chapter illustrations as a guide.
2. In class or on a separate sheet of paper, discuss the devices revealed by your analysis.

1. Bartók: *Boating* from Mikrokosmos, vol. V, no. 125, mm. 1–10.

2. Ives: *The Alcotts* from the Second ("Concord") Piano Sonata, m. 2.

3. Hindemith: "Un Cygne" ("A Swan") from *Six Chansons*, mm. 1–5.

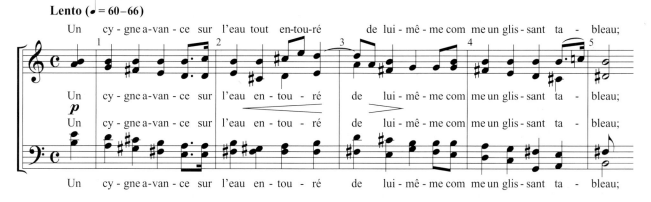

Assignment 33.2   Make a complete analysis of the following *March* for piano duet using the same approach as the analysis of *Marche du Soldat*. Discuss the the similarities and differences between the two marches and create an outline of your findings. Be sure to listen to a live performance or recording of this work before attempting the analysis.

Stravinsky: *March* from *Three Easy Pieces*.

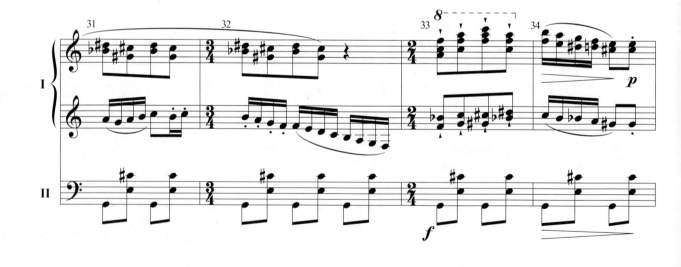

Assignment 33.3

1. Using the following three compositional devices (found in *Marche du Soldat*), write a short composition of 16 to 30 measures:

   Changing meters
   Ostinato
   Bitonality (polytonality)

2. Write for any combination of instruments played by class members.
3. Perform the composition in class.
4. The class should discuss each composition, its strengths and weaknesses, its resemblance to the style of the *Marche du Soldat,* and its general musical qualities.

Assignment 33.4 The following short song by Stravinsky includes musical devices found in his ballet, *The Rite of Spring*. Analyze the song by identifying the various techniques and procedures. Before preparing the analysis, have two students perform the composition in class or listen to a recording until the work is thoroughly familiar.

Stravinsky: "La Petite Pie" ("The Magpie") from *Three Little Songs: Recollections of My Childhood*.

CHAPTER 34

Pitch-Class Set Theory

Topics	Set Theory	Set	Normal Order
	Pitch Class	Inversion	Prime Form

Important Concepts

As we learned in the previous chapter, music of the early twentieth century frequently presents challenges that cannot be addressed by an individual analytical system. In Chapter 16, the identification of compositional devices was used as the mode of analysis. In this chapter, *set theory* is introduced as a means for classifying collections of pitch structures.

Set Theory

Set theory analysis is based on a collection of pitch classes. A *pitch class* is any particular pitch (such as C or F) in any octave. Thus, pitch-class G refers to the pitch G, regardless of the octave in which it may appear.

In set theory, pitch classes with enharmonic spellings are considered to be equivalent. This means that pitch classes such as C♯ and D♭, for example, are interchangeable and should be considered a single entity in a set.

Set

The term *set* means an unordered group of pitch classes such as C, D, and E. A set may contain any number of pitch classes from 2 through 12 (Figure 34.1).

Figure 34.1

The advantage of the system as applied to a non-tonal composition lies in its capacity to include groupings of pitch classes (sets) outside the traditional diatonic scales. (The diatonic scales may also be thought of as sets. See below.) As an example, the first five notes of the *Chromatic Invention* are A, G♯, E♭, D, and G—notes that, taken together, do not conform to any of the diatonic scale systems.

Set Types

Sets are classified according to the interval between the first pitch class of the set and each successive pitch class expressed as the number of half steps in the interval (Figure 34.2).

Figure 34.2

Some typical sets:

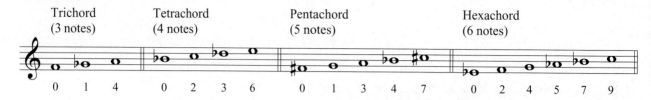

The "0" indicates the lowest pitch class in the set, and the remaining pitches are named by the interval they form with the lowest pitch class. For example, the 0 1 4 trichord contains the following:

Interval	From	To
0	F	F
1	F	G♭
4	F	A

The major scale can be considered a heptachord—a seven-tone set (Figure 34.3).

Figure 34.3

Major scale

Numbers refer to half-step intervals
above the first note (C)

Sets are usually written with the pitch classes in ascending order, but in compositions they are often transposed or written in different orders. Figure 34.4 shows the tetrachord 0 1 2 5 followed by the same set reordered and transposed.

Figure 34.4

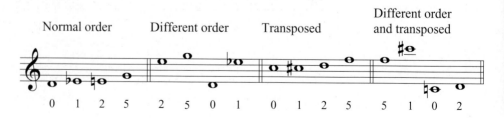

Sets, like chords, can be inverted. In *inversion,* the original direction of the intervals is turned upside down. Consider the three-note set in Figure 34.5.

Figure 34.5

Set 0 2 5

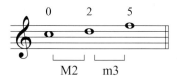

The inversion of this set is shown in Figure 34.6.

Figure 34.6

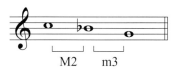

Because sets are usually written starting with the lowest note, the inversion set would be written in reverse order, as shown in Figure 34.7.

Figure 34.7

The pentachord and its inversion shown in Figure 34.8 are found in the *Chromatic Invention* by Bartók.

Figure 34.8

0 1 5 6 7 pentachord   Its inversion, 0 1 2 6 7

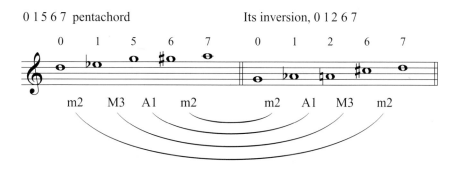

To find out whether one set is the inversion of another (e.g., the 0 1 5 6 7 pentachord in Figure 34.8), do the following:

1. Subtract all the numbers of the set from 12. This procedure will invert all the intervals, just as the inversion of a major 2nd (two half steps) is a minor 7th (10 half steps):

Inversion of 0 1 5 6 7

12	12	12	12	12
−0	−1	−5	−6	−7
12	11	7	6	5

2. These numbers represent the inversion, but they are confusing because the set does not begin with "0." To convert the set to the lowest possible numbers, just subtract from all the numbers the lowest one. Here the lowest number is 5:

12	11	7	6	5
−5	−5	−5	−5	−5
7	6	2	1	0

3. Now, put the numbers in order from the lowest to highest, and the inversion of
    $0\ 1\ 5\ 6\ 7 = 0\ 1\ 2\ 6\ 7$.

Normal Order

As mentioned before, composers employ sets in a variety of configurations. To understand the compositional techniques employed, it is necessary to trace the derivation and development of such structures. The fundamental ordered form of a set is the *normal order*. To reduce a set to its normal order, do the following:

1. Begin with any note in the set and rearrange the remaining notes in ascending order within an octave. Change the order of the notes as needed (Figure 34.9).
2. At the end of the set, add the first note an octave higher.

Figure 34.9

Set as it appears in a composition

Set rearranged within an octave

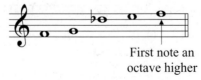

First note an
octave higher

3. Bracket the largest interval, as in Figure 34.10.

Figure 34.10

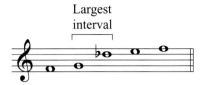

4. Begin the set with the second note of the bracketed interval, and the set will be in its normal order, as shown in Figure 34.11.

Figure 34.11

Normal order

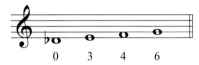

0   3   4   6

Prime Form

Occasionally a set will contain two larger intervals of the same size. Add the numbers (interval classes) of both possibilities. The *best normal order* or *prime form* is the arrangement of a set with the lowest total (i.e., the most small intervals at the beginning of the set). Another way of thinking of the prime form is the arrangement that is most densely packed to the left of the set. Both the original set and its inversion need to be considered when determining the prime form (Figure 34.12).

Figure 34.12

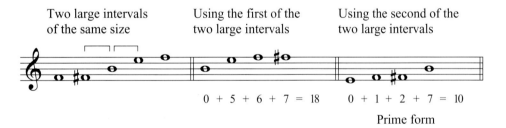

Two large intervals of the same size

Using the first of the two large intervals

Using the second of the two large intervals

$0 + 5 + 6 + 7 = 18$

$0 + 1 + 2 + 7 = 10$

Prime form

Set theory was initially developed by such theorists as René Leibowitz, Milton Babbitt, and Allen Forte to analyze compositions that are not based on diatonic scales but exhibit a great deal of internal consistency of musical materials. For a more complete treatment of set theory, refer to Allen Forte, *The Structure of Atonal Music* (New Haven, Conn.: Yale University Press, 1973); John Rahn, *Basic Atonal Theory* (New York: Longman, 1980); or Joseph Straus, *Introduction to Post-Tonal Theory* (Upper Saddle River, N.J.: Pearson Prentice Hall, 2005).

To illustrate pitch-class set procedures, Béla Bartók's *Chromatic Invention* from *Mikrokosmos,* volume 3, no. 91 follows.

A composer of considerable stature in the twentieth century, Béla Bartók was born in a farming region of Hungary and emigrated to the United States in 1940. He was beset most of his life with financial difficulties and eventually died almost penniless in a New York hospital in 1945. Almost all his music is in some way influenced by folk music material. He collected in excess of 6,000 Magyar, Slovak, Transylvanian, and Rumanian folk tunes, and they often appear in his works. Bartók developed his own unique compositional techniques, working and experimenting as he went along. He avoided the twelve-tone technique, did not imitate major composers of his own era, and showed only passing interest in the native styles of America. Important works include *Music for Strings, Percussion and Celesta* (1936), *Concerto for Orchestra* (1943), and six string quartets, which are regarded among the greatest twentieth-century works for that medium.

Application

The series of compositions known as the *Mikrokosmos* is a group of 153 piano compositions in six volumes, graded from easy to difficult. The *Chromatic Invention* is from the third volume of this set. These works are often assigned as "teaching pieces" and illustrate in miniature form the compositional techniques Bartók used in his larger works. The *Mikrokosmos* was written in an 11-year period (1926–1937).

Chromatic Invention
by Béla Bartók

Because Bartók's *Chromatic Invention* is homogeneous in its materials, it will be given an analysis based on set theory. Figure 34.13 shows the distribution of the sets found in the composition: the 0 1 5 6 7 set; its inversion, the 0 1 2 6 7 set; and the 0 1 2 set.

Figure 34.13

Bartók: *Chromatic Invention* from *Mikrokosmos,* vol. III, no. 91.

The sets in this composition could be analyzed in a variety of ways. We have chosen the following analysis because it accounts for every single note in the composition.

The Theme

The composition is based entirely on one theme, shown in Figure 34.14.

Figure 34.14

Complete theme

The theme is divided into two sections, with each containing five notes, as shown in Figure 34.15.

Figure 34.15

Theme — first section   Theme — second section

Theme First Section

The first section of the theme is made up of the 0 1 5 6 7 pentachord (five notes). Its inversion, 0 1 2 6 7, also occurs in the composition (Figure 34.16).

Figure 34.16

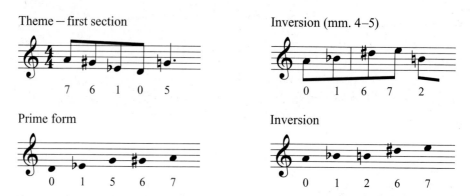

Theme — first section   Inversion (mm. 4–5)

      7 6 1 0 5   0 1 6 7 2

Prime form   Inversion

      0 1 5 6 7   0 1 2 6 7

In Figure 34.17, the notes of the 0 1 5 6 7 and 0 1 2 6 7 (inversion of 0 1 5 6 7) sets as they appear in the composition are extracted on the upper staff, and the prime form of each is listed on the staff beneath it.

Figure 34.17

Measure 1   Measures 1–2   Measures 2–3   Measure 3

  0 1 5 6 7   0 1 5 6 7   0 1 5 6 7   0 1 5 6 7

Measures 4–5   Measure 5   Measures 6–7   Measure 7

  0 1 2 6 7   0 1 2 6 7   0 1 2 6 7   0 1 2 6 7

Theme Second Section   The second section of the theme is made up of the 0 1 2 trichord (Figure 34.18).

Figure 34.18

Theme — second section

Prime form

Note that the 0 1 2 trichord fills in pitch classes not found in the 0 1 5 6 7 pentachord to form a chromatic set. Thus the aggregate (combination) of both sets is a chromatic scale from D to A (Figure 34.19).

Figure 34.19

Whole notes: theme — first section
Black notes: theme — second section

Theme — first section:	0	1				5	6	7
Theme — second section:			0	1	2			
Theme — complete:	0	1	2	3	4	5	6	7

Figure 34.20 shows each instance of the second section of the theme in the composition. The notes of the 0 1 2 set (with occasional added half steps) as it appears in the first six measures of the composition are extracted on the upper staff, and the prime form of each is listed on the staff beneath it.

Figure 34.20

Measures 1–2   Measure 2   Measures 3–4   Measures 5–6

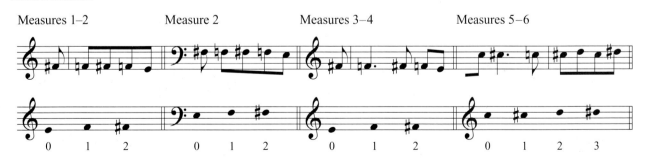

Figure 34.21 shows a further analysis of Bartók's *Chromatic Invention*.

Figure 34.21

Bartók: *Chromatic Invention* from *Mikrokosmos,* vol. III, no. 91.

Imitation is used in the composition (Figure 34.21) as follows:

1. With the exception of measure 11 and parts of measures 10 and 12, the entire composition utilizes canonic imitation.
2. Imitation in the first 10 measures is by similar motion.
3. Imitation in the last seven measures is by contrary motion (melodic inversion).
4. Most of the composition employs imitation at the octave, but imitation at the M6th, M9th, and P4th also occurs.

Influence of the Tritone

The tritone relationship is prominent in the composition.

1. The tritone is one of the intervals contained in the first section (0 1 5 6 7) of the theme.
2. Indicated in the score along with the imitation are four conspicuous step progressions that emphasize the tritone. Each outlines portions of the whole-tone scale, which is rich in tritone relationships.

Form

The composition divides neatly into three sections as follows:

Measures	Description
1–6	The complete theme occurs six times, four times derived from the prime form and twice from the inversion.
6–11	Canon at the octave with overlapping entrances of the first section of the theme. The second section of the theme is found only at the end, in measures 10 and 11.
11–17	The complete theme occurs three times in the upper voice, whereas the lower voice, containing an inversion of the theme, occurs in canon (by contrary motion) with the upper voice.

The sections are not set apart from each other. Each contrasts with the others through the compositional techniques employed.

Tonality

Naming the tonal center of the *Chromatic Invention* is a hazardous venture indeed. Certainly there are few clues—no highly organized key system present, no long pedal tones to influence a decision—and the highly chromatic nature of the theme renders little assistance. Thus a definitive answer, acceptable to all, is unlikely.

One might argue that because the theme outlines a perfect 4th (see Figure 34.22), a suggestion of tonality might be gained from that relationship. Although the *Chromatic Invention* begins with the theme clearly stated, the ending (mm. 15–17) seems bent on destroying any tonal hints that might have accrued up to that point.

Figure 34.22

Theme outlines P4th

A   E

Conclusions

A unique and highly organic invention, the *Chromatic Invention* is held together through a single theme constructed from the 0 1 5 6 7 pentachord, along with its inversion, the

0 1 2 6 7 pentachord, and its chromatic complement, the 0 1 2 trichord. These sets, with some extensions of the 0 1 2 trichord, are used exclusively throughout. Imitation, both in similar and contrary motion, further helps to weld the work into a tightly knit and eminently unified whole.

Summary

Collections of pitch classes that allow for interchangeable enharmonic spellings are known as pitch-class sets. A set can have as few as 2 pitch classes (thereby forming an interval class) or as many as 12. Although sets can be organized in a variety of ways (normal order, different order, transposed, and inverted), the prime form is the fundamental ordered form of the set. The prime form occurs when the pitch classes are organized by ascent within an octave and with the pitch classes packed most densely to the left.

Practice

To become proficient at reducing sets to their prime form, begin by practicing with very small sets. Take two pitch classes and write them as closely together as possible. After you have reduced the interval class to its smallest form, identify the lowest note as "0" and count half steps as you ascend upward to determine the upper number. Figure 34.23 provides an example of this simple process.

Figure 34.23

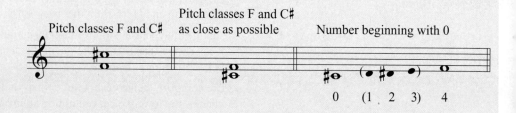

Assignment 34.1   Beneath each of the following intervals, write the number representing the interval.

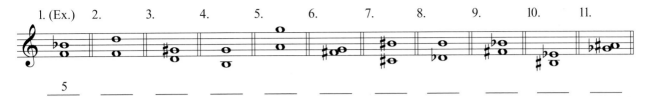

_____5_____   _____   _____   _____   _____   _____   _____   _____   _____   _____   _____

Assignment 34.2   Furnish the interval numbers for each of the following sets.

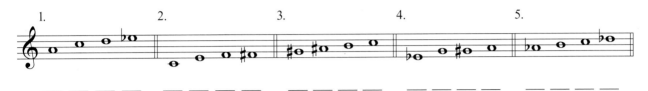

__ __ __ __   __ __ __ __   __ __ __ __   __ __ __ __   __ __ __ __

Assignment 34.3   Following are six tetrachords. Three are inversions of the remaining three. Indicate the pairs.

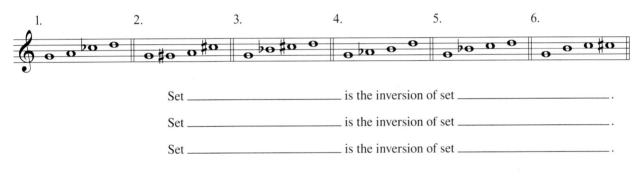

Set _____ is the inversion of set _____ .

Set _____ is the inversion of set _____ .

Set _____ is the inversion of set _____ .

Assignment 34.4   Following are five sets in scrambled order. Find the prime form of each set.

    1. Rearrange the notes of the above sets within an octave and bracket the largest interval:

    2. Write the prime form on the blanks below.

____ ____ ____   ____ ____ ____   ____ ____ ____   ____ ____ ____   ____ ____ ____

Assignment 34.5

1. On a separate sheet of paper, make a complete analysis of the following composition, using the same approach as is used for the *Chromatic Invention* of Bartók.

2. The violin duo is based on a tetrachord. Trace its development throughout the composition.

3. As an alternative analysis, consider the two sets that occur simultaneously as a single eight-pitch set (an octachord). Do you recognize the scales formed by these eight-pitch sets?

4. Before preparing the analysis, have two students perform the composition two or three times in class, or listen to a recording until the work is thoroughly familiar.

Bartók: *Song of the Harvest,* no. 33 from *Forty-Four Violin Duets.*

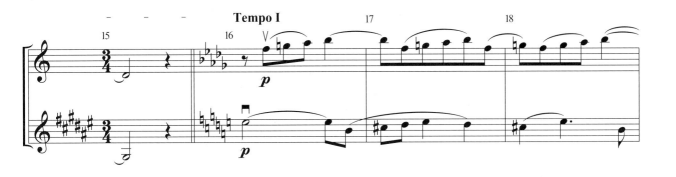

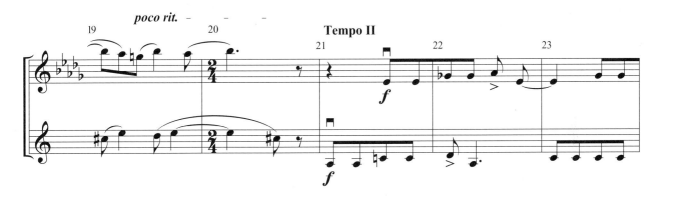

Assignment 34.6

1. Using the following compositional techniques (found in the *Chromatic Invention*), write a short two-voice composition (16 to 30 measures):
   a. Asymmetric divisions of the meter.
   b. A tetrachord or pentachord as a basis.
   c. Transpositions of the theme or motive.

2. Write for any combination of instruments played by class members.

3. Perform the composition in class.

4. After each student composition is performed, members of the class should enumerate (from listening only) some of the various devices employed in the work.

Assignment 34.7

Analyze a section of Debussy's *La Cathédrale engloutie* (p. 679) using set theory analysis. As a beginning point, convert the melodic motives shown in Figure 32.32 (p. 687) into set form and trace these sets through a section of the composition. How well does set theory account for the pitch-class material of this work?

Twelve-Tone Technique

Important Concepts

Twelve-tone technique, a method of composition based on a fixed order of the 12 chromatic tones, was widely adopted by composers during the mid–twentieth century. It was developed by Arnold Schoenberg around 1920 as a means of providing a coherent basis for highly chromatic music. According to Schoenberg, "The method of composing with twelve tones grew out of necessity. In the last hundred years the concept of harmony has changed tremendously through the development of chromaticism. The idea that one basic tone (the root) dominated the construction of chords and regulated their succession—the concept of *tonality*—had to develop first into the concept of *extended tonality*. Very soon it became doubtful whether such a root still remained the center to which every harmony and harmonic succession must be referred. Furthermore, it became doubtful whether a tonic appearing at the beginning, at the end, or at any other point really had a constructive meaning." Schoenberg saw clearly that innovations of the post-romantic period had had the effect of weakening the constructive force of functional harmony. He sought a means to return order to music, to replace the lost power of tonal harmony that had been used to regulate the relationships among tones. He said, "After many unsuccessful attempts during a period of approximately twelve years I laid the foundations for a new procedure in musical construction which seemed fitted to replace those structural differentiations provided formerly by tonal harmonies. I called this procedure the *Method of Composing with Twelve Tones Which Are Related Only with One Another*."

Twelve-Tone Technique

Schoenberg provided the following guides for his twelve-tone technique (dodecaphonic composition):

Order

The set of all 12 tones contained within the octave in a particular order (tone row) forms the basis for the method. Except for immediate repetitions, there is no return to a particular tone until all the succeeding tones in the row have been sounded.

Register

The tones of the series (tone row) may appear in any octave.

Forms

The tone series may appear in any of the following four forms:

Symbol		Form	Description
P	=	Prime	The series as it is originally constructed.
R	=	Retrograde	The prime series sounded in reverse order.
I	=	Inversion	Starting with the first tone of the prime series, the direction (up or down) of each successive interval is inverted.
RI	=	Retrograde Inversion	The inversion of the series is sounded in reverse order.

Transposition

Any of the four forms of the series can be transposed. The prime form untransposed is P^0, one half step up is P^1, another half step up P^2, and so on. As a further illustration, note the following:

P^8 = Prime form of the series transposed up eight half steps (m6th).
R^8 = Retrograde form of the series transposed up eight half steps (m6th).
RI^2 = Retrograde inversion transposed up two half steps (M2nd).
I^{11} = Inverted series transposed up 11 half steps (M7th).

Row or Series

The term *row* is a literal translation of the German word *Reihe*. Later authors, who believe that *row* denotes certain properties not in keeping with the true nature of the original German term, use another term, *series*. Despite controversies over subtleties in translation, *row* and *series* are used synonymously in this book.

Numbering

Earlier writers also numbered the series from 1 to 12, but later theorists adopted a numbering system from 0 to 11 to facilitate mathematical calculation.

Pitch Class

Pitch class is another term frequently found in contemporary writing. This term is used in preference to *tone* or *pitch* because it is broader in meaning and includes a single pitch together with its octave duplications.

Matrix

A *matrix* is a convenient analytical device for showing all forms and transpositions of a row. Schoenberg did not invent the matrix (described in detail later), but its use by later writers has made it a standard device for analysis of twelve-tone music.

History

Schoenberg invented twelve-tone technique around 1920. This development was preceded by the independent invention of a similar method in 1919 by Josef Matthias Hauer that was based on unordered sets of six pitches that he called *tropes*. Anton Webern (1883–1945) was a student of Schoenberg from 1904 until 1910. He adopted twelve-tone technique around 1924, and his work fully exploits the potential of the system. Webern wrote in such a concentrated style that most of his works are quite brief, and his complete works can be played in less than six hours (any two of Wagner's operas would consume more time). Alban Berg (1885–1935), another student of Schoenberg, also adopted twelve-tone technique but with much less rigor. Schoenberg, Webern, and Berg were at the center of artistic and intellectual circles in Vienna, and their work was a major force in the development of musical style in the mid–twentieth century.

Application

As an example of twelve-tone technique, a detailed analysis of the song "Wie bin ich froh!" by Anton Webern is presented in Figure 35.1.

Figure 35.1

Webern: "Wie bin ich froh!" ("How Happy I Am!"), no. 1 from *Drei Lieder* (Three Songs), op. 25.

The following matrix shows the possible series forms and their transpositions (48 possibilities in all). This particular matrix represents the series that is the basis of Webern's "Wie bin ich froh!" (Figure 35.1).

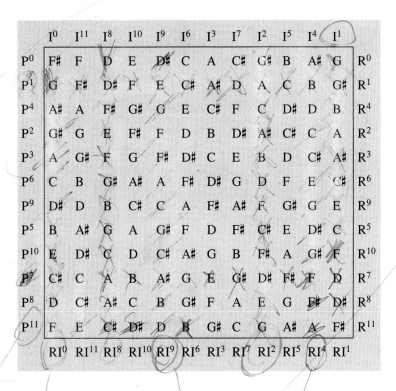

The matrix is created by first listing the P⁰ form along the top:

List the inversion beginning with the first pitch of the original row down the left side of the chart:

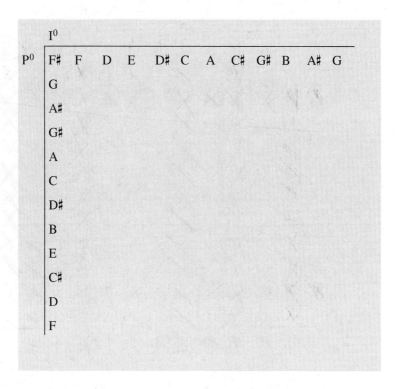

	I^0											
P^0	F♯	F	D	E	D♯	C	A	C♯	G♯	B	A♯	G
	G											
	A♯											
	G♯											
	A											
	C											
	D♯											
	B											
	E											
	C♯											
	D											
	F											

Label the left side of the chart beginning with P^0 according to the number of half steps each tone of the I^0 series is above the first tone:

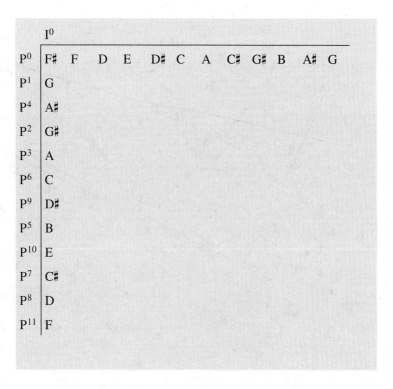

	I^0											
P^0	F♯	F	D	E	D♯	C	A	C♯	G♯	B	A♯	G
P^1	G											
P^4	A♯											
P^2	G♯											
P^3	A											
P^6	C											
P^9	D♯											
P^5	B											
P^{10}	E											
P^7	C♯											
P^8	D											
P^{11}	F											

Write the P^1 series, which will be one half step above the P^0 series:

	I^0										
P^0	F♯	F	D	E	D♯	C	A	C♯	G♯	B	A♯	G
P^1	G	F♯	D♯	F	E	C♯	A♯	D	A	C	B	G♯
P^4	A♯										
P^2	G♯										
P^3	A										
P^6	C										
P^9	D♯										
P^5	B										
P^{10}	E										
P^7	C♯										
P^8	D										
P^{11}	F										

Fill in the remaining transpositions in order (P^2, P^3, etc.). Each row will be one half step above the previous row:

	I^0										
P^0	F♯	F	D	E	D♯	C	A	C♯	G♯	B	A♯	G
P^1	G	F♯	D♯	F	E	C♯	A♯	D	A	C	B	G♯
P^4	A♯										
P^2	G♯	G	E	F♯	F	D	B	D♯	A♯	C♯	C	A
P^3	A	G♯	F	etc.							
P^6	C										
P^9	D♯										
P^5	B										
P^{10}	E										
P^7	C♯										
P^8	D										
P^{11}	F										

Finally, add the remaining labels (I, R, and RI) to complete the matrix:

	I^0	I^{11}	I^8	I^{10}	I^9	I^6	I^3	I^7	I^2	I^5	I^4	I^1	
P^0	F#	F	D	E	D#	C	A	C#	G#	B	A#	G	R^0
P^1	G	F#	D#	F	E	C#	A#	D	A	C	B	G#	R^1
P^4	A#	A	F#	G#	G	E	C#	F	C	D#	D	B	R^4
P^2	G#	G	E	F#	F	D	B	D#	A#	C#	C	A	R^2
P^3	A	G#	F	G	F#	D#	C	E	B	D	C#	A#	R^3
P^6	C	B	G#	A#	A	F#	D#	G	D	F	E	C#	R^6
P^9	D#	D	B	C#	C	A	F#	A#	F	G#	G	E	R^9
P^5	B	A#	G	A	G#	F	D	F#	C#	E	D#	C	R^5
P^{10}	E	D#	C	D	C#	A#	G	B	F#	A	G#	F	R^{10}
P^7	C#	C	A	B	A#	G	E	G#	D#	F#	F	D	R^7
P^8	D	C#	A#	C	B	G#	F	A	E	G	F#	D#	R^8
P^{11}	F	E	C#	D#	D	B	G#	C	G	A#	A	F#	R^{11}

RI⁰ RI¹¹ RI⁸ RI¹⁰ RI⁹ RI⁶ RI³ RI⁷ RI² RI⁵ RI⁴ RI¹

11 10 9 8 7 6 5 4 3 2 1 0

For prime series (P), read from left to right.
For inverted series (I), read down.
For retrograde series (R), read from right to left.
For retrograde-inversion series (RI), read up.

Selected Forms and Transpositions

Webern selected the series forms and transpositions (from the preceding matrix) seen in Figure 35.2 for "Wie bin ich froh!"

Figure 35.2

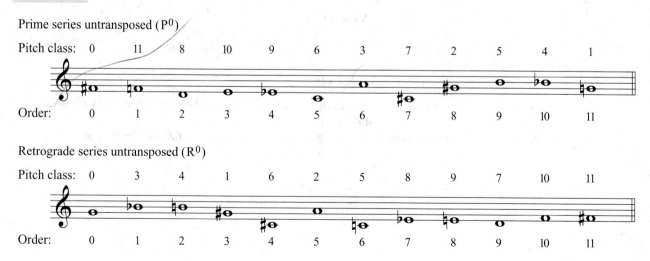

Prime series untransposed (P^0)

| Pitch class: | 0 | 11 | 8 | 10 | 9 | 6 | 3 | 7 | 2 | 5 | 4 | 1 |
| Order: | 0 | 1 | 2 | 3 | 4 | 5 | 6 | 7 | 8 | 9 | 10 | 11 |

Retrograde series untransposed (R^0)

| Pitch class: | 0 | 3 | 4 | 1 | 6 | 2 | 5 | 8 | 9 | 7 | 10 | 11 |
| Order: | 0 | 1 | 2 | 3 | 4 | 5 | 6 | 7 | 8 | 9 | 10 | 11 |

Inverted series transposed up one whole step (I^2)

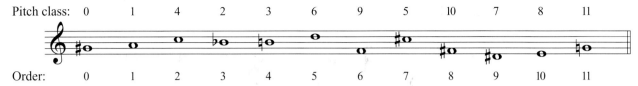

Inverted series in retrograde transposed up one whole step (RI^2)

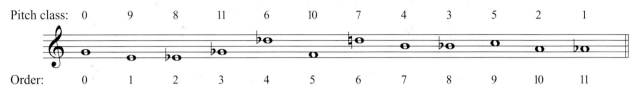

Segments

The series itself is very carefully planned to include a three-tone figure (trichord) with two transpositions. The second and fourth trichords are transpositions of the first (Figure 35.3).

Figure 35.3

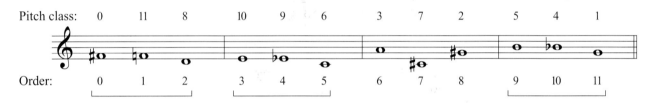

The Text

The basis for the composition is a poem of two strophes by Hildegard Jone:

Wie bin ich froh!
noch einmal wird mir alles grün
und leuchtet so!
noch über blühn die Blumen mir die Welt!
noch einmal bin ich ganz ins Werden hingestellt
und bin auf Erden.

How happy I am!
Once more all around me grows
green and shimmers so!
Blossoms still cover the world for me!

Once again I am at the center
of Becoming
and am on earth.

Strophes

The voice line is divided as follows:

First strophe: The retrograde inversion (RI) of the series followed by the first four notes of the same

Second strophe: The retrograde of the original series followed by the complete retrograde inversion

Form	While an internal balance and symmetry in the voice line is obtained through the use of RI^2, then R^0, and finally a return to the RI^2, a two-part form emerges from the two strophes of the poem:	

Strophe	Section	Measures
1	A	1–5
2	B	6–12

Accompaniment

The selection of series forms and transpositions in the accompaniment is as follows:

Strophe 1	Strophe 2
P^0 RI^2 P^0 RI^2	R^0 I^2 I^2 P^0 R^0

Notice that the accompaniment is created from complementary forms of the row in the two strophes—P^0 vs. R^0, RI^2 vs. I^2, etc.

Rhythmic and Harmonic Figures

The accompaniment consists for the most part of three figures, two of which are rhythmic and the other harmonic (Figure 35.4).

Figure 35.4

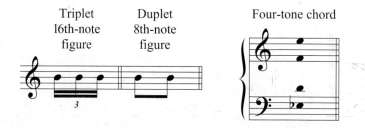

Triplet 16th-note figure   Duplet 8th-note figure   Four-tone chord

The 16th-Note Triplet Figure

A direct relationship exists between the figures and the pitches contained in them (Figure 35.5). All 16th-note triplet figures are based on a minor 2nd plus a minor 3rd (the 0 1 4 set).

Figure 35.5

Measure:	Pickup to 1	2	3	4	4	5	5
Series type:	P^0	RI^2	RI^2	P^0	P^0	RI^2	RI^2

Series number:	0 1 2	0 1 2	9 10 11	5 6 7	9 10 11	6 7 8	9 10 11

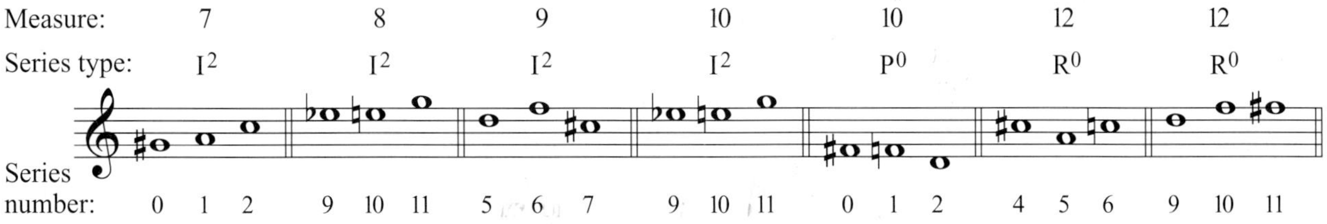
Measure: 7 8 9 10 10 12 12
Series type: I2 I2 I2 I2 P0 R0 R0
Series number: 0 1 2 9 10 11 5 6 7 9 10 11 0 1 2 4 5 6 9 10 11

The 8th-Note Figure

Most two-tone eighth-note figures are made up of half-step intervals, with the exception of two examples indicated by an asterisk (*) in Figure 35.6.

Figure 35.6

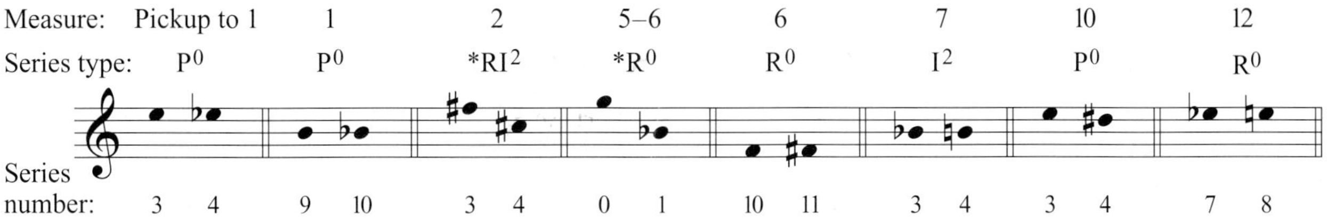
Measure: Pickup to 1 1 2 5–6 6 7 10 12
Series type: P0 P0 *RI2 *R0 R0 I2 P0 R0
Series number: 3 4 9 10 3 4 0 1 10 11 3 4 3 4 7 8

The Four-Tone Chord Figure

In most four-tone chord figures, the lower two tones form a major 7th (with the exception of m. 2) and the upper two tones form a major 7th (with three exceptions) (Figure 35.7).

Figure 35.7

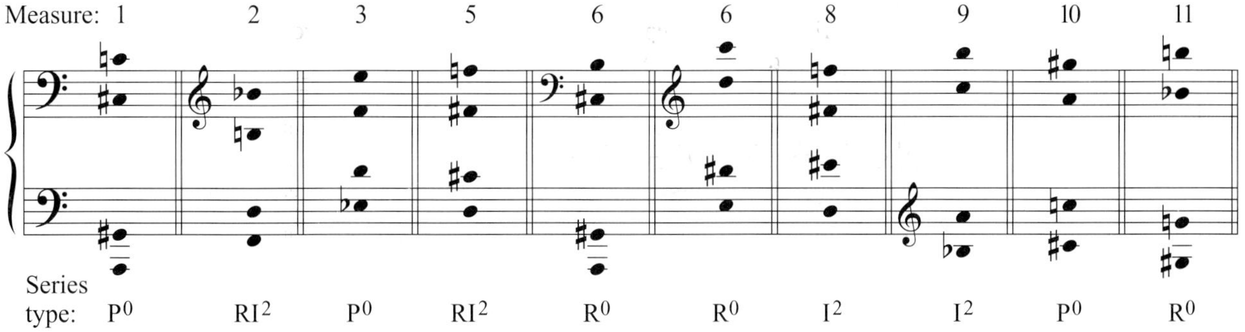
Measure: 1 2 3 5 6 6 8 9 10 11
Series type: P0 RI2 P0 RI2 R0 R0 I2 I2 P0 R0

Dynamics and Tempo Indications

The dynamics and tempo indications follow this pattern:

1. The third line of each strophe is marked with a soft dynamic.
2. The first line of each strophe begins loud and ends soft.
3. For each strophe, accompaniment begins loud and ends soft.
4. The tempo is usually slowed at the end of each line or strophe.

Summary

The method of composition developed by Schoenberg using all 12 pitch classes contained within the octave is known as twelve-tone technique. The set of 12 tones is organized in a specific order called the prime form, and other than immediate repetitions, the entire tone series is required to sound before a tone is allowed to return. In twelve-tone technique, the tone series appears not only in its prime form, but also in retrograde, inversion, and retrograde inversion. The analytical tool used to list all forms and transpositions of a twelve-tone series is called a matrix.

Practice

The ability to construct a matrix will have an impact on your understanding of twelve-tone technique. As you follow the instructions on pp. 743–746 for creating a matrix, remember that the series of 12 tones is simply a large pitch-class set (see Chapter 34). To find the inversion of the prime form, all you need to do is subtract the interval numbers from 12 (Figure 35.8).

Figure 35.8

1. Assign pitch-class numbers to each tone of the series.

P^0	F#	F	D	E	D#	C	A	C#	G#	B	A#	G
Set	0	11	8	10	9	6	3	7	2	5	4	1

2. Subtract the pitch-class numbers from 12 to identify the inversion numbers.

	12	12	12	12	12	12	12	12	12	12	12	12
P^0	−0	−11	−8	−10	−9	−6	−3	−7	−2	−5	−4	−1
Inversion	12	1	4	2	3	6	9	5	10	7	8	11

3. Write the inversion numbers in the first left-side column and convert the numbers to pitch-class names in the neighboring column.

I^0

12 = 0 =	F#	F	D	E	D#	C	A	C#	G#	B	A#	G
1 =	G											
4 =	A#											
2 =	G#											
3 =	A											
6 =	C											
9 =	D#											
5 =	B											
10 =	E											
7 =	C#											
8 =	D											
11 =	F											

Assignment 35.1

On a separate sheet of paper, make a complete analysis of the following composition using the same approach as for "Wie bin ich froh!"

Before preparing the analysis, have a singer and an accompanist from the class perform the composition two or three times, or listen to a recording until the work is thoroughly familiar.

This work is based on the same twelve-tone row as the song analyzed in the chapter. The matrix on p. 743 can be used. (This song begins with a statement of RI^7.) As an alternative, you may consider the row presented in measures 1 to 3 in the piano to be a new row and create a matrix for it.

Webern: "Des Herzens Purpurvogel fliegt durch Nacht" ("The Heart's Purple Eagle Flies by Night"), no. 2 from *Drei Lieder* (Three Songs), op. 25, mm. 1–22.

Assignment 35.2

1. On a separate sheet of paper, make a complete analysis of the Theme from Schoenberg's *Variations for Orchestra,* op. 31, using the same approach as for "Wie bin ich froh!"
2. The prime row (P⁰) for this work is as follows:

3. Make a matrix for this row, following the instructions on p. 743.
4. Before preparing the analysis, listen to a recording until the work is thoroughly familiar.

Schoenberg: Theme from *Variations for Orchestra,* op. 31, mm. 34–57.

Assignment 35.3

1. On a separate sheet of paper, make a complete analysis of the Trio from Schoenberg's *Suite für Klavier,* op. 25, using the same approach as for "Wie bin ich froh!"
2. Make a matrix for this composition, following the instructions on p. 743.
3. Before preparing the analysis, listen to a recording until the work is thoroughly familiar.

Schoenberg: Trio from *Suite für Klavier,* op. 25.

Assignment 35.4

1. Write a short song with text for solo voice and piano employing the following twelve-tone series:

P0

    0   1   2   3   4   5   6   7   8   9   10   11

2. Examine the series for motivic cells that might lend themselves to the kind of technique found in Webern's "Wie bin ich froh!"

3. Prepare a matrix for this series (see p. 743).

4. Select four compatible series forms.

5. Prepare (without score paper) a plan for the form of the composition. Use techniques discovered in the Webern song analyzed in this chapter.

6. Select two rhythmic figures for the accompaniment.

7. Sketch in the voice part and add the accompaniment.

8. Add dynamics and other marks of interpretation as well as phrasing.

9. Perform the composition in class.

10. After each performance, the composer will lead a discussion concerning the techniques employed in the composition.

POSTLUDE

Music Since 1945

The years since 1945 have witnessed the greatest stylistic changes and most extensive exploration of new techniques in the history of Western music. In the popular music field, the most important development has been rock music. In art music, composers have explored new media and new methods to a greater extent than at any other time. Although it is still too early to make a definitive judgment, it appears that two distinct periods may be observed. These periods are distinguished not so much by style as by attitude.

Musical Developments from 1945–1970

The first of these two periods lasted from about 1945 to 1970. This era, dominated by the philosophy of the avant-garde, emphasized the exploration of new techniques and highly regarded innovation and experimentation. The primary paths of exploration were serialism, indeterminacy, electronic and computer music, sound mass, and extended vocal and instrumental techniques. Several of these new directions might be observed in a single work.

Serialism

Serialism (sometimes called *total serialism*) began in the years 1920–1945 as an extension of the twelve-tone technique of the Viennese atonalists, especially Anton Webern. As you saw in Chapter 18, Webern's music is characterized not only by use of a pitch series but also by carefully controlling the number of rhythmic motives in the piano accompaniment. Webern was the primary inspiration for composers who chose to order or serialize other elements of music, such as rhythm, dynamics, articulations, and tone colors.

Perhaps the most important serialist is Milton Babbitt (1916–2011), who composed *Three Compositions for Piano* in 1947. An excerpt from the *First Composition* is found in Figure 36.1.

Figure 36.1

Babbitt: First Composition from *Three Compositions for Piano,* mm. 1–6.

The *rhythmic series* Babbitt employs in this piece consists of the numbers 5 1 4 2. This series is used to articulate a rhythmic division in the statement of each hexachord. In the first measure, the lower voice consists of a group of five notes ending on C, which is the first long note and fifth pitch of the hexachord, hence the "5" (note brackets in illustration) of the rhythmic series 5 1 4 2. The single remaining note (D-flat) in this measure represents "1" in the rhythmic series. The same 5 1 rhythmic grouping may be observed in the upper voice in measure 1, although the long note ending the first rhythmic subdivision of this hexachord is only an eighth note in duration.

Diagram of Rhythmic Series

P	(prime)	5 1 4 2
R	(retrograde)	2 4 1 5
I	(inversion)	1 5 2 4
RI	(retrograde inversion)	4 2 5 1

In the next measure, a long note—the fourth in the hexachord—breaks the sixteenth-note continuity of the hexachords of each voice. This produces a 4 2 grouping that completes the 5 1 4 2 statement, the prime form (P) of the rhythmic series.

The retrograde form (R) of the series, 2 4 1 5, is found in the upper voice of measures 3 and 4. The inversion form (I), 1 5 2 4, derived by subtracting each number of the P form from 6 (the number of pitches in a hexachord), appears in measures 5 and 6, lower voice. The retrograde-inversion form (RI), 4 2 5 1, occurs in the lower voice of measures 3 and 4.

The dynamic series is much simpler, associating each form of the pitch set with a different dynamic:[1]

Set Form	=	Dynamic
P		Mezzo piano
R		Mezzo forte
I		Forte
RI		Piano

Babbitt's approaches to rhythmic and dynamic serialism are only some of the nonpitch elements that have been serialized. Composers have experimented with articulations, timbres, and numerous other aspects of music.

Indeterminacy

Another important concept explored by composers of this period was *indeterminacy,* sometimes also called *aleatory* or *chance music.* The following characteristics are essential to indeterminacy:

1. Some aspect or aspects of the composition, the performance, or both are beyond the composer's control.
2. Some musical decisions are unpredictable or left to chance.

The stage at which chance enters the music-making process varies from work to work.

Always an innovator, the American composer John Cage (1912–1992) thoroughly explored methods by which chance could be incorporated into composition and performance. Cage's *Music of Changes* (1951), for piano, is traditionally notated but was composed in an untraditional fashion. He made all musical decisions (pitches, rhythm, and dynamics) by consulting the *I Ching* (pronounced "e Jing"), an ancient Chinese method of soothsaying.

A very different type of indeterminacy is represented by Cage's *Aria* (1958) (Figure 36.2). This work for solo voice is composed in graphic notation. Vertical contoured lines represent relative pitch; horizontal contours give the relative durations. Each page was intended to last about 30 seconds. The soloist can determine eight different singing styles, and the black squares indicate other sounds of the performer's choice. Because each performer has the major responsibility for interpreting the precise meaning of the symbols, performances vary greatly. The singer also has the option of performing the work simultaneously with either of two other Cage compositions: *Fontana Mix* (1958) for magnetic tape or instruments, or *Concert for Piano and Orchestra* (1957–1958).

---

[1] This analysis owes a great deal to George Perle, *Serial Composition and Atonality,* 4th ed. (Berkeley: University of California Press, 1977), pp. 132–341, and David Cope, *New Directions in Music,* 6th ed. (Madison, Wisconsin: Brown & Benchmark Publishers, 1993), pp. 41–44.

Figure 36.2

Cage: *Aria*.

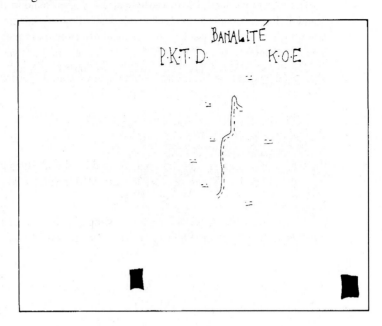

Improvisation

Improvisation is the spontaneous realization of any or all aspects of a composition and has been employed throughout most of Western music history. Beethoven's concerts, for instance, often featured his improvisations. Today, the most familiar forms of improvisation are those used in jazz performance.

Improvisation differs from other types of indeterminacy in that the composer predetermines a desired musical effect rather than detailing the notation. The performer is free to spontaneously interpret any or all of the composition.

For Pauline Oliveros (1932–2016), spontaneity is a philosophy whose benefits transcend the performed sounds. She breaks with many long-held notions of what a composition can or cannot do. As a result of her democratic philosophy, she creates music accessible to all. *Sonic Meditations I*, "Teach Yourself to Fly," is an example of a therapeutic, relaxing work in which anyone—not just trained musicians—can participate (Figure 36.3).

Figure 36.3

Pauline Oliveros: *Sonic Meditations I*, "Teach Yourself to Fly," 1974 Smith Publications, Baltimore, Maryland.

> *Any number of persons sit in a circle facing the center. Illuminate the space with dim blue light. Begin by simply observing your own breathing. Always be an observer. Gradually allow your breathing to become audible, then gradually introduce your voice. Allow your vocal chords to vibrate in any mode that occurs naturally. Allow the intensity to increase very slowly. Continue as long as possible naturally, and until all others are quiet, always observing your own breath cycle. Variation: Translate voice to an instrument.*

Electronic and Computer Music

Although efforts to create *electronic music* date back to the turn of the twentieth century, serious development came after World War II with the invention of plastic magnetic recording tape. Early composers worked primarily on tape, in contrast to live performance, and used either live or electronically generated sources.

Musique Concrète

Preferred by French composers, *musique concrète* (which was intended to denote a music that used natural or "concrete" sounds) used sounds recorded from the environment. Sounds were processed or modified in the following ways:

1. Splicing—cutting and rearranging the tape.
2. Playing the tape backward.
3. Varying the speed and pitch of the tape.
4. Tape loops—cutting and splicing the tape in an endless loop.
5. Tape delay—a means of creating artificial echo by rerecording a sound multiple times.

These taping techniques ranged from simple reordering of familiar sounds to complete transformations, making the original sound sources unidentifiable to the listener.

Electronic Music

The first German composers of *electronic music* generated sounds with equipment previously found in physics laboratories: oscillators, pulse generators, filters, and ring modulators. This music required even more splicing than the works of *musique concrète*.

Two of the greatest early masterpieces of electronic music combined both electronic and *concrète* techniques. It is interesting that one of these works, *Gesang der Jünglinge* (Song of the Youths in the Fiery Furnace) (1955–1956), is by the German Karlheinz Stockhausen (1928–2007) and that the other, *Poème Electronique* (1956–1958), was composed by the French-born American Edgard Varèse (1885–1965), thus demonstrating that the distinction between the two styles was not the nationality of the composer. Because a performance of either work consists of playing a tape recording, neither has a score in the conventional sense.

Live Performance with Tape

Any arbitrary limitations on the use of electronic media were short-lived. From the early years of electronic music, composers began to combine taped sounds with live instrumental or vocal performance. One of the greatest contributions to this genre is the series of six *Synchronisms* of the Argentinian-American Mario Davidovsky (1934–2019) (Figure 36.4).

Figure 36.4

Davidovsky: No. 3 for Cello and Electronic Sound from *Synchronisms*.

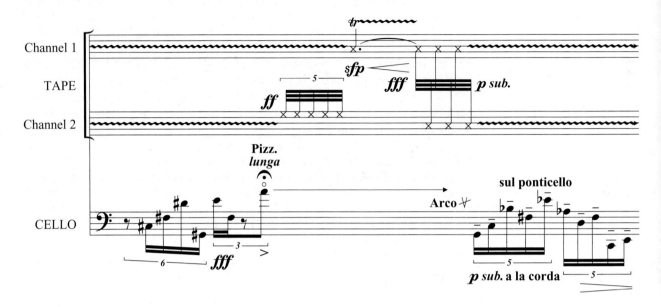

The taped sounds used in the *Synchronisms* were entirely electronically generated. The scores transcribe only as much of the tape as is needed for the synchronization of the instrumentalists.

Live Electronic Music

Although it seems that most electronic music composers preferred to work with tape, many used electronics in live performance. Alvin Lucier's (b. 1931) *I Am Sitting in a Room* (1970) required only a microphone, two tape recorders, an amplifier, and a loudspeaker. The text Lucier provided for this work is a technical description of what the audience hears (Figure 36.5).

Figure 36.5

Lucier: "I Am Sitting in a Room" (1969), p. 30.

"I am sitting in a room different from the one you are in now.
"I am recording the sound of my speaking voice and I am going to play it back into the room again and again until the resonant frequencies of the room reinforce themselves so that any semblance of my speech, with perhaps the exception of rhythm, is destroyed.
"What you will hear, then, are the natural resonant frequencies of the room articulated by speech.
"I regard this activity not so much as a demonstration of a physical fact, but more as a way to smooth out any irregularities my speech might have."

Voltage-Controlled Synthesizers

The *voltage-controlled synthesizer,* introduced in the 1960s, generated and processed sound by a series of control voltages. This allowed the composer to move instantaneously rather than gradually from one setting to another. If, for example, a composer desired a melody from a nonsynthesizer oscillator, each pitch would have to be recorded separately and then spliced together. On a voltage-controlled synthesizer, a melody could be played on an oscillator by a series of voltages from a keyboard or some other controlling device.

Computer-Assisted Composition

Composers have been using computers in a variety of ways since the late 1950s. The earliest use of computers in composition was as an aid in writing works for traditional instruments. Greek composer Iannis Xenakis (1922–2001) employed his Stochastic Music Program (stochasticism is a mathematical system based on the calculus of probabilities) to supply the precise details of pitch, rhythm, and timbre in a series of complex, densely textured works.

Computer Synthesis

A more popular application of computer technology was sound synthesis. A computer could generate electronic or traditional instrumental sounds in either of two ways: through the sampling of natural sounds or through spectrum analysis and resynthesis. The American composer Charles Dodge (b. 1942) created a series of works featuring the electronic simulation of singing and speaking voices (Figure 36.6).

Figure 36.6

Dodge: *In Celebration* (based on a poem by Mark Strand), mm. 1–3.

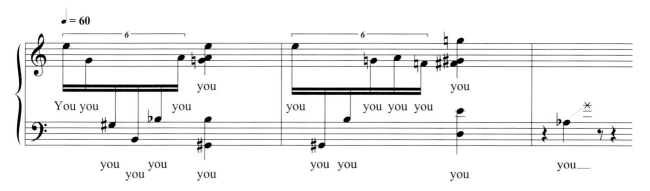

Sound Mass

Sound mass denotes a texture of such density and complexity that the musical effect resides in the whole rather than in the delineation of individual parts. A listener need not, and often cannot, easily distinguish between shifts in pitch, timbre, and dynamics.

Chord clusters, which have been used since the beginning of this century, form a large part of the tonal language of sound-mass compositions. Some works also employ the many-voiced, rhythmically intricate, highly chromatic counterpoint known as *mikropolyphonie.*

One of the best-known sound-mass compositions, *Threnody to the Victims of Hiroshima* for fifty-two strings (1960) by the Polish composer Krzysztof Penderecki (b. 1933), uses both clusters and mikropolyphonie (Figure 36.7).

Figure 36.7

Penderecki: *Threnos Den Opfern von Hiroschima (Threnody to the Victims of Hiroshima).*

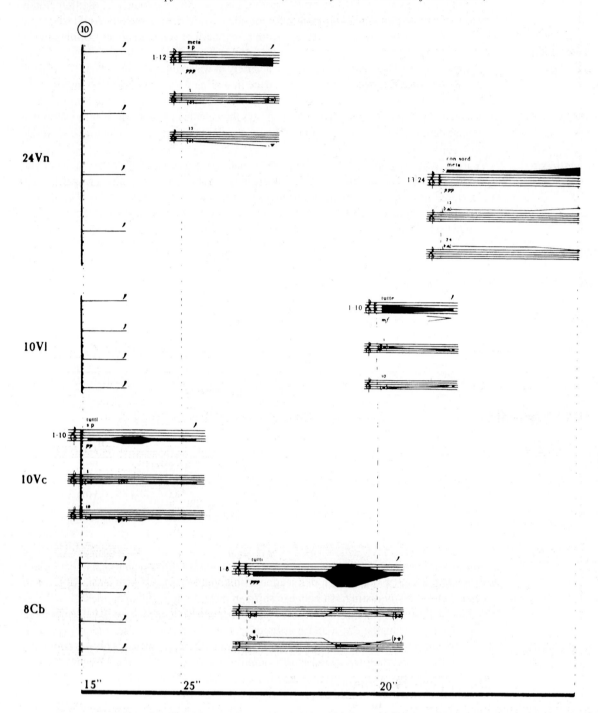

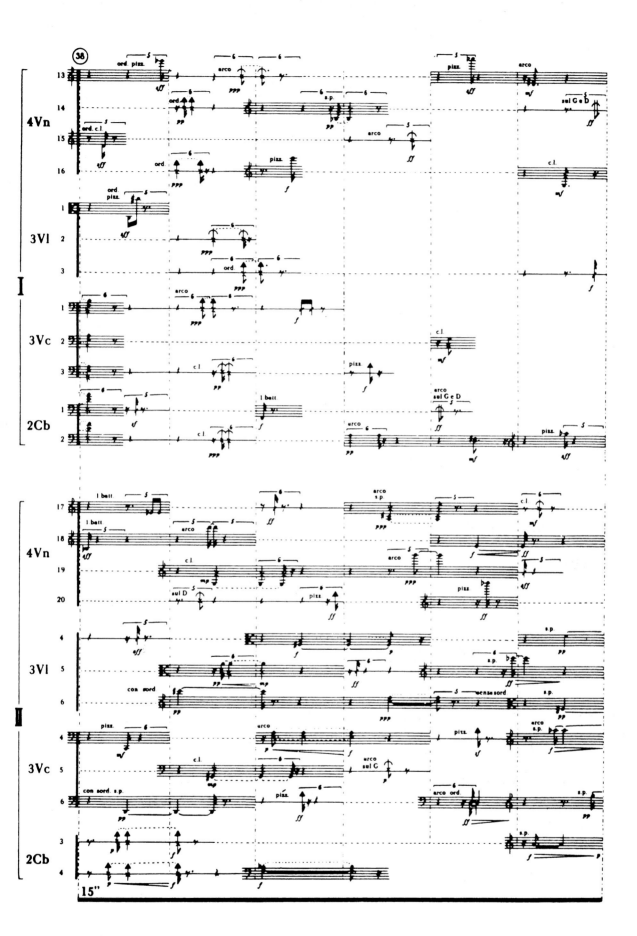

Extended Techniques

Throughout the twentieth century, composers explored new instrumental and vocal timbral possibilities. This search for innovative techniques is an extension of a type of instrumental exploration begun much earlier in the century, most notably by Webern, who used unusual combinations of instruments rather than standard chamber ensembles. The choice of instruments has become as much a part of the creative process as the choice of pitches and rhythms. The labeling of any technique as extended is always provisional because every technique, including pizzicato and vibrato, was unusual when it first appeared. Some *extended techniques* follow:

1. Western instruments played in unusual ways, such as muting piano strings or playing piano strings with a metal instrument.
2. Unfamiliar or newly invented instruments.
3. Noninstruments such as sirens or auto horns.
4. Additional apparatus such as amplifiers.
5. Extended vocal techniques: tongue clicking, humming, whispering, etc.

Rock 'n' Roll and Rock Music

The dominant form of white-American popular music in the period from 1955 to 1960 was *rock 'n' roll,* which fused the African-American popular music called rhythm and blues with white popular music (Tin Pan Alley and country-and-western) and a hard-driving rhythm dominated by the bass drum and electric bass. The best-known performer of the late 1950s was Elvis Presley (1935–1977), whose records sold far more than other rock 'n' roll musicians. The term *rock 'n' roll* became an umbrella term for all popular music of the late 1950s and was gradually shortened to *rock* in the early 1960s. The rock music of the 1960s was an electronic medium, relying extensively on amplification, distortion, and ultimately on electronic synthesis of sound. Recording technology began to dominate rock music in the later sixties, and many bands curtailed live performance in favor of issuing albums. In the mid-sixties, the first wave of the "British Invasion" bands brought white versions of late-1950s African-American rhythm-and-blues hits back to the United States. The best known of these bands was the Beatles. Their album *Sgt. Pepper's Lonely Hearts Club Band* (1967), which incorporated sophisticated studio techniques and many extra musicians (including the London Symphony Orchestra), set the tone for the age.

Music Since 1970

Although none of the new musical trends of the years 1945–1970 has disappeared, it is apparent that at about 1970 a shift in attitude took place. This new musical philosophy, called *post-modernism,* emphasizes the musical experience of the listener over innovation and experimentation.

Eclecticism

Like the avant-garde, eclectic composers experiment, but only as a tool to produce meaningful musical results. Using the cultural creations of all eras and all places, eclectic composers create unusual and fascinating combinations, borrowing passages from earlier music and freely mixing styles.

No discussion of *eclecticism* can be complete without reference to Luciano Berio (Italian, 1925–2003). His early post-modern five-movement masterpiece, *Sinfonia* (1968), uses a barrage of quotations from Bach, Ravel, Mahler, Stockhausen, and his own work. The vocalists sing in jazz syllables or sing and speak a collage of texts as eclectic as the music itself.

New Accessibility

Several new styles and genres have emerged in the post-modern era. One feature that unites many of these approaches is their accessibility. The works of David del Tredici (b. 1937), George Rochberg (1918–2005), Henryk M. Gorecki (1933–2010), and others have been called neoromantic, partly because of their return to tonality. The audiences who often felt shut out by the avant-garde can comprehend and enjoy these new styles.

Minimalism

Minimalism is the gradual process of unfolding a very limited body of motivic material, often with an unprecedentedly high degree of literal repetition. Although the motivic material may be anything, it is most often simple, tonal or modal, and largely diatonic. Many minimal works owe a great deal to the influences of African and Asian music.

Steve Reich (American, b. 1936) is one of the most important of the minimalists. His *Four Organs* for four electric organs and maracas (1970) consists entirely of a single chord whose individual tones are gradually augmented while maracas keep a steady eighth-note pulse (Figure 36.8).

Figure 36.8

Reich: *Four Organs,* mm. 1–4.

The maraca part consists of steady unbroken eighth notes played throughout the piece thus:

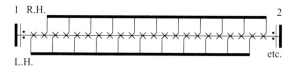

Because the maracas must be clearly heard over the four organs, it is suggested that two pairs be used, one pair in each hand.

Performance Art

Performance art is art that is performed (in contrast to object art, such as painting and sculpture). It is, like opera, a multimedia genre that may involve costumes, staging, movement or dance, video, words, and, of course, music. Laurie Anderson (American, b. 1947) is trained, as are many performance artists, in the visual arts; however, she is now known mostly as a composer/performer and has wide followings among both concert and rock music listeners. Anderson's compositions are intended specifically for her own performances, no two of which are alike. Her music tends to be modal, minimal, and rhythmically driving in the manner of rock music, and she frequently uses ostinato. Her creations involve electronics, live performance, and movement. She describes herself as a storyteller and says that "the gadgets don't matter if the emotional center, and the words, aren't there . . ."

MIDI Technology

In the early 1980s, digital technology was increasingly applied to portable keyboard synthesizers, culminating in 1983 in the establishment of an industry standard for connecting digital musical instruments called *MIDI* (Music Instrument Digital Interface). This development has facilitated the interfacing of personal computers with digital keyboards, and much software now exists for creating, editing, storing, and manipulating musical information in computer-readable form. The implications of MIDI networks involving synthesis equipment, computers, and analog or digital recording technology on the future direction of music are now being explored, but the impact has already been felt on commercial music applications, in instructional applications, and in music publishing. In recent years a thriving international community of MIDI-based musicians has formed on the worldwide web (www), sharing MIDI files of their compositions and arrangements with one another and the world at large.

Computer-Assisted Composition

Computer-assisted composition has largely shifted from large mainframe computer systems to MIDI networks using personal computers, putting this technology in the hands of individual composers. In the 1980s, computer programs such as *M, Jam Factory, Music Mouse,* and *Cybernetic Composer* were developed and marketed, moving computer-assisted composition out of the realm of experimentation and into the mainstream (Figure 36.9). Many amateur musicians now engage in computer-assisted composition as a form of recreation.

Figure 36.9

Macintosh keyboard controls map for *Music Mouse—An Intelligent Instrument.*

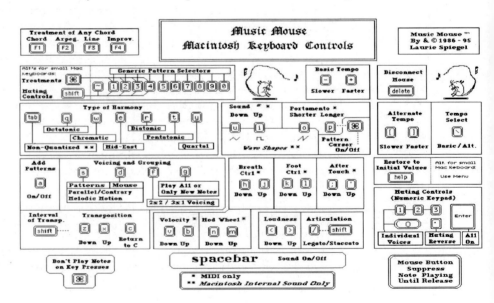

The development of the *CD-ROM* (Compact Disc Read-Only Memory) has allowed composers such as Morton Subotnick (b. 1933) to create multimedia compositions involving video and audio materials that the listener can interact with in real time using personal computers. His *All My Hummingbirds Have Alibis* and *5 Scenes from an Imaginary Ballet,* both produced on CD-ROM, are examples of this interactive medium. The advent of *CD-I* (Interactive Compact Discs) in the mid-1990s allows listeners to interact with prerecorded music played on home audio equipment to change such elements as tempo, relative intensity of various elements, and other large-scale aspects of the music they are listening to. It would seem that audience interaction and participation, long a goal of the avant-garde, is well on its way to fruition through the strides made in digital technology.

Sampling Systems

An outgrowth of digital recording technology, *sampling systems* produce their sounds by recording and playing back acoustic sounds. This makes possible the electronic simulation of all acoustic instruments. The full potential of this technology was first explored in commercial music, but these systems have made their way to the concert hall in recent years. Libby Larsen (b. 1950) has employed sampling synthesizers in orchestral works such as *Ghost of an Old Ceremony* and *Schöenberg, Schenker, and Schillinger.* With the development of computer software to sample and record sounds, virtually any sound can be recorded and manipulated to create music. Composers wanting to create *musique concrète* (see p. 763) compositions now have powerful digital tools at their disposal.

Post-1970 Rock

By the early 1970s, the term *rock* was used for all popular music, regardless of style. During the 1970s and 1980s, rock music employed a basic instrumentation consisting of electric guitars, bass, keyboards, and drums. (These instruments have been gradually augmented or replaced by digital instruments with the advent of MIDI instrumentation.) Much of this music was sophisticated, being derived in part from the style of the late Beatles albums. A blending of jazz and rock began in the 1970s, resulting in a style called *fusion.* In the later 1970s, new types of rock (*punk* and *new wave*) represented a return to the simplicity and directness of rock 'n' roll. At the same time, a more commercial type of rock-based music, called *pop,* arose. The advent of music videos, MTV, and other video programs in the 1980s marked a radical departure for all commercial popular music, and popular music has become conceived in visual as well as aural terms. In the late 1980s, a type of African-American street poetry was fused by inner-city disk jockeys (DJs) with background music derived from a late-seventies African-American style known as *funk* to form a style known as *rap.* These background sounds were originally done by mixing sounds from recordings in a live setting, either in the studio or in concert. More recently, there has been an extensive use of sampling synthesizers to produce rap music.

New Age Music

In the 1980s, elements of minimalism, jazz, and electronic music were fused into a genre that has come to be called *new age,* or "space," music. This largely instrumental music is characterized by a static or very slow harmonic rhythm and an interest in complex textures with sensuous appeal; it has relaxation or reflection as its goal. Composers who have contributed to this eclectic popular music include minimalists such as Phillip Glass (b. 1937), Terry Riley (b. 1935), and Harold Budd (b. 1936); jazz composers such as Keith Jarrett (b. 1945), Paul Winter (b. 1939), and Pat Metheny (b. 1954); experimentalists such as David Hykes (b. 1953); commercial musicians such as Chip Davis (b. 1947) (Mannheim Steamroller, Fresh Aire); and electronic composers such as Wendy Carlos (b. 1939) and Kitaro (b. 1953).

Ambient Music

Spearheaded by the work of Don G. Campbell (1946–2012) and based on the work of French physician and psychologist Alfred A. Tomatis (1920–2001), some composers are producing compositions whose purpose is to create feelings of well-being and even to effect changes in the physical and mental health of listeners.

World Music

In the 1980s, as a direct result of the availability of recordings and the tremendous increases in worldwide communication and travel, the concept of *world music* began to develop. Popular music of the West (primarily England and the United States) had been disseminated to and imitated in many countries in Asia and Africa, often superseding the traditional music of these cultures. Now the traditional music of Asia and Africa has begun to seriously influence the popular music of the West. Musicians such as Paul Winter (b. 1939), David Amram (b. 1930), Brian Eno (b. 1948), and Paul Simon (b. 1941) have incorporated much non-Western music into their compositions. Even in the concert hall, the last bastian of western European art music, composers such as John Corigliano (b. 1938), Kay Gardner (1941–2002), Toru Takemitsu (1930–1996), and R. Murray Schafer (b. 1933) have contributed works that are strongly influenced by non-Western music. Many people see the gradual emergence of a new international style, understood and appreciated by people all over the world, as a result of the musical cross-fertilization that is now taking place.

Conclusions

Today's music is rich in diversity. It appears that the rigorous experimentation of the avant-garde has yielded the center stage to post-modernism, a philosophy that tolerates not only the uncompromisingly original but also innovative combinations of tradition and invention, tonality and atonality, Eastern and Western music, popular music and art music, and trained and untrained musicians.

Audiences enjoy the new music, and composers enjoy the attention. Although no one can predict which recent developments will retain their importance in the future, we can all be grateful for the enormous variety of music that is available to us now.

APPENDIX G

Summary of Part-Writing Practices

Stylistic Practices

Triads

These refer to special part-writing situations that occur often.

1. **Root Position.** When two roots lie a P5th or P4th apart, keep the common tone and move the remaining two upper voices stepwise to the chord tones of the next triad. If handled correctly, the roots of the chords will be doubled.

2. **Root Position.** When two roots lie a P5th or P4th apart, especially when the soprano voice descends scale degrees $\hat{2}$ to $\hat{1}$, move all three upper voices in similar motion to the nearest chord tone. If handled correctly, the roots of the chords will be doubled.

3. **Root Position.** When roots lie a third apart, keep both common tones and move the remaining voice stepwise. If handled correctly, the roots of the chords will be doubled.

4. **Root Position.** When roots lie a second apart, move the three upper voices in contrary motion to the bass, and make sure that each voice moves to the nearest chord tone of the next chord. If handled correctly, the roots of the two chords will be doubled. An exception is the progression V to vi or VI. In this case, double the third factor of the vi or VI triad. Only two upper voices will move in opposite direction to the bass.

5. **Any Position—Repeated Chords.** Maintain proper doubling and range of voices, and keep the usual order of voices (soprano, alto, tenor, and bass). Otherwise, you are quite free to exchange chord factors among voices. Sometimes a change of position takes place (example: I to I^6).

6. **First Inversion.** Double any triad factor that facilitates smooth voice leading. Favored notes are the soprano (found often) and bass (slightly less common). Never double the leading tone (seventh scale degree). Observe general recommendations regarding voice ranges, order of voices, and spacing.

7. **First-Inversion (vii°⁶).** Double the third (bass note) or fifth factor. The bass note is preferred. Move all voices with as much stepwise movement as possible. Avoid melodic skips of a tritone.

8. **First-Inversion (ii°⁶).** Double the third (bass note) or the root, which will be in an upper voice. When approaching or leaving the ii°⁶ triad, make voice leading stepwise whenever possible and avoid melodic tritones.

9. **Second Inversion.** No established voice-leading pattern, but double the bass note and use only the four types of $^6_4$ chords described in volume 1, Chapter 9.

Dominant Seventh Chords

10. Resolve the seventh of the V^7 chord down one scale degree in the same voice. In the few instances where the resolution tone is not present, either keep the seventh as a common tone or move it by the smallest melodic interval possible.

11. All four factors of the V^7 chord are usually present, but for smoothness of voice leading, the fifth may be omitted and the root doubled.

Leading-Tone Seventh Chords

12. Resolve the seventh factor of the vii^{ø7} or vii$^{°7}$ (and inversions) down one diatonic scale degree.

13. Resolve the root of the vii^{ø7} and vii$^{°7}$ upward to the tonic note.

14. Resolve the seventh factor of nondominant seventh chords one diatonic scale degree down to the third factor of the next chord (in circle progressions). Otherwise, resolve the seventh factor down one step if its resolution is a part of the following chord.

15. Altered tones are seldom doubled. Otherwise, follow the guidelines for all borrowed chords as they appear in the parallel minor or major keys.

16. Double the bass note (3rd of chord) whenever possible. Move upper voices in contrary motion with the bass, and avoid chromatic voice leading in leaving the N^6. When the N^6 proceeds to i_4^6, watch out for parallel 5ths.

17. Resolve the augmented 6th interval outward (in contrary motion) by half step to an octave. Neither of the two tones forming the augmented 6th interval is ever doubled. In the Italian 6th, double the 3rd above the bass note.

18. To avoid parallel 5ths, Gr^6 proceeds to i_4^6 or I_4^6 instead of V.

19. In major keys, when the German 6th progresses to I_4^6, the P5 above the bass is spelled as a doubly augmented 4th to avoid chromatic spelling of the resolution (upward to the 3rd of the tonic chord).

20. For V^9, the root, 3rd, 7th, and 9th are usually present. The 7th and 9th resolve down to the 3rd and 5th of the tonic triad.

21. For V^{11}, the root, 7th, 9th, and 11th are usually present. The 11th is retained as a common tone (tonic note), and the 7th and 9th resolve down to the 3rd and 5th of the tonic triad.

22. For V^{13}, the root, 3rd, 7th, and 13th are usually present. The 13th is usually in the soprano and resolves a 3rd downward to the tonic factor of I or i. The 7th resolves down by step to the 3rd of the tonic triad.

23. Resolve the altered 5th in the direction of the alteration—raised pitches up, lowered pitches down. Remember to resolve the 7th of the chord downward by step, even if it results in a nonstandard doubling of the tonic triad. Altered tones are almost never doubled.

24. Double the root of chromatic mediants, even if this results in doubling an altered tone. Resolve as smoothly as possible, even if chromatic voice leading results.

25. Resolve the altered tones upward by a half step. Remember to keep the common tone.

There are no exceptions to these practices under any conditions:

1. Avoid parallel perfect octaves (P8ths), parallel perfect fifths (P5ths), and parallel unisons (P1s).

2. Never double the leading tone of the scale.

3. Do not write pitches outside the range of a particular voice.

4. Avoid the melodic augmented second (A2) and fourth (A4) in all voices.

Observe these practices carefully unless particular situations permit no other alternative:

5. Avoid crossing voices.

6. Spacing between adjacent voices should not exceed an octave in the three upper voices.

7. Do not overlap two adjacent voices more than a whole step.

8. Do not move in the same direction to perfect intervals in the two outer voices.

9. Unequal fifths, P5ths to d5ths, or vice versa, should be used sparingly.

10. The melodic descending d5th appears sometimes in bass voices, but rarely in the soprano. The d4th may be written in isolated situations.

11. The leading tone should progress upward to the tonic when it is in an outer voice.

Macro Analysis Symbols

Macro analysis is a flexible, elective analytical technique. It can be used by itself or in conjunction with Roman numerals. The system consists of two basic types of analysis labels: letter symbols and slurs. For most chords, the root and the quality of a chord are identified by letter symbols (augmented 6th and quartal chords are exceptions). Circle progressions are labeled with a solid slur; leading-tone progressions are labeled with a dotted slur.

An introduction to the system is presented in volume 1. The following is a summary and continuation of the system's symbols.

Symbol	Illustration	Symbol Meaning	Examples
Capital letter	C	Major triad	
Capital letter with $^+$	C^+	Augmented triad	
Lowercase letter	c	Minor triad	
Lowercase letter with $^\circ$	c°	Diminished triad	
Capital letter with ^{7}	C^7	Major-minor 7th chord	
Capital letter with ^{M7}	C^{M7}	Major-major 7th chord	
Lowercase letter with ^{7}	c^7	Minor-minor 7th chord	

Symbol	Illustration	Symbol Meaning	Examples
Lowercase letter with $^{\circ 7}$	$c^{\circ 7}$	Diminished-diminished 7th chord	$g^{\circ 7}$ $f\sharp^{\circ 7}$ $eb^{\circ 7}$
Lowercase letter with $^{\varnothing 7}$	$c^{\varnothing 7}$	Diminished-minor 7th chord	$g^{\varnothing 7}$ $f\sharp^{\varnothing 7}$ $eb^{\varnothing 7}$
Capital letter with ^{9}	C^{9}	Major-minor 7th chord with a 9th	G^{9} $F\sharp^{9}$ Eb^{9}
Capital letter with ^{11}	C^{11}	Major-minor 7th chord with an 11th	G^{11} $F\sharp^{11}$ Eb^{11}
Capital letter with ^{13}	C^{13}	Major-minor 7th chord with a 13th	G^{13} $F\sharp^{13}$ Eb^{13}
Lowercase letter with ^{9}	c^{9}	Minor-minor 7th chord with a 9th	g^{9} $f\sharp^{9}$ eb^{9}
Lowercase letter with ^{11}	c^{11}	Minor-minor 7th chord with an 11th	g^{11} $f\sharp^{11}$ eb^{11}
Lowercase letter with ^{13}	c^{13}	Minor-minor 7th chord with a 13th	g^{13} $f\sharp^{13}$ eb^{13}
Capital letter with ^{5b} or $^{7}_{5b}$	C^{5b}, C^{7}_{5b}	Altered dominant chord with a lowered 5th	G^{5b} $F\sharp^{7}_{5\natural}$ Eb^{7}_{5bb}
Capital letter with $^{+7}$	C^{+7}	Altered dominant chord with a raised 5th	G^{+7} $F\sharp^{+7}$ Eb^{+7}
Solid slur	⌣	Circle progression	D G D^{7} g
Dotted slur	⌣ (dotted)	Leading-tone progression	$f\sharp^{\varnothing 7}$ G $f\sharp^{\circ 7}$ g

Popular Music Chord Symbols

Following is a comprehensive list of chords found in jazz and popular song accompaniments. All are based on C but may be transposed to any other tone. This chart is a synthesis of the symbols presented in *The New Real Book* series (Sher Music Co.) and represents adaptations of the recommendations made by Carl Brandt and Clinton Roemer in *Standardized Chord Symbol Notation.*

Alternative chord symbols for some common chords:

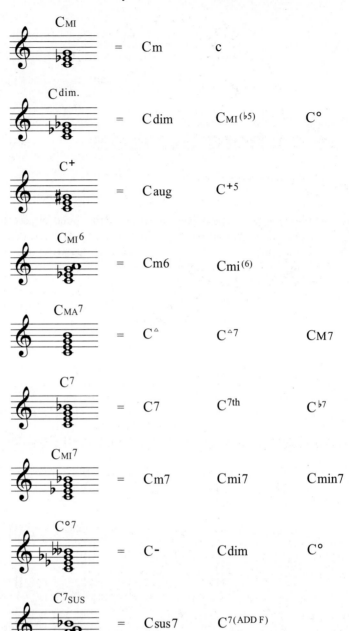

C_{MI} = Cm	c	

Chord inversions are shown by the addition of a diagonal line to the right of the basic chord symbol, followed by the letter denoting the bass note for the inversion. The diagonal line can also be used to indicate a bass note that is dissonant with the chord above.

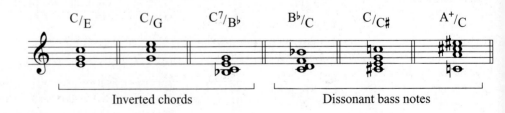

Glossary

Aggregate   The total. (Example: The first six tones of a twelve-tone series form an aggregate with the second six tones.)

Aleatory (also Aleatoric)   Interchangeable with indeterminacy. See *indeterminacy.*

Altered chord   A chord that contains one or more factors that are not part of the prevailing diatonic system.

Altered dominant   A dominant triad or a 7th chord that contains a raised or lowered 5th and sometimes a lowered 3rd. (Example: G B D♯ F = altered dominant [V^{+7}] in C major.)

Analog   An exact representation of something in a medium different from that of the original.

Answer (in a fugue)   Imitation of the fugue subject usually at the interval of a P5th higher or P4th lower.

Answer—real   See *real answer.*

Answer—tonal   See *tonal answer.*

Asymmetric meter   Meter in which the beats are not grouped into units divisible by two or three (Examples: $\frac{7}{8}$ and $\frac{5}{4}$ meters). Also known as *irregular* or *combination* meter.

Augmentation   A melody in increased (usually doubled) note values. (Example: In augmentation, a melody in quarter notes becomes a melody in half notes.)

Augmented 6th chords   A type of altered chord that contains the interval of an augmented 6th. The three most common types (up from the lowest-sounding tone): (1) *Italian*—M3rd and A6th; (2) *German*—M3rd, P5th, and A6th; and (3) *French*—M3rd, A4th, and A6th. The bass note is most frequently a M3rd below the tonic. Symbols: It^6, Gr^6, and Fr^6.

Avant-garde   Music or composers characterized primarily by unorthodox or experimental ideas. Applies as well to other art media.

Basso continuo   Same as *figured bass.* Usually performed by a cello, viola da gamba, or bassoon playing the bass line while a harpsichordist or pianist plays the bass notes and adds the chords as indicated by the figures (numbers).

Basso ostinato   See *ground.*

Best normal order   If a set of pitches contains two larger intervals of the same size, the best normal order is the arrangement that is most densely packed to the left of the set. See *normal order.*

Bitonality   See *polytonality.*

Borrowed chord   A chord borrowed from the parallel major or minor key. (Example: A C E♭ is a borrowed chord [from G minor] in G major.)

Bridge (in a fugue)   A short passage in the exposition of a fugue between entrances of the subject or answer. Acts as a modulatory passage for return to the tonic of the subject that ends in the dominant.

Bridge passage   Another term for "transition." Connects two themes. See *transition.*

Cadence—linear   See *linear cadence.*

Chance music   Interchangeable with indeterminacy. See *indeterminacy.*

Changing meters   Meter changes within a composition to show rhythmic patterns more clearly than could a single constant meter.

Chord cluster   A chord with three or more factors of which each is no more than a whole step from its adjacent factor. (Example: C C♯ D E when sounded together is a chord cluster.)

Chords of addition and omission   Chords with added or deleted tones. (A common example of an added tone chord: C E G A—the A is an added tone. Example of a chord of omission: C G C—the 3rd is omitted from the triad.)

Chromatic mediant chords   The altered mediant and submediant triads and 7th chords on occasion. (Example: E G♯ B = III in C major.) Not common in any style, but found most often in the late romantic period.

Clausula vera   The most common cadence in two-voiced, sixteenth-century choral writing. The voices either expand to an octave (from a 6th) or contract to a unison (from a 3rd).

Cluster   See *chord cluster.*

Coda   Technically an expanded cadence. Occurs at the end of a composition and traditionally brings the composition to a convincing conclusion. May consist of a few measures or an entire subdivision in itself.

Combination meter   See *asymmetric meter.*

Combinatoriality   The combination of the first hexachords (first six tones) of two different set forms to produce all 12 tones. (Example: When the first six tones of a particular P^0 and the first six tones of I^9 are combined, the result is all 12 tones of the series with no duplications.) See *aggregate.*

Contrary motion   See *inversion—melodic.*

Countermotive   Counterpoint accompaniment to the motive in an invention. In some inventions the countermotive is utilized in ensuing developmental material.

Countersubject (of a fugue)   The continuation of counterpoint in the voice that has just completed the subject. In actuality, it should be called *counteranswer* because it appears with the answer. In most fugues, the countersubject is a fertile source of material for the remainder of the composition.

Derived set   A twelve-tone set different in order from another but retaining some particular characteristics of the original. (Example: Deriving a twelve-tone set from a prime with a particular trichord type, 0 1 6, as its first segment. The derived set might be manipulated to contain a series of four 0 1 6 trichords.)

Development (in a fugue)   The subject, answer, or possibly countersubject are stated in various keys connected by episodes (brief sections that contain neither the subject nor the answer) after the exposition has been completed.

Development (of a sonata form)   The middle section of a movement or composition in sonata form. The function of this division is to depart from the tonality at the end of the exposition and to form a transition to the tonic of the recapitulation, thereby providing an opportunity to develop the themes of the exposition through variation, alteration, fragmentation, modification, and mutation. The development section is characterized by restless modulation, agitation, and increased tension.

Diminution   A melody in decreased (usually halved) note values. (Example: In diminution, a melody in quarter notes becomes a melody in eighth notes.)

Dodecaphonic   Term used to describe twelve-tone serial writing.

Dual modality   Simultaneous use of major and minor mode or combinations of church modes. Usually the two modes have the same tonic or final.

Duodecuple scale   See *scale—duodecuple.*

Dyad   Two pitches. Generally used when describing segments of a twelve-tone series. Has both melodic and harmonic connotations.

Eclecticism   Derives from the word *eclectic.* In music it refers to the borrowing of devices or ideas from many existing styles.

Electronic music   Music that is electronically produced and processed.

Eleventh chord   A superposition of five 3rds—one 3rd above the 9th of a 9th chord. (Example: G B D F A C = V^{11} in C major.)

Episode   A short interlude in the development section of a fugue that does not contain the subject or answer but connects entrances of either in various keys. Most development sections contain a number of episodes.

Equivalences   A trichord or tetrachord in two or more arrangements or registrations but having the same intervallic content.

Exposition (of a fugue)   The first section of a fugue. Consists of an entrance in all voices of either the fugue subject or answer. When all voices have entered, the exposition gives way to the development.

Exposition (of a sonata form)   The first large section of sonata form containing at least two contrasting key relationships and more often two or three contrasting themes set apart by transitions.

Expressionism   A reaction to impressionism. Its proponents hoped to create music that would be an expression of their inner world in contrast to the impressionists, who sought to represent their impressions of the external world.

Extended technique   Usually refers to traditional instruments that are played in unusual ways, but may also include amplifiers and noninstruments such as sirens and auto horns. Examples include plucking piano strings, striking a harp with the knuckles, and singing into the piano with the damper pedal down.

Free atonality   A kind of atonal writing that allows free use of the 12 tones of the chromatic scale but does not order or prescribe the arrangement as in serial technique.

Free tonality   Term used to designate music that contains a definite tonal center but is not related to traditional major or minor keys. In contrast to chromaticism, which also utilizes a variety of tones but is placed in a setting of functional harmony where each scale degree (and its chromatic alterations) has a traditional role in the operation of key-centered tonality.

French augmented 6th chord   See *augmented 6th chords.*

Fugue   A contrapuntal composition in two or more voices, based on a subject (theme) that is introduced at the beginning in imitation and recurs frequently in the course of the composition. A monothematic composition, except for double or triple fugues that contain two or three subjects.

Fusion   A form of popular music beginning in the 1970s that blended elements of jazz and rock.

German augmented 6th chord   See *augmented 6th chords*.

Graphic notation   A score where musical textures and events are implied through the use of graphic analogs (analogies). A dark area on a score may imply loud sounds, whereas a white area suggests silence.

Ground   A short melodic figure of four to eight measures maintained in the lowest voice and repeated throughout the composition. Same as basso ostinato.

Hexachord   Six pitches. In the Middle Ages and the Renaissance, it referred to a six-tone segment of the total diatonic range, or gamut. Generally used when describing segments of the twelve-tone series. Has both melodic and harmonic connotations.

Hocket (thirteenth century)   Adjacent notes and rests alternating among different voices or parts in such a way that one voice is silent while the other sings.

Hocket (sixteenth century)   The overlapping of phrases at the cadence point where one voice rests and then immediately begins the new phrase.

Imitation   The restatement in close succession of melodic figures in different voices in polyphonic textures.

Indeterminacy   Indefinite or uncertain. Refers in music to some aspect of a composition that the composer places beyond his conscious control and that is thus left to chance.

Interval class   Intervals (not including the unison) may be grouped in six interval classes by the number of half steps between the two pitch classes. In this system only the numbers 1 through 6 are used, and intervals of greater than six half steps are grouped with their inversions. (Example: Interval class 1 contains both the m2 and the M7.)

Inversion (of a twelve-tone series and pitch-class set)   The reversal of the direction (up or down) of each successive tone of the prime series, starting with the first tone (symbol: I^0). Transposed up a half step, the inversion becomes I^1, another half step up I^2, and so on.

Inversion (of the vertical order of voices)   A device in counterpoint in which the vertical order of two simultaneous voices is reversed. When the counterpoint is purposely contrived to sound as well in the "upside down" order, it is known as *invertible counterpoint*. Inversion of vertical order is not to be confused with melodic inversion in which the direction (up or down) of a single melody is reversed.

Inversion—melodic   Reversal of melodic direction. Upward direction in the original becomes downward direction in the inversion, an ascending 6th becomes a descending 6th, and a descending 3rd becomes an ascending 3rd. In tonal music, the inversion is usually diatonic rather than exact. Melodic inversion is synonymous with *contrary motion*.

Invertible counterpoint   Two-voiced counterpoint that is purposely contrived to sound as well in reversed (upside down) order. Inversion may be at any interval, but the octave is most common.

Irregular meter   See *asymmetric meter*.

Italian augmented 6th chord   See *augmented 6th chords*.

Linear cadence   Melodic lines that converge or diverge at the cadence point. Oblique motion is also possible.

Linear harmony   Harmony that results from melodic motion without regard for traditional (functional) harmonic progression.

Melismatic   Describes a style of vocal writing in which several or many pitches are set to a single syllable of a text.

Melodic doubling   The doubling of melodic lines to create parallel movement. Also called *melodic parallel*.

Melodic inversion   See *inversion—melodic*.

MIDI   Musical Instrument Digital Interface, a communications standard for connecting synthesizers to computers and other synthesizers.

Mikropolyphonie   A contemporary musical style featuring many-voiced, rhythmically intricate, highly chromatic counterpoint.

Minimalism   The gradual process of unfolding a very limited (minimal) body of motivic material, often with a high degree of literal repetition. The material is often simple, tonal/modal, and largely diatonic. A typical minimal composition, Steve Reich's *Four Organs*, consists entirely of a single chord whose individual tones are gradually augmented.

Modal mixture   A blending of the resources of the parallel major and minor scales that often results in modal ambiguity.

Monophony   A single line of melody with no accompaniment. (Example: Gregorian chant or folk melodies that do not require a supporting accompaniment.)

Movement   A unit of a larger work that may stand by itself as a complete composition. Such divisions are usually self-contained. Most often the sequence of movements is arranged fast-slow-fast or in some other order that provides contrast.

Musica ficta   Accidentals added to modal compositions of the sixteenth century and earlier. Such accidentals were not included by the composers but were added by singers to eliminate tritones and provide leading tones for the modes that lacked them. Now musica ficta accidentals are usually written above the staff.

Musique concrète   Employs "live" sounds from the environment that are recorded and processed or modified by tape techniques such as splicing and varying the speed of the tape. One of the early types of electronic music.

Nationalism   The use of materials that are identifiably national or regional in character, including folk music, folk stories, myths, or literature.

Neapolitan 6th chord   A major triad based on the lowered 2nd degree of the major or minor scale. (Example: Db F Ab = N in C major.) Because the chord is most often found in first inversion, it is called the Neapolitan 6th.

Neoclassicism   A reaction to the freedom and lack of order in the form and content of compositions of the romantic period. A return to discipline, form, and symmetry of the classical period. Immediately followed the post-romantic and impressionistic period. Representative composer: Paul Hindemith.

New age music   A form of popular music in the 1980s and 1990s consisting of a blend of minimalism, jazz, and electronic music. Also called *space music.*

Ninth chord   A superposition of four 3rds—one 3rd above the 7th of the 7th chord. (Example: G B D F A = V^9 in C major.)

Nonaccentual rhythms   Absence of dynamic accents.

Nonfunctional harmony   Harmony that is more the result of voice leading than of harmonic progression within a major or minor key. See *linear harmony.*

Normal order   In set theory, the term indicates the ascending order of intervals (from small to large) of a trichord, tetrachord, pentachord, or hexachord. (Example: A trichord in normal order = 0 1 6 as against 0 6 1.)

Nota cambiata   A common dissonant melodic device of sixteenth-century vocal music. The decoration of a descending 3rd. The figure consists of four tones: a dotted half note that descends one step to a quarter note (the nota cambiata) and then descends a 3rd to a half note and up a step to another half note.

Octatonic scale   A scale of eight tones. The traditional octatonic scale is a pattern of alternating whole and half steps.

Order number   The number that represents the position of any given tone in the twelve-tone series. (Example: The 3rd tone in a given series is *order number* 2—remember that the first tone is always 0.)

Ostinato   A short musical pattern that is repeated again and again. Ostinato is often used as an accompaniment device but may be the central element in some folk music and in twentieth-century minimalism.

Palindrome   A literary term referring to a sentence that reads the same backward as forward. (Example: "Madam, I'm Adam.") In the context of twelve-tone serial music, it denotes a series with the same interval content forward and backward.

Pandiatonicism   The use of the tones of a diatonic scale in such a way that each tone is stripped of its usual function in the key.

Parallel chords   Chords in which all factors or voices move in parallel motion. Parallel chords are sometimes diatonic (Example: C E G to D F A) and sometimes chromatic (Example: C E G to B D♯ F♯).

Parameter   Variables that are independent of each other. In music the word *parameter* most often refers to such basic components as pitch, melody, rhythm, timbre, and so on. As an example, pitch is a parameter that is independent of timbre—a given pitch may have a particular timbre, but no matter what timbre is selected the pitch remains the same.

Pentachord   Five pitches. Generally used when describing segments of the twelve-tone series or pitch-class set. Has both melodic and harmonic connotations.

Pentatonic scale   A five-tone scale. (Example: C D E G A [C].)

Permutation   A term used in connection with the twelve-tone series and involving a change of the order of a set.

Pitch class   A more recent term for a pitch. Considered broader because pitch class includes octave duplications, whereas a pitch designates only a single sound.

Planing   See *parallel chords.*

Polychord   Simultaneous use of two chords. Spacing is important in the use of polychords because the chords must be spaced sufficiently apart to be heard as two distinct entities.

Polyphony   Simultaneous interacting melodies. A texture of independent but compatible melodic layers sounding at the same time. (Examples: A Bach fugue, a Bach two-part invention, a Palestrina mass.) Music of both the Renaissance and the baroque period was predominantly polyphonic. The terms *polyphony* and *counterpoint* are used interchangeably.

Polytonality   Simultaneous use of two or more tonalities.

Portamento   A common dissonance found in sixteenth-century vocal writing, resembling the anticipation of harmonic counterpoint in the eighteenth century. Most often of quarter-note value in $\frac{3}{2}$ meter. Approached by step and left by repetition.

Pre-dominant   Any chord in functional harmony that normally resolves to the dominant chord. (Examples: IV, ii, N^6, Gr^6, etc.)

Prime series (in twelve-tone technique)   The twelve-tone series as it is originally constructed (symbol: P^0). The same series transposed up a half step is P^1, another half step is P^2, and so on.

Primitivism   A reaction to the refined and fragile music of such composers as Debussy. Its proponents sought to eliminate the subtlety and gentility of previous music and emphasize the mechanistic, the violent, the animal nature, and the more earthy aspects of music.

Quartal chords   Chords constructed through a super-position of 4ths rather than the conventional 3rds as in tertian harmony. (Example: B E A or B E A D.)

Quintal chords   Chords constructed through a super-position of 5ths rather than the conventional 3rds as in tertian harmony. (Example: D A E B or A E B.)

Real answer   An exact transposition (usually interval by interval, but in any case by diatonic interval) of a fugal or other contrapuntal subject, usually at the P5th above or P4th below.

Recapitulation (of a sonata form)   The third section of a movement or composition in sonata form. Contains the return of the themes stated in the exposition. Conventionally, all themes in the recapitulation are returned to the tonic key.

Recapitulation (of a fugue)   The third and final part of the fugue containing the return of the subject and/or answer in the tonic key of the composition. Not all fugues have recapitulations, and in some the recapitulation is quite abbreviated.

Retransition   A transition at the end of the development section in sonata form that leads back to the first theme of the recapitulation.

Retrograde   A melody, subject, motive, and so on, in reverse order or backward. (Example: A melody C D G E F in retrograde is F E G D C.) *Cancrizans* is another term meaning "retrograde."

Retrograde (of a twelve-tone series)   The prime series sounded in reverse order from last to first. Symbol for the retrograde set is R^0, transposed up a half step it is R^1, transposed up another half step it is R^2, and so on. It is important to remember that R^0 begins on the last pitch of P^0.

Retrograde inversion (of a twelve-tone series)   The inversion of the prime series in reverse order from last pitch to first. Symbol for the retrograde inversion is RI^0, transposed up a half step it is RI^1, transposed up another half

step it is RI^2, and so on. It is important to remember that the RI form begins on the last tone of I^0.

Rock music   The primary form of popular music in the mid-twentieth century characterized by a heavy bass beat. Beginning as "rock 'n' roll" in the 1950s, rock came to mean any form of popular music in the 1970s. See *fusion.*

Romanticism   The period of musical writing from roughly 1825 to 1900. Characterized by a tendency to accentuate the impulsive, the unusual, the adventuresome, the impetuous, and the passionate attitudes toward musical composition.

Scale—duodecuple   The 12 tones of the octave each with equal status. Although the older term *chromatic scale* also denotes 12 tones, its relation to key and tonal systems makes it inappropriate for present-day purposes. The term *duodecuple* is used in connection with serial music.

Serialism   An extension of the twelve-tone technique. An example is Milton Babbitt's composition *Three Compositions for Piano,* where other parameters such as rhythm, dynamics, articulations, and timbres (as well as pitch) are given a specific order.

Set   A collection of pitch classes, usually without regard to their order. See *normal order.*

Set type   Sets are classified according to the interval between the first pitch class of the set and each successive pitch class. The lowest pitch is assigned the number 0, and the other pitches are assigned numbers indicating their distance in half steps above the lowest pitch.

Shifted tonality   Sudden tonality change without preparation or modulation in the traditional sense.

Sonata   A composition usually in three or four movements for (1) piano or harpsichord solo or (2) solo instrument and accompaniment. These multimovement compositions developed in the seventeenth century and attained their classic form in the mid-eighteenth century.

Sonata form   A compositional structure used most often in the first movement of a sonata, symphony, trio, string quartet, and so on. It consists of three main sections: an exposition, a development, and a recapitulation.

Sound mass   Denotes a texture of such density and complexity that the parts cannot be distinguished individually.

Space music   See *new age music.*

Stochastic music   Music written according to a system based on a probability distribution. After the probabilities have been set by the composer, random selections for various musical parameters are then chosen, usually by a computer. These selections are then used to write the composition.

Stretto (in a fugue) Overlapping of subjects (or answers) in different voices. A subject in one voice is not completed before the same subject is introduced in another voice.

Subject (of a fugue) A short melody that is used as the basis for a fugue.

Syllabic Describes a style of vocal writing in which one pitch is used for each syllable of a text. It contrasts with melismatic writing, which employs many notes per syllable.

Tetrachord Modern interpretation: a four-tone scale segment. (Example: C D E F is the lower tetrachord of the C major scale.) The term was adapted from Greek music, where it referred to a four-tone scale segment in descending order.

Third relationship Relationship of a 3rd between roots of adjacent chords. When prominent progressions employ 3rd relationship in concentration or in succession, particularly ascending, tonal emphasis is decreased.

Third relationship cadence A cadence in which the roots of the two chords lie in 3rd relationship. (Example: E G♯ B progresses to C E G in a cadence.)

Thirteenth chord A superposition of six 3rds—one above the 11th of an 11th chord. (Example: G B D F A C E = V^{13} in C major.)

Tonal answer The subject (of a fugue) transposed usually to the P5th above or the P4th below. However, slight modifications are made in a tonal answer so that the intervallic distance is not always the same as in the subject. The modifications generally entail replacing dominant implications with tonic. Thus, if a fugue subject begins on the dominant tone, the answer begins on the tonic.

Total serialism All (or at least most) of the elements or dimensions of a twelve-tone serial composition are serialized. (Example: Serialization of pitch, intensity, duration, and timbre.)

Transition A passage that provides a musical link between one theme and the next. The term is used most often to designate passages in the exposition and recapitulation of sonata form that furnish a smooth connection between themes.

Trichord Three pitches. Generally describes segments of twelve-tone sets. Has both melodic and harmonic connotations. *Trichord* is used in place of *triad* by contemporary composers and theorists because triad has key and tonal implications.

Tritone The common name for the A4 or d5 interval. Usually avoided in earlier practice, it became an important structural element in much twentieth-century music.

Twelve-tone row Same as *twelve-tone series*. *Series, set,* and *row* are used synonymously. Authors and composers of the 1960s and 1970s prefer the term *set.*

Variation—continuous A type of composition employing variation techniques in which the variations are fused together in the continuous flow of the music. The most common type employs a ground (basso ostinato).

Variation—principle The transformation of a melody, harmony, or rhythm with changes or elaborations. A modification of a melody, harmony, or rhythm, especially using one of the techniques developing the potential of the theme or subject material.

Variation—theme and variations A genre in which a theme, usually in sectional form, is stated simply and ends with a cadence. Variations follow this theme, maintaining sufficiently the character and form of the original to identify them as variations.

Whole-tone scale The harmonic or melodic use of a six-tone scale in which each degree is a whole step from the next. (Example: C D E F♯ G♯ A♯ [C].)

Credits

CHAPTER 28

Assignment 28.5 PRELUDE I (ALLEGRO BEN RITMATO E DECISO) By GEORGE GERSHWIN. Copyright © 1927 (Renewed) WB MUSIC CORP. in the U.S. Rights throughout the World excluding the U.S. and British Reversionary Territories. Controlled by NEW WORLD MUSIC COMPANY (LTD.) and Administered by WB MUSIC CORP. Rights throughout the British Reversionary Territories Controlled by CHAPPELL & CO., INC. All Rights Reserved. Used By Permission of ALFRED MUSIC.

CHAPTER 30

Figure 30.16 Barbershop Honor Society, "In the Good Old Summertime." Used with permission. All rights reserved.

CHAPTER 32

Figure 32.1 CHANTY (from POEMS OF THE SEA) by Ernest Bloch. Copyright © 1923 by G. Schirmer, Inc. (ASCAP) International Copyright Secured. All Rights Reserved. Used by Permission.

Figure 32.2 Trittico Botticelliano. Music by Ottorino Respighi. Copyright © 1928 by Casa Ricordi S. r. l. - Milan, Italy. All rights reserved. Reproduced by kind permission of Hal Leonard Euorpe S. r. l. - Italy.

Assignment 32.2 Je garde une médaille de'elle. Music by Lili Boulanger. Copyyright © by Éditions Durand - Paris, France. All rights reserved. Reproduced by kind permission of Hal Leonard Europe S. r. l. - Italy and Centre International Nadia et Lili Boulanger.

CHAPTER 33

Figure 33.1 Sonata For Two Pianos by Igor Stravinsky, © 1945 Boosey & Hawkes Inc. Copyright Renewed. All Right Reserved. Used With Permission.

Figure 33.3 "Mikrokosmos" by Béla Bartók © 1940 by Hawkes & Son (London) Ltd. All Right Reserved. Used With Permission.

Figure 33.4 PIANO SONATA NO. 8 IN 8 FLAT MAJOR, OP. 84 By Sergei Prokofiev Copyright © 1946 (Renewed) by G. Schirmer, Inc. (ASCAP) International Copyright Secured. All Rights Reserved. Reprinted by Permission.

Figure 33.7 A THREE SCORE SET By William Schuman. Copyright © 1944 (Renewed) by Associated Music Publishers, Inc. (BMI). International Copyright Secured. All Rights Reserved. Used by Permission.

Assignment 33.1 "Mikrokosmos" by Béla Bartók © 1940 by Hawkes & Son (London) Ltd. All Right Reserved. Used With Permission.

Assignment 33.1 THE ALCOTTS (from CONCORD SONATA). Words and music by Charles Ives. Copyright © 1976 by Associated Music Publishers (BMI) International Copyright Secured. All Rights Reserved. Used by permission.

CHAPTER 34

Figure 34.13 "Mikrokosmos" by Béla Bartók © 1940 by Hawkes & Son (London) Ltd. All Right Reserved. Used With Permission.

Figure 34.21 "Mikrokosmos" by Béla Bartók © 1940 by Hawkes & Son (London) Ltd. All Right Reserved. Used With Permission.

Assignment 34.5 "44 Violin Duets" by Béla Bartók © 1933 Boosey & Hawkes, Inc. Copyright Renewed. All Right Reserved. Used With Permission.

POSTLUDE

Figure 36.2 Aria by John Cage. Copyright © 1960 by Henmar Press, Inc. All Rights Reserved. Used by permission of C.F. Peters Corp.

Figure 36.3 Pauline Oliveros. Sonic Meditations I, "Teach Yourself to Fly," Reprinted with permission of Smith Publications.

Figure 36.4 Mario Davidovsky: No. 3 for Cello and Electronic Sound from Synchronisms. Reprinted with permission of McGinnis and Marx.

Figure 36.5 "I Am Sitting in a Room" (1969) by Alvin Lucier. Reprinted from Chambers © 1980 by Alvin Lucier, Wesleyan University Press of University Press of New England.

Figure 36.6 In Celebration (based on a poem by Mark Strand) by Charles Dodge. © 1975 Charles Dodge, North Cape Music. Used with permission.

Figure 36.7 THRENODY FOR THE VICTIMS OF HIROSHIMA By KRZYSZTOF PENDERECKI. Copyright © 1961 (Renewed) EMI DESHON MUSIC, INC. Exclusive Worldwide Print Rights Administered by ALFRED MUSIC. All Rights Reserved. Used By Permission of ALFRED MUSIC.

Figure 36.8 "Four Organs" by Steve Reich. © 1980 By Hendon Music, Inc. A Boosey & Hawkes Company. All Right Reserved. Used With Permission.

Figure 36.9 Reprinted with permission of Laurie Spiegel.

Musical Example Index

Subject Index

Frescobaldi, Girolamo, 527
Fugue, 459–478
  answer, 459, 472, 783, 784
  augmentation, 464
  bridge, 461
  countersubject, 460, 461, 462, 467, 471, 473
  defined, 780
  diminution, 464–465
  episodes, 473
  exposition, 459, 462
  final part of, 466
  form, 472
  history of, 466–467
  link, 461
  melodic inversion, 466
  retrograde (cancrizan), 465–466
  stretto, 463–464
  subject, 459, 464, 473
  variants of subjects and answers in an entry, 463–468
Functional harmony, 448, 479, 687, 739
Funk, 771
Fusion, 771, 781

G

Gapped scale, 666–667
Gardner, Kay, 772
German 6th chord, 509, 510, 511, 515, 516–517, 643–645, 658, 774, 781
Gershwin, George, 633
Glass, Phillip, 771
Gorecki, Henryk M., 768
Graphic notation, 781
Gregorian mode, 697
Ground bass, 529–531

H

Harmonic figures, 748–749
Harmonic intervals, 450
Harmonic motive, theme and variation, 534–535
Harmonic progression, 449, 676, 775, 776
Harmonic rhythm, 449
Harmonic structure, 567
Harmony
  change of, 534
  clusters, 702, 779
  early twentieth-century music, 697–702
  nonfunctional, 638, 655, 671, 782
  polychords, 700–701, 782
  quartal chords, 671–672, 701–702, 783
  quintal chords, 671–672, 783
  sonata form, 554–567
  theme and variation, 534
  See also Chromatic harmony; Non-harmonic tones
Hauer, Josef Matthias, 740
Heptachord, 724
Hexachord, 724, 760, 761, 781
Hexatonic scale, 666
Hidden octave, 449–450
Hidden 5ths, 449–450
Hindemith, Paul, 697
History
  altered dominants, 616
  augmented 6th chords, 513–515

borrowed chords, 484–488
chromatic mediants, 625–627
eighteenth-century counterpoint, 448
fugue, 466–468
late Renaissance music, 1428
Neapolitan 6th chords, 497–499
rondo, 578
sixteen-century polyphony, 448
sonata form, 554
9th, 11th, and 13th chords, 601–604
theme and variation and continuous variation, 536
twelve-tone technique, 740
Hocket, 424, 432, 781
Homophonic texture, 711
Hykes, David, 771

I

I Ching, 761
Imitation, 20, 733, 734, 781
Impressionistic Period, 669–696
  cadences, 672–675
  chords, 668–672
  scales, 665–668, 678
  texture, 675–677
  See also Post-Romantic and Impressionistic Period
Improvisation, 762
Indeterminacy, 761–762, 781
International music, 772
Interval class, 781
Inversion, 613, 773
  augmented 6th interval, 513
  melodic, 62, 781
  at the octave, 450
  set, 725–726, 733
  twelve-tone series, 740, 760, 761, 781
  of vertical order of voices, 781
Invertible counterpoint, 461, 781
Ionian mode, 415
Italian 6th, 509, 510, 511, 516, 774, 781
Ives, Charles, 697

J

Jam Factory, 770
Jarrett, Keith, 771
Javanese gamelan, 678
Jazz and Popular Music (1900–present), 634, 777
  altered dominants, 616
  improvisation, 762
  9th, 11th, and 13th chords, 603, 605
  See also Popular music
Jeppesen, Knud: The Style of Palestrina and the Dissonance, 428
Jone, Hildegard, 747

K

Kitaro, 771

L

Lassus, Orlande de, 413, 428
Leading tone, 416, 567, 640, 773
Lead sheets, 605
Leibowitz, René, 727
Letter symbols, macro analysis, 775–776

Linear cadence, 672–673, 687, 781
Linear harmony, 781
Link, 461
Live electronic music, 764
Live performance with tapes, 763
Lower neighboring tone, 418–419
Lully, Jean-Baptiste, 527
Lydian mode, 415, 416, 417

M

Macro analysis symbols, 775–776
  chromatic harmony, 479–480
  letter symbols, 775–776
  macro analysis slurs, 776
Mahler, Gustave, 655
Manet, Édouard, 665
Mass media, 634
Matrix, 740, 743–746
Mediants, chromatic, 597, 623–632, 635
Melismatic, 432, 781
Melodic cadences, 714
Melodic contour, 451
Melodic doubling in parallel, 675–676, 781
Melodic inversion, 466, 474, 781
Melody
  in early twentieth-century music, 711
  in sixteenth-century choral music, 422, 431–432
  theme and variation, 532
Meter
  change of, 532
  early twentieth-century music, 715
  See also Rhythm and meter
Metheny, Pat, 771
Microtonal systems, 697
MIDI technology, 770, 771, 781
Mikropolyphonie, 765, 781
Minimalism, 768–769, 781
Mixolydian mode, 415, 416, 417, 675
Modal mixture, 481, 635, 638, 781
Modes, 415–417, 431
  musica ficta, 415–416, 431
  theme and variation change of, 533–534
  transposed, 416–417
Modulating subject, 460
Modulation, 625, 636, 704
Monet, Claude, 665
Monophony, 781
Monothematic, 549
Motive, 441–442, 443, 474
  early twentieth-century music, 711–712
  harmonic, 534–535
  repeated, 535
MTV, 634, 771
Multimedia compositions, 771
Musica ficta, 415–416, 431, 782
Music Mouse, 770
Musique concrète, 763, 771, 782

N

Nationalism, 782
Neapolitan 6th, 495–508, 635, 774, 782
  characteristics, 495–499
  defined, 782

Neapolitan 6th (continued)
doubling, 500
history, 497–499
part-writing practices, 774
voice-leading, 500
Neighboring tone, 450, 641
Neoclassicism, 697, 782
Neoromantic, 768
New accessibility, 768
New Age music, 634, 771, 782
The New Real Book series (Sher Music Co.), 605, 777
New Wave, 771
9th chords, 597, 599–612, 635, 639, 669
characteristics, 599–601
defined, 782
history, 601–604
macro analysis, 776
part-writing, 774
popular music chord symbols, 605, 777
voice leading, 604
Nonaccentual rhythms, 703, 782
Nonfunctional harmony, 638, 655, 671, 782
Nonharmonic tones, 599, 639, 656
accented passing tone, 418, 450
chromatic, 638
consonant 4th, 422
lower neighboring tone, 418–419
nota cambiata, 420, 448, 782
portamento, 418, 419, 420, 448, 782
suspensions, 418, 419, 448, 450
in two-voice counterpoint, 450
unaccented passing tone, 418, 450
unresolved dissonance, 637
Nonoverlapping phrases, 566
Nonsynthesizer oscillator, 765
Normal order, 724, 726–727, 782
Nota cambiata, 420, 448, 782
Numbering, twelve-tone technique, 740

O

Octatonic scale, 782
Octave, hidden, 449–450
Omitted-tone chord, 668–670
Omnibus progression, 658–659
Order
normal, 724, 726–727, 782
twelve-tone technique, 739
Order number, 782
Ostinato, 714, 770, 782
Overlapping phrases, 715

P

Palestrina, Giovanni Pierluigi da, 413, 428
Palindrome, 782
Pandiatonicism, 698, 704, 782
Parallel chords (planing), 426–427, 676–677, 701, 782
Parallel intervals
3rds, 450
4ths, 701
5ths, 448, 449, 461, 516
6ths, 450
Parallel motion, 426–427
Parallel perfect intervals, 448, 774
Parallel unisons, 774

Parameter, 782
Part-writing practices
stylistic practices, 773–774
altered dominant chords, 774
augmented 6th chords, 774
borrowed chords, 774
chromatic-mediant chords, 774
common-tone diminished 7th chords, 774
dominant seventh chords, 773
leading-tone seventh chords, 773
Neapolitan 6th chords, 774
nondominant seventh chords, 774
9th, 11th, and 13th chords, 774
triads, 773
unstylistic departures, 774
Passacaglia, 530
Passamezzo, 536
Passing tone, 418, 450, 638, 638–639, 641
Pedal tone, 448, 450, 688, 713
Pentachord, 724, 725–726, 730, 731, 733, 782
Pentatonic scale, 666–667, 678, 782
Performance art, 770
Period construction, 565
Permutation, 782
Phrase extension, 713
Phrase members, 565–566
Phrases, 565–566
overlapping, 566, 567, 715
in sonata form, 565–566
Phrygian mode, 415, 416, 666
Picardy 3rd chord, 484, 488
Pitch class, 723–724, 731, 734, 740, 749, 782
Pitch series, 759
Plagal cadences, 426, 432
Planing, 676–677, 782
Polychords, 700–701, 782
Polyphony, 415–440, 441, 782
consonance, 417–418
modes, 415–417
rhythm and meter, 422–425
text setting, 427
See also Counterpoint
Polyrhythms, 704
Polytonality, 698, 704, 782
Popular music, 633
African American, 768, 769
augmented 6th chords, 515
chord symbols, 605, 777–778
rock music, 759
rock 'n' roll, 768
Portamento, 418, 419, 420, 448, 782
Porter, Cole, 633
Position
altered dominants, 613
borrowed chords, 481–482
chromatic mediants, 624
Neapolitan 6ths, 495
9th, 11th, and 13th chords, 599
Post-1945 music. See Contemporary Period (1920–Present)
Post-Romantic Period, 633, 659–664
augmented 6th chords, 515
augmented triads, 660

blurred cadence, 659–660
borrowed chords, 485–486
chromatic mediants, 627
Neapolitan 6th chords, 499
nonfunctional harmony, 657–659
omnibus progression, 658–659
tonal instability, 655–657, 659
Pre-dominant effects, 783
Presley, Elvis, 768
Prime, 740, 760
Prime form, 727, 734
Prime series, 783
Primitivism, 697, 783
Progression
altered dominants, 613–615
augmented 6th chords, 510–512
borrowed chords, 482
chromatic mediants, 624–625
circle, 449, 479, 480, 482, 484, 485, 495, 566, 567, 600, 613, 637, 656, 774, 775, 776
common-tone diminished 7th chords, 641–643
Neapolitan 6th chords, 495–499
omnibus, 658–659
9th, 11th, and 13th chords, 600–601
Punk, 771

Q

Quadruple meter, 422–423, 448
Quartal chords, 671–672, 701–702, 783
Quintal chords, 671–672, 783

R

Ragtime, 515
Raison, André, 530
Rameau, Jean-Philippe, 527
Ramuz, C. F., 704
Rap, 634, 771
Ravel, Maurice, 665
Real answer, 459, 779, 783
Recapitulation
fugue, 466, 783
sonata, 547, 552, 564, 566, 783
Refrain (rondo theme), 577, 578, 579–580, 582, 583
Renaissance Period
consonances and dissonances, 418
form, 428
function of music in, 413
melody in choral music, 422
musica ficta, 415–416, 431, 782
parallel motion, 426–427
polyphony, 415–440
rhythm and meter, 422–424
rondeau, 578
text setting, 427
Renoir, Auguste, 665
Repeated motive, 535
Resolution
altered dominants, 617
augmented 6th chords, 513, 516
borrowed chords, 483, 485, 486–488
chromatic mediants,
common-tone diminished 7th chords, 641–642

Tone rows, 704, 739
Tonic chord, 484, 497, 566, 624, 637, 641, 656, 659
Tonic key, 443, 466
Total serialism, 759, 784
Transition
    rondo, 577
    sonata form, 548, 784
Transposed modes, 416–417
Transposition, twelve-tone, 740, 746–747
Tredici, David del, 768
Triads, 10, 700
    augmented, 660
    dominant, 613
    stylistic practices, 773
    tonic delayed, 566
Trichord, 724, 731, 747, 784
Triple meter, 422, 448
Tritone, 733, 784
Tropes, 740
Twelve-tone row, 784
Twelve-tone technique, 697, 739–758
    history, 740
    matrix, 740, 743–746
    numbering, 740
    order, 739
    pitch class, 740

    row or series, 740
    transposition, 740, 746–747
Twentieth century, early
    analytical methods, 704
    harmony, 700–702
    history, 703–704
    major styles, 697–698
    rhythm, 702–703
    tonal basis, 698–700
Two-part inventions, 441
Two-voice counterpoint, 441–458, 531
    melodic intervals to avoid, 451
    rhythm, 451
    writing, 448–452

U

Unaccented neighboring tone, 450
Unaccented passing tone, 418, 450
Unresolved dissonance, 637

V

Variation technique, 529–547, 784
    continuous variation, 529–531, 784
    theme and variation, 531–536, 784
Vertical dissonance, 418, 432
Vertical sonority, 448

Victoria, Tomás Luis de (1548–1611), 413, 428
Viennese atonalists, 759
Voice, theme and variation, 536
Voice leading, 486–488, 500, 516, 773
    altered dominant chords, 617, 774
    augmented 6th chords, 516, 774
    borrowed chords, 486–488, 774
    chromatic mediants, 628, 774
    common-tone diminished 7th chords, 774
    Neapolitan 6th chords, 500, 774
    9th, 11th, and 13th chords, 604, 774
Voltage-controlled synthesizers, 765

W

Wagner, Richard, 655, 665, 678
Weak interior cadences, 426
Webern, Anton, 704, 740, 759, 768
Whole-tone scale, 667–668, 733, 784
Winter, Paul, 771, 772
Wolf, Hugo, 655
World music, 772

X

Xenakis, Iannis, 765